Using Digital Information Services in the Library Workplace

LIBRARY SUPPORT STAFF HANDBOOKS

The Library Support Staff Handbook series is designed to meet the learning needs of both students in library support staff programs and library support staff working in libraries who want to increase their knowledge and skills.

The series was designed and is written by Hali Keeler and Marie Shaw, both of whom teach in support staff programs and have managed libraries.

The content of each volume aligns to the competencies of the required and elective courses of the American Library Association-Allied Professional Association (ALA-APA) Library Support Staff Certification (LSSC) program. These books are both textbooks for library instructional programs and current resources for working library staff. Each book is available in both print and e-book versions.

Published books in the series include:

1. *Foundations of Library Services: An Introduction for Support Staff*
2. *Library Technology and Digital Resources: An Introduction for Support Staff*
3. *Cataloging Library Resources: An Introduction*
4. *Working with Library Collections: An Introduction for Support Staff*
5. *Communication and Teamwork: An Introduction for Support Staff*
6. *Supervision and Management: An Introduction for Support Staff*
7. *Foundations of Library Services: An Introduction for Support Staff, Second Edition*
8. *Using Technology in the Library Workplace: An Introduction for Support Staff*
9. *Using Digital Information Services in the Library Workplace: An Introduction for Support Staff*

Using Digital Information Services in the Library Workplace

An Introduction for Support Staff

Marie Keen Shaw

ROWMAN & LITTLEFIELD
Lanham • Boulder • New York • London

Published by Rowman & Littlefield
An imprint of The Rowman & Littlefield Publishing Group, Inc.
4501 Forbes Boulevard, Suite 200, Lanham, Maryland 20706
www.rowman.com

6 Tinworth Street, London SE11 5AL, United Kingdom

British Library Cataloguing in Publication Information Available

Library of Congress Cataloging-in-Publication Data Available

ISBN 978-1-5381-4539-5 (cloth)
ISBN 978-1-5381-4540-1 (pbk.)
ISBN 978-1-5381-4541-8 (electronic)

To Jiayi, Joe, Sarah, and Ken
Users of Digital Information Services Who Better the World through
Pharmaceuticals, Biotechnology, Education, and Environmental Science

Contents

List of Figures ix

List of Tables xi

Preface xiii

Acknowledgments xix

Editorial Advisory Board xxi

PART I Databases, Discovery Services, and Digital Collections

Chapter 1. Digital and Visual Literacies 3

Chapter 2. Subscription Databases 17

Chapter 3. Library Discovery Services 31

Chapter 4. Primary Sources 45

Chapter 5. Digital Collections and Libraries 59

Chapter 6. Archives and Preservation 75

PART II Web Services, E-Books, Responsibilities, and Media

Chapter 7. Searching the Internet 91

Chapter 8. Metadata and Searching 105

Chapter 9. Website Services 117

Chapter 10. E-Books 131

CHAPTER 11. DIGITAL RIGHTS AND RESPONSIBILITIES 143

CHAPTER 12. MEDIA AND STREAMING SERVICES 155

PART III Social Networks, Mobility, Education, and Future

CHAPTER 13. SOCIAL NETWORKS AND MOBILE SOLUTIONS 169

CHAPTER 14. LEARNING AND DIGITAL INFORMATION SERVICES 183

CHAPTER 15. FUTURE OF DIGITAL INFORMATION SERVICES 195

GLOSSARY 209
INDEX 217
ABOUT THE AUTHOR 223

Figures

1.1	Truck in Deep Water	11
2.1	Collection Data Analysis	19
2.2	Promote Databases	25
3.1	Representation of Discovery Services Process	33
3.2	Linking Discovery Services	38
3.3	Primo Search Screen	39
3.4	Discovery Search	40
4.1	Groton Public Library History Room	48
4.2	Day After Lunar Landing—July 21, 1969	49
4.3	Catalog Search	50
5.1	Black Magick	69
5.2	100 Poems by 100 Poets	71
6.1	Archival and Preservation Supplies	79
6.2	Letter from Abraham Lincoln	82
7.1	Searching the Web	96
8.1	Example of PastPerfect	111
8.2	Library Card Catalog	113
9.1	Planning the Library Website	120
9.2	Example of Accessible Library Website	122
10.1	E-Book Reader	134
10.2	Child Reading an E-book	137
11.1	Copyright Protection	147
11.2	Libraries Lend Materials	150

12.1   Live Streamed Performance   157
12.2   Site License Permits Audience Viewing   162
13.1   Facebook, Preston Public Library   173
13.2   Accessing Library Using Smartphone   176
13.3   Twitter, Wolcott Public Library   178
14.1   Digital Learning Environment   187
14.2   Online Learning   189
15.1   Digital Fluency   200
15.2   Digital Information Using Virtual Reality   204

Tables and Textboxes

TABLES

1.1	Paper vs. Screen Self-Test	8
2.1	Reliability of Databases	21
4.1	Examples of Primary Sources Found in Libraries	46
4.2	Examples of Secondary Sources	51
4.3	File Format Standards	53
4.4	Steps for Digitization	54
5.1	Comparative Strategies with Libraries	65
6.1	Prevent Deterioration	78
6.2	How to Search the Online 1940 Census	83
7.1	Business Directories	94
7.2	Advanced Shortcuts	99
7.3	Words for Levels of Searches	100
8.1	Dublin Core Metadata Elements	110
9.1	Key Design Elements	122
10.1	Examples of E-Book Services	138
11.1	Potential Digital Copyright Situations	150

TEXTBOXES

| 2.1 | Federated Searching | 23 |
| 5.1 | Personal Digital Assets | 61 |

8.1   Best Metadata Practices   108
9.1   Planning Process   119
15.1 Digital Information is Accessible When It Is . . .   197
15.2 Ways LSS Can Enhance Digital Fluency   201

Preface

Librarians use information that is coded, scanned, or otherwise created into digital content. What is common to all digital content is that it requires some type of computing device to interpret the information into text, sound, or visuals.

This text uses the term digital information services to describe the digital content libraries offer their users. These services could be e-books, e-journals, subscription databases, discovery systems, media, and many other formats of digitization that support users' need to seek information or to enjoy reading, listening, or viewing with e-books, e-journals, audio, and streaming video.

Library Support Staff (LSS) who know the general trends and developments in digital information services enhance library functions and services for users. LSS must be ready to use, support, and help others successfully navigate a seemingly endless amount of digital content.

Aligned with the revised national American Library Association Library Support Staff Certification (ALA-LSSC) competency standards, *Using Digital Information Services in the Library Workplace: An Introduction for Support Staff* provides clear explanations about digitization and how Library Support Staff (LSS) can keep current and best use an array of products and services to enhance library service. In today's libraries LSS use a variety of digital information services in their work. They also are expected to be able to instruct, support, and problem solve many of the issues around patrons' acquiring their information needs.

This book is aimed to add to the knowledge and skills LSS need to use digital information services to support how patrons find, read, and view information. The text is divided into three parts; part I provides readers an introduction to essential "Databases, Discovery Services, and Digital Collections" that are mainstays of information found today in libraries. In the first six chapters LSS learn the essentials of digital literacy and how these skills are essential for locating, selecting, and using information today. The need for libraries to acquire access to databases and discovery systems is discussed. Not only do libraries purchase rights to these services, but today LSS can have key roles in the creation of local digital collections as well as the digital archiving and preservation of information.

The second section of the book, part II, "Web Services, E-Books, Responsibilities, and Media," provides practical techniques and approaches to enhance LSS ability to successfully use the internet as a tool. With an understanding of the fundamentals of metadata, they are better able to conduct thorough searches for themselves and others. LSS learn in chapters 7 through 12 best practices to use the internet to enhance information opportunities through quality websites, e-books, media, and streaming services. Digital rights of both vendors and users, as well as the responsibilities we all have to ensure the integrity of how we use digital information, are discussed. Digital information services are also essential to the successful functioning and use of assistive technologies, making information available to all.

The final section of this book, part III, discusses the impact of digital information on our "Social Networks, Mobility, Education, and Future." How people communicate with each other in real time through social networks rapidly evolves with the continual advances of digitization technologies. Likewise, libraries must constantly rethink how they use their budgets and staff to provide the digital information services patrons seek. As technology has developed for increased mobility, so libraries must also find means to offer information for personal devices on the go. At the same time, digital information has rapidly become the primary format for educational and learning resources. During the pandemic, schools and colleges were able to quickly adapt to virtual online learning because curricula and resources were available digitally. The final chapter discusses the advances of digitization LSS may encounter in the not-too-distant future, how they may impact their work, and how users will seek information.

This book is essential for those who work in libraries who need to know and apply the fundamental strategies to locate, select, and help others use digital information services and programs. It is also essential for those LSS who have undertaken or will be undertaking technical or leadership roles and responsibilities for ensuring the library remains competitive and in the forefront as an information provider. Embedded throughout the book are tables and textboxes that provide examples or give easy-to-understand information about a concept or related topic. At the end of each chapter is an extensive list of online references and suggested readings for further exploration of library digital information services. This important handbook is geared to improve the reader's knowledge and skills so that the library can provide equity and reliable access to information found both locally and globally.

Each chapter is broken down into short subheadings to make complex topics easy to find, read, and understand. Tables and illustrations are abundantly used throughout the text to present key ideas simply and clearly.

The text is written for three intended audiences: working library staff, college instructors, and students in college library certificate or degree programs. No matter the type of library, there is even greater need today for LSS to understand how digitization supports the information needs of its customers and provides libraries a means to share local collections across the internet.

There is a shortage of practical texts written for LSS on digital information services. Other books on this topic are written at a level that is aimed for professional librarians or are highly technical in other areas of business that do not address the library workplace. Written in clear language, this text enables LSS to understand the context behind the functions and uses of library digital information services through many examples and practical suggestions. Students who are training to work in libraries and those who currently are employed as LSS will want this book because it provides understandable explanations about today's challenges and updated accepted practices of finding and using digitized information. At the end of each chapter there are discussion questions and guided practice exercises for current issues LSS may encounter.

Professors in library technology certificate or associate degree programs will want this book as a primary instructional resource. With extensive chapter bibliographies, this book supports the curriculum and instruction in teaching current issues and practices in digital resources in LSS academic programs.

Students will find this a useful text for the way the information is presented in clear, non-technical language. An abundance of tables, textboxes, and figures make concepts easier to understand. Suggested websites and readings at the end of each chapter can further students' knowledge of topics that are introduced in the book. Many references are from academic journals that are cited for further reading.

The structure of each chapter begins with the specific ALA-LSSC technology competency standard it will address. Following subchapter headings are definitions of key terms that explain how the term applies to digital information services. Each chapter has an introduction where the upcoming topics and content are foreshadowed. Background knowledge, practical examples, and many step-by-step instructions abound in every chapter. The aim of this book is to describe digital information services in clear and direct ways so that the reader has both a basic understanding and the immediate knowledge of how to apply successful strategies and processes to their work. This book has broad appeal because of its topic coverage and practical suggestions. The reader can immediately put into practice many of the ideas and skills gleaned from each chapter.

The scope of the book addresses many different aspects of digital information services staff should know about and be able to perform in their working with others. Sequenced in fifteen chapters, this book contains the following.

PART I: DATABASES, DISCOVERY SERVICES, AND DIGITAL COLLECTIONS

Digital and Visual Literacies—Digital and visual literacy skills are essential to interpreting, analyzing, and drawing conclusions when using online sites and information. By practicing how to improve comprehension when reading online, LSS become better able to help patrons locate, interpret, use, and create information. LSS use visual literacy skills to view images from digital information services more carefully and critically. LSS with digital literacy skills support the role and responsibility of libraries to provide and enable to patrons to use digital information services.

Subscription Databases—Subscription databases are a core information resource in all types of libraries. Users today expect to obtain information digitally and automatically seek the internet for answers. LSS have important roles in the selection, evaluation, and acquisition processes of subscription databases. Working directly with the public and being attentive to their information needs, LSS can introduce, demonstrate, and support patrons' use of high-quality subscription databases on a wide variety of general and subject-specific knowledge.

Library Discovery Services—Any database has the potential to be searched by discovery, making it imperative that LSS are knowledgeable of best practices to guide users to searches and to help them select resources from overwhelming numbers of results. LSS who know the role of technology in creating, identifying, retrieving, and accessing information resources and demonstrate facility with appropriate information discovery tools can effectively use discovery services in both their personal lives for themselves and in their work with others.

Primary Sources—LSS can support the use of primary sources in many ways. They locate firsthand information for patrons and create scanned images of texts, photographs, and artifacts for local library digital collections. With advancements in scanning technology and the internet, items that were once in reserve collections or not for circulation can now be shared with patrons through the library website. LSS who are knowledgeable in searching and competent in the use of technology can apply their skills to create digital collections of local primary sources.

Digital Collections and Libraries—Digital libraries are an ever-growing important information source in library information services that are not necessarily found through a typical internet search. LSS who become users of digital collections can apply their knowledge and experience to helping others locate digital assets for research, education, and enjoyment. LSS who are knowledgeable of how to locate and are experienced users of digital collections support their role and responsibility for introducing relevant applications of technology, including digital literacy, to the public.

Archives and Preservation—LSS who understand the importance of archiving and preserving important records and artifacts and are able to perform the work of digitization support the role and responsibility of libraries for introducing relevant applications of technology to find, select, and use digital collections and archives to the public. LSS who have digital and archive training are able to create, identify, retrieve, and help others access information resources from national, state, and local archives and digital libraries.

PART II: WEB SERVICES, E-BOOKS, RESPONSIBILITIES, AND MEDIA

Searching the Internet—Search engines are tools for locating information on the web. Like any tool, knowledge of its capabilities and practice using it improves work performance. LSS who know the concepts and issues concerning the use of search engines and web browsers support searching by different user groups. LSS are able to assist and train users to connect to the internet to find quality web pages that meet their needs by using a variety of search strategies and techniques.

Metadata and Searching—Metadata is the foundation of aggregated searching, federated searching, and discovery services. LSS catalogers are already familiar with metadata when they catalog items for library collections in MARC 21 using basic bibliographic information such as the title, author, publisher, date, and so on. However, metadata are also elements of detailed descriptions and associations. LSS demonstrate flexibility when they adapt to using metadata management systems and are able to help others with their searches. LSS support users to better search the internet and use databases and library digital collections for specific requests and information needs.

Website Services—LSS are often responsible for aspects of the library website that is a portal to its online resources. LSS support digital literacy when they apply assistive technology guidelines and strategies that ensure equitable web accessibility for all users.

E-Books—LSS who are informed users of e-books are able to assist and train others to access library e-book services on a variety of e-readers and mobile devices from remote locations. LSS perform basic troubleshooting of technical problems with e-books and resolve or refer those problems as appropriate. They also know how to use the basic assistive technologies of e-books to ensure that all users have equitable access to this technology.

Digital Rights and Responsibilities—LSS who know and apply the basic principles and best practices to adhere to copyright help to ensure the integrity of data and the confidentiality of user activities. When LSS understand copyright concepts and issues concerning digital rights management, they can support appropriate use of technology and digital content by different user groups.

Media and Streaming Services—In less than a decade DVDs have rapidly been replaced both in homes and in libraries with streaming video. LSS are able to assist and train users to select streamed content offered either free or through the library subscriptions by connecting to the internet and downloading appropriate apps. LSS know how streaming is currently changing how people across the globe retrieve and access audio and visual information resources and are able to help others in its use.

PART III: SOCIAL NETWORKS, MOBILITY, EDUCATION, AND FUTURE

Social Networks and Mobile Solutions—LSS demonstrate flexibility in supporting the library use of social media to communicate to its users and promote its services. Those who are knowledgeable of and familiar with mobile devices and apps are able to assist and train users to access library services from remote locations. LSS have an important role in planning, implementing, and supporting the use of social media and mobile apps in order to enhance the library programs, events, and information resources in its community.

Learning and Digital Information Services—Learning, education, and digital information services are intertwined. Our future lies with how people are able to use digital information to solve problems and for the benefit of society. LSS who know the general trends and developments in digital information services and technology applications enhance library functions and services for users. LSS who access and use all of the digital information services of their library and learn how to use basic assistive technologies help to ensure that all users have equitable access to information for formal and informal learning.

Future of Digital Information Services—This text provides LSS the general trends and developments in technology applications for library digital information services and how they may change in the future. Digital equity is critical to the social, economic, educational, and health success of all people and places. LSS who demonstrate flexibility in adapting to new technology influence the critical and essential role libraries have to be providers of digital information services to their communities.

Using Digital Information Services in the Library Workplace: An Introduction for Support Staff covers new ground with its content aligned with the technology competencies established by the American Library Association Library Support Staff Certification Program (ALA-LSSC). Each chapter addresses one or more of the competencies so that the reader can understand each requirement in real and practical applications and examples. In this book the technology competencies are turned into examples of library practice that LSS can absorb and practice daily at work.

This text provides a different perspective than most books or materials written for library professionals. Simply put, the majority of library literature is aimed at professional librarians. Works are often highly theoretical and not practical. Other books on the topic of digital information services are written at a level that is aimed at professional librarians and not support staff. However, 85 percent of library support staff do not hold professional degrees yet will assume many of the functions and responsibilities of providing accurate and high-quality information. The many examples within this book can help the reader become more proficient and confident using the functions of digitized resources. At the end of each chapter are discussion questions that are written to refocus the reader to the more important or salient ideas presented within the chapter. There is a learning activity at the end of each chapter that an instructor can use with a class or the reader can work through independently or with other staff to gain experience or additional practice with ideas or processes described in the text. Using this handbook as a guide, LSS will be able to apply the ALA-LSSC standards of technology and demonstrate their understanding of these important competencies that relate to digital information services in their daily practice and work performance.

Acknowledgments

I acknowledge the librarians, educators, and academic mentors who in the early days of educational technology guided and supported my own learning, experimentation, and practice using digital information services.

With special appreciation I acknowledge my editorial advisory board, who provided me with important feedback during the stages of writing this book.

I thank my executive editor, Charles Harmon, for his confidence in me and for his supportive advice throughout my writing process with this book and its predecessors in the Library Support Staff Handbook Series.

Editorial Advisory Board

PART I

Databases, Discovery Services, and Digital Collections

CHAPTER 1

Digital and Visual Literacies

Library Support Staff know the role and responsibility of libraries for introducing relevant applications of technology, including digital literacy, to the public.

Topics Covered in This Chapter
Analog vs. Digital
Digital Literacy
Cognitive Digital Literacy Skills
   Reading
   Comprehension
   Writing
Visual Literacy
   Visual Literacy Skills
Chapter Summary

Key Terms
Analog—Libraries circulate books, tapes of sound and film, and other continuous formats. Recorded in a continuous line with a beginning and end, analog media formats have rapidly been replaced with digital.

Binary code—Using the numbers zero and one (0 and 1), this code used in programming operates computers and other digital devices.

Cognition—These are the processes of thinking and how the human brain stores and processes information to make sense of the world.

Digital literacy—This is the ability to use information and communication technologies to find, evaluate, create, and communicate information, requiring both cognitive and technical skills.

Library Support Staff—LSS or library paraprofessionals are involved in library operations at all levels. The range and complexity of their duties varies with each position, the size and type of the library, and each library's specific needs.

Literacy—This is the ability and skills of a person to read, write, and perform mathematics. The term also defines having knowledge and expertise in a particular field of study.

Nonlinear text—This refers to words or sentences that are neither in consecutive order nor follow a left-to-right, line-by-line arrangement. Nonlinear text may be words in any vertical or horizontal manner and may not appear connected to each other.

Technology standards—Clear expectations of outcomes of achievement define what students should know how to do with technology to support their learning.

Visual literacy—This is the ability to interpret information and inferences from photographs, pictures, or illustrations, whether they are still or animated.

ANALOG VS. DIGITAL

The invention of the modern computer introduced digital to the world. While libraries continue to circulate and use many **analog** or linear systems, such as print books, magazines, and archival microforms, digital collections have equally become the norm. Libraries provide customers digital magazine subscriptions, e-books, databases, streaming video, and other computerized educational and entertaining content.

Analog information is presented in a continuous transmission that has a start and a finish, while digital information is stored using a series of ones and zeros organized in **binary code**. The number one represents "on" and zero represents "off." These are called a bit (think of just a little bit). Strings of eight bits are called a byte. Bytes are represented by this sequence of numbers, doubling beginning with the number one to number 128 read from right to left:

128	64	32	16	8	4	2	1
0	1	0	1	1	1	1	1

The programmer turns bytes on (with 1) or off (with 0). In order for a computer to use the number 95, the bytes 64, 16, 8, 4, 2, and 1 are on. Bytes 128 and 32 are off:

$$64 + 16 + 8 + 4 + 2 + 1 = 95$$

Alphabets are coded in 1s and 0s. For example, the letter *A* is represented by the number 65 or the binary code of 01000001 (64 +1). Letter *B* is represented by the number 66 or the binary code of 01000010. Binary code, while simplistic, represents incredible amounts of data. CDs and DVDs can be used to store and play high-quality sound and video data coded in 1s and 0s.[1] Digital library services are built around products and practices that rely on computers to operate devices and provide information.

Digital information services continue to be developed. As technology rapidly evolves and changes, so does the way libraries use products. Examples of products are

subscription databases,
index discovery tools,
archives and digital collections,
digital libraries,
e-books,
LibGuides,
media and streaming services,
virtual reality devices, and
machine learning systems.

New products require new learning. This text is about these and other digital information services and the skills and practices LSS need to support effective services. Examples of digital information practices learned from this text are

perfecting digital and visual literacy skills,
improving searching techniques,
understanding the Internet of Things,
using metadata,
organizing web content,
complying with digital copyright,
communicating on social networks,
finding mobile solutions, and
applying online learning strategies.

The remainder of this chapter will address the first practice of literacy skills.

DIGITAL LITERACY

This chapter delves into two of the many types of literacies: **digital literacy** and **visual literacy**. *Literacy* is associated with reading and writing proficiency as well as possessing knowledge, skills, and education. **Library Support Staff** (LSS) develop cognitive and technical skills in literacies so that they, in turn, can help others. LSS have a critical role to assist patrons' use of digital information services. Librarians and educators encounter several types of literacies in their work:[2]

- *Academic Literacy*—being able use advanced vocabulary; understand academic texts; distinguish between essential and nonessential information, fact and opinion, cause and effect; classify, categorize, and handle data that make comparisons.[3]
- *Information Literacy*—being able to recognize when information is needed and to have the ability to locate, evaluate, and use it effectively.
- *Media Literacy*—being able to critically use non-textual formats.

- *Mathematical Literacy*—the ability to use mathematics to problem solve, analyze, and reason.
- *Digital Literacy*—the ability to use information and communication technologies to find, evaluate, create, and communicate information, requiring both cognitive and technical skills.[4]
- *Privacy Literacy*—the ability for learners to understand how their private information will be stored, used, or distributed, combined with their personal philosophy about what information should be public or private.[5]
- *New Literacies*—the ability to learn using multiple modalities such as text, sound, and film, as well as exploration, simulation, kinetic movement, and technologies with others.
- *Visual Literacy*—the ability to analyze, interpret, and understand the context of information depicted in pictures, photographs, and other visual means of expression.

Literacy dates back to 3500 BC with the Sumerians in Mesopotamia, who developed the earliest known writing communication system called cuneiform. Only a small number of people learned to read and write cuneiform; they held public performances of their skills. The first known books originated in Rome, around 23 BC. Books were also developed in the Middle East and several Asian nations around this time. Initially, books were quite rare and expensive, until the invention of the printing press in the fifteenth century. As printed books became more common, literacy rates began to rise. In Colonial America, the Puritans placed a high value on reading for spiritual edification, and some colonial governments required citizens be literate in order to vote. The ability to sign one's name and the importance of literacy grew in early America, and those who learned to use a signature set themselves apart from their less-educated peers. The Industrial Revolution brought more changes to the advancement of literacy. Paper production greatly reduced the cost of books, and literacy became a primary goal in U.S. public education, with literacy rates reaching 70 percent in some parts of the United States in the 1920s.[6]

A key difference between digital information services and traditional library books is how we read, view, and use the information contained therein. Because books are the primary medium used to teach reading, LSS assume that users select library books based on their reading skills and interests. Do not assume this is the case with digital information services. Readers and users of traditional print books and texts have a different experience and may struggle with digital information services.

The ability to read, interpret, use, and create information are higher-level skills. Teachers grapple to teach phonics and other techniques as tools for independent reading.[7] Learning to read is difficult, not only for the sounding of words, but for contextual meaning. Children learn to read primarily using books with much instructional support, yet they are expected to seamlessly transfer to screen reading on their own. Nonfiction books are fairly predictable, beginning with a table of contents and ending with an index. Text appears in a uniform font and size. While illustrations and photography vary from book to book, within a book there is often a consistent appearance. Young adult and children's books have great variation in length of text, illustrations, and placement, but young readers can count on a linear format with the story beginning on page one and progressing to the last pages of the book. Is reading from a book the same as reading on a computer monitor, smartphone, or tablet screen? It is not.

Reading onscreen presents many different challenges. Text size and color are not always uniform. Words may be moving in animation. Placement of words often is not in traditional typeset columns or pages. Screen sizes vary in size and shape. Ask yourself, how does technology influence your ability to read text and view pictures for context and meaning?

The goal of this chapter is to answer these questions for ourselves so that we, in turn, can support our patrons who seek information from digital information services. Our world is digital, and libraries have dramatically adapted their collections and services to keep current with e-content. Technology requires people to read, write, view, and use information differently than the traditional methods they once learned in school.

If literacy is the ability to read and write in traditional ways with paper and pencil, digital literacy is the ability to read and write using computer technology. A digitally literate person successfully uses computer technology to read, write, and effectively communicate information. A digitally illiterate person struggles with the expectations of today's **technology standards**.[8]

Digitally literate LSS have expertise with technology; they are able to operate and use technology for research, problem solving, and innovation, adhering to legal and ethical requirements. They use technologies, regardless of platform or format, to work a variety of digital information services. The transfer of traditional literacy is not automatic; it takes work to achieve digital literacy proficiency both technically and cognitively.

COGNITIVE DIGITAL LITERACY SKILLS

Cognition is how the human brain thinks and the processes it uses to store and process information to make sense of the world. In addition to technology skills, digital literacy requires cognitive skills for people to find, evaluate, create, and communicate information. Digital literacies are challenging and require different cognitive practices.

Prior to personal computers, people primarily read from two-dimensional paper books, journals, or documents. Occasionally reading occurred for a brief message on a TV or movie screen. With the onset of computers, there was an assumption that reading skills would automatically transfer to technology. How different could reading be online?

Reading

E-books, e-journals, websites, and other digital products provide a vast amount of information. Researching online often is faster than print research, and the cost of comprehensive databases is much lower than purchasing individual texts. Online tools such as dictionaries, thesauri, and writing supports are plentiful as well as embedded media, charts, and other data presentations.[9]

The relationship between the act of reading and the work of the human brain is complex. The Dartmouth College Reading Brains Lab suggests the following processes must be in place as they work together in reading:

- *orthographic processing*—the visual look of a word or string of letters;
- *phonological processing*—the sounds of language;
- *morphological processing*—differences between similar words;
- *semantic processing*—the meaning of words; and
- *syntactic processing*—the order and arrangement of words in phrases and sentences.[10]

Syntactic processing, how sentences are understood, relates to some of the issues of reading on a screen. We learn to read line by line. When we read in linear sentences, we are able to comprehend more from the text. Our eyes focus on a larger amount of text, and we preread ahead and reread behind to get deeper meaning and context from the paragraphs. Reading on a computer is often **nonlinear** because sentences appear in unpredictable places all over the screen. Neuroscience has found we use different parts of the brain when reading from a piece of paper than from a screen.[11]

Comprehension

Words and sentences do not fall into linear, predictable representations on a screen. Our brains have to work harder for depth of understanding. The speed of reading complex text may decrease dramatically, bogging down the reader, explaining why people are more likely to read Twitter feeds and short news or magazine articles online than long passages of complex text. Sustained reading is often interrupted by flipping between screens to preread and reread sentences. Take the self-test found in table 1.1 and compare your results between the processes of reading new research material on paper versus screen.

What can LSS do to support patrons' reading and comprehension online? When introducing a patron to a database, be sure features such as keyword searching,

Table 1.1. Paper vs. Screen Self-Test

Step	Action
1	Create two T-charts. Make each T-chart by simply writing a very large letter *T* on a full piece of paper. The vertical line of the *T* divides your paper into two columns. On the top line of the *T* write "Positives" on the left side of the page and "Negatives" on the right side of the top of the page.
2	Go to the Pew Research Internet Project found at http://www.pewinternet.org/.
3	Select two of the current reports on internet and technology that are about equal in length. One report you will read on the screen, the other report you are to print and read on paper.
4	As you read each report, list five positive ideas you found in the article on the left side of T-chart. On the right side of your T-chart list five negative ideas from the article. By doing this you are going to have to read deeply.
5	Get a timer and read each article and T-chart. What were your results? Which format was more successful?

relevance or date sort, and downloadable texts are understood. Ask if the patron would like to read the article online or would prefer a print copy. The print copy moves the patron back into the familiar realm of traditional reading where she can highlight and make notes near meaningful content. Some techniques, such as highlighting text, do not transfer as meaningfully to the brain when reading online as they do on paper.[12]

Research shows people spend less than one minute per webpage, and only 16 percent say they read every word. Making a mental map of where information lies on a page is an important step in reading comprehension that is not taking place with online reading.[13] LSS can explain to users that reading more slowly online than they would normally do with print potentially increases comprehension. LSS may also offer to help the patron set up a simple table in a document for notetaking and citing important websites. Online readers need to give the brain time to file important information for later use to increase comprehension.

Writing

Digital literacy is also defined by the ability to write with technology. While LSS may not support the writing process of patrons, it is interesting to note, similar to the reading process, different centers of the brain, such as motor skills and memory that aid cognition, are activated when we write by hand compared to keyboarding.[14] Yet there is a tradeoff of efficiency with keyboarding, and many schools no longer teach cursive writing in order to teach keyboarding. The engagement of the brain during handwriting results in better recall of information. Experiment with taking notes by hand to see if your recall is improved. Below are ways LSS support digital literacy with patrons.

1. Take the self-test several times. Find techniques that augment your reading on the screen, such as prereading or skimming ahead or changing font size to accommodate full sentence size. By analyzing the differences between your reading on paper and reading on a screen, you can provide firsthand experiences that may be helpful to others.
2. Well-constructed and authored digital information sources are more likely to be created in ways that will support reading on a screen. Share websites that offer clean representations of linear text over those that may be harder to navigate.
3. Provide print copies to patrons whenever possible, especially if they are doing research.
4. If you create or contribute to making library web pages, think about creating linear text in appropriate places. A crowded and unorganized webpage is not helpful to the reader. Do not make your readers skim and jump to multiple places when they could read text in the recognizable form of a paragraph.
5. If you create digital resources or collections, in the planning discuss with others the issues of digital literacy that will improve the reading for users.
6. Nonfiction more likely requires deeper reading than fiction. Newspaper and popular magazine articles are easier to read online than academic or research journal articles. As you help patrons find digital or electronic resources, guide

them to use screens for lighter, less intense reading. Suggest patrons use their devices or screens for fiction or popular reading and paper for research or deep reading.

7. Practice will improve reading on screens and awareness of the work the brain must do will help readers sustain their efforts for the hard work of reading online.

VISUAL LITERACY

Today it is common for libraries to create local digital collections by scanning primary source documents, artifacts, and other treasures not typically available to their patrons. Images are now readily available to patrons in digital files. Visual literacy is the ability to interpret information and inferences from photographs, pictures, or illustrations, whether they are still or animated. LSS who have visual literacy skills look carefully at images for important information that otherwise would be skipped or overlooked. Key visual literacy concepts are

1. the ability to focus on important details in a photograph or picture that provides rich or historical context or setting;
2. the ability to draw information from photographs, pictures, or illustrations; and
3. the ability to extract a greater sense of meaning or purpose than text provides from a picture or photograph.

The Association of College and Research Libraries says these essential skills equip a learner to understand and analyze the contextual, cultural, ethical, aesthetic, intellectual, and technical components involved in the production and use of visual materials. A visually literate individual is both a critical consumer of visual media and a competent contributor to a body of shared knowledge and culture.[15]

Look closely to obtain subtle information such as the context, setting, time period, or purpose of people in a photograph. Clothing styles, innovations, architecture, and other cultural cues can assist with the reference of a photograph. Kaplan and Mifflin suggest there are three levels of awareness of visual literacy:

1. Superficial awareness—this is our first glance or look at a photograph, film, or other media. We ask ourselves what is the picture *of*? Most of our viewing is done at the superficial level as images confront us constantly in our lives. We often take in just enough information from the picture that we need to get by.
2. Concrete awareness—what is the picture *about*? At this second level of awareness, we focus on details of the photograph or media. Here we determine things such as setting, time period, faces, actions that occur, and other information that gives us a frame of reference about what is going on.
3. Abstract awareness—what is the *context*? What did the creator intend to evoke in his or her audience with this picture? Is there deeper meaning or inferences that can be made from the image? At this level we study the picture and make connections with our own base of knowledge or experience. As with deep reading, at the abstract awareness level we need to think hard about the intended

message in a more meaningful context than concrete awareness. At the abstract level the creator of the photograph or media wants to convey to the viewer a subtle but important message.[16]

Carefully look at figure 1.1. At superficial awareness, it is a truck traveling through high water. At level two, concrete awareness, the truck is painted in military camouflage. The boxes are stacked high and all similar, suggesting some kind of supplies. The passenger may be wearing a short-sleeved work shirt. At the front bumper there is some kind of flotation device to keep the engine from stalling in the water. Looking at the background, there are trees inundated in the waters; perhaps the truck is not on a road?

Abstract awareness requires some research. LSS could discover that this is a National Guard truck. If the labels on the boxes could be magnified, it would be learned that these supplies are heading to the Superdome for people taking shelter after Hurricane Katrina in New Orleans. With this information the photo is no longer one of a truck in high water but a National Guard unit called into action after one of the worst natural disasters in the United States.

Figure 1.1. Truck in Deep Water. *Stocktreck Images/Stocktreck Images Via Getty Images*

Visual Literacy Skills

Visual literacy skills are paramount to using information and communicating with others. Children are expected to read and view online as Chromebooks and other devices have become learning tools. Schools offer specialized curricula in visual graphics. A visually literate person uses skills to read and research information as suggested by Helena Zinkham.[17]

How to Read Photographs:

1. Note first impressions.
2. Name everything you see.
3. Look again at the picture.
4. Write a description about meaning, including reading accompanying text, describing what the photograph shows, and listing any assumptions you can make about the photograph.

How to Research Photographs:

1. Confirm your caption information by verifying its date, title, names, and so on.
2. Ask colleagues to look at the photograph. What do they see that you missed?
3. Study the frame, housing, and any other written information.
4. Research and describe any information about the location and time period.
5. What events led to the photo's creation?
6. What is the photograph's style, form, and genre?
7. Research physical features such as the type of photography, processes used to take the photo and develop it, print formats, sizes, color or black and white.
8. What are the types of image mounts used and image bases—film, glass, metal, paper?

Additionally, when looking at a photograph, LSS can ask the following questions:

1. Is this image in its original state (i.e., no manipulation or "doctoring")?
2. How do the subjects of the photograph relate to each other?
3. What is the main idea or argument the image expresses?
4. In what context or under what conditions was this image originally created? Displayed?
5. Is emotion or tension displayed? Be specific about the source and instigator.
6. Is there a larger context of which this image is a part?
7. What place in the photo is your attention most immediately drawn to? Why?
8. What is the smallest detail that says the most?
9. What do we need to know to read the image successfully?
10. If this image was altered, who did it and why?

All of these questions can provide not only clues but, more importantly, the information or story the photographer intended to communicate. LSS who practice these skills for improving their visual literacy will be able to help patrons find and interpret visual information more accurately from both print and digital photographs of historical and other value from local library collections.

CHAPTER SUMMARY

Digital and visual literacy skills are essential to interpreting, analyzing, and drawing conclusions when using online sites and information. By practicing how to improve comprehension when reading online, LSS become better able to help patrons locate, interpret, use, and create information. LSS use visual literacy skills to view images from digital information services more carefully and critically. LSS with digital literacy skills support the role and responsibility of libraries to provide and enable patrons to use digital information services.

DISCUSSION QUESTIONS

1. In what ways has the change from analog to digital changed library services?
2. What are some of the similarities and differences between traditional literacy and digital literacy?
3. In what ways can LSS help support patrons' digital literacy?
4. What are the three types of visual awareness and how does each step affect how we view a photograph?
5. What steps can a person take to interpret and use information from a photograph?

ACTIVITY: VISUAL LITERACY—
PHOTOGRAPHIC INVESTIGATION AND INTERPRETATION

Photographs reveal multiple pieces of information. Select five photographs from the collection of the George Eastman Museum that convey contextual or subtle information. The collection is found at https://www.eastman.org/photography.

For each photograph describe at least three "hidden" or subtle parts of the photo that tell the viewer more about the time period, people, working conditions, climate, and so on. In other words, identify pieces of visual information that go beyond the surface of the picture. Use the questions in the Visual Literacy Skills section above to help hone those skills.

NOTES

1. Sharpened Productions, "Digital Definition," *Tech Terms*, last modified 2020, accessed February 25, 2020, https://techterms.com/definition/digital.

2. Madison College Libraries, "Information Literacy: Guide for Students: What is Information Literacy?" Last modified March 25, 2020, accessed April 26, 2020, https://libguides .madisoncollege.edu/InfoLitStudents.

3. Community College of Baltimore County, "What Is Academic Literacy?" *Academic Literacy*, last modified 2020, accessed April 26, 2020, https://www.ccbcmd.edu/Resources -for-Students/Tutoring-and-Academic-Coaching/Writing-Center-and-Online-Writing-Lab/Aca demic-Literacy.aspx.

4. "Issues and Trends," *American Libraries*, Special issue (2020), https://www.ala.org/news /state-americas-libraries-report-2020/issues-trends.

5. Christina L. Wissinger, "Privacy Literacy: From Theory to Practice," *Communications in Information Literacy* 11, no. 2 (2017): 387–89, accessed September 12, 2021, https://pdx scholar.library.pdx.edu/comminfolit/vol11/iss2/9/.

6. University of Texas, Arlington Online, "A Brief History of Literacy," *Education Archives*, last modified September 9, 2015, accessed September 12, 2021, https://academicpartnerships .uta.edu/articles/education/brief-history-of-literacy.aspx.

7. Jen Ogden, "How I Learned to Teach Reading," *Educational Leadership* 77, no. 5 (February 2020): 28–30, https://search.ebscohost.com/login.aspx?direct=true&db=aph&AN =141670215&authtype=cookie,cpid&custid=csl&site=ehost-live&scope=site.

8. International Society for Technology in Education, "Skills Learners Need to Thrive in Work and Life," *ISTE Standards*, last modified 2020, accessed April 26, 2020, https://www .iste.org/standards.

9. Liane Hughes, "Reading Academic Articles: Paper v. Screen," *Fine Print* 42, no. 1 (2019), https://search.ebscohost.com/login.aspx?direct=true&db=aph&AN=136193649&authtype =cookie,cpid&custid=csl&site=ehost-live&scope=site.

10. Dartmouth College, "Reading Development," Reading Brains Lab, last modified 2006, accessed April 27, 2020, https://readingbrains.host.dartmouth.edu/ResearchFiles/reading.html.

11. T. J. Raphael, "Your Paper Brain and Your Kindle Brain Aren't the Same Thing," *Technology*, last modified September 18, 2014, accessed April 27, 2020, https://www.pri.org/sto ries/2014-09-18/your-paper-brain-and-your-kindle-brain-arent-same-thing.

12. Raphael, "Your Paper Brain."

13. Michael S. Rosenwald, "Why Do Digital Natives Prefer Reading in Print?" *Washington Post*, February 23, 2015, accessed April 27, 2020, https://search.proquest.com/washington post/docview/1657262425/CF8A4AD6B7DB4007PQ/1?accountid=46995.

14. Laura Deutsch, "Is It Better to Write by Hand or Computer?" *Psychology Today*, last modified October 2, 2017, https://www.psychologytoday.com/us/blog/memory-catcher/201710 /is-it-better-write-hand-or-computer.

15. American Library Association, "Keeping Up With . . . Visual Literacy," ACRL, last modified 2020, accessed April 27, 2020, http://www.ala.org/acrl/publications/keeping_up_with /visual_literacy.

16. Elisabeth Kaplan and Jeffrey Mifflin, "Mind and Sight: Visual Literacy and the Archivist," *Libraries Digital Conservancy*, last modified 1997, accessed April 27, 2020, https://con servancy.umn.edu/handle/11299/46590.

17. Helena Zinkham, "Reading and Researching Photographs," Prints and Photographs Reading Room, last modified 2007, accessed April 28, 2020, https://www.loc.gov/rr/print /resource/researchertool.html.

REFERENCES, SUGGESTED READINGS, AND WEBSITES

American Library Association. "Keeping Up With . . .Visual Literacy." ACRL. Last modified 2020. Accessed April 27, 2020. http://www.ala.org/acrl/publications/keeping_up_with /visual_literacy.

———. "Resources for Library Support Staff." Library Support Staff Education. Last modified 2020. Accessed April 27, 2020. http://www.ala.org/aboutala/offices/library-sup port-staff-education-and-training.

Community College of Baltimore County. "What Is Academic Literacy?" *Academic Literacy*. Last modified 2020. Accessed April 26, 2020. https://www.ccbcmd.edu/Resources-for-Stu dents/Tutoring-and-Academic-Coaching/Writing-Center-and-Online-Writing-Lab/Academ ic-Literacy.aspx.

Dartmouth College. "Reading Development." Reading Brains Lab. Last modified 2006. Accessed April 27, 2020. https://readingbrains.host.dartmouth.edu/ResearchFiles/reading.html.

Deutsch, Laura. "Is It Better to Write by Hand or Computer?" *Psychology Today*. Last modified October 2, 2017. https://www.psychologytoday.com/us/blog/memory-catcher/201710/is-it -better-write-hand-or-computer.

EBSCO. "Training at Your Library: We Asked, You Answered." *Novelist*. Last modified October 12, 2017. https://www.ebscohost.com/novelist-the-latest/blog-article/training-at -your-library-we-asked-you-answered.

Hughes, Liane. "Reading Academic Articles: Paper v. Screen." *Fine Print* 42, no. 1 (2019): 3–7. https://search.ebscohost.com/login.aspx?direct=true&db=aph&AN=136193649&auth type=cookie,cpid&custid=csl&site=ehost-live&scope=site.

International Society for Technology in Education. "Skills Learners Need to Thrive in Work and Life." *ISTE Standards*. Last modified 2020. Accessed April 26, 2020. https://www.iste .org/standards.

"Issues and Trends." *American Libraries*, Special issue (2020): 14–27. https://www.ala.org /news/state-americas-libraries-report-2020/issues-trends.

Kaplan, Elisabeth, and Jeffrey Mifflin. "Mind and Sight: Visual Literacy and the Archivist." *Libraries Digital Conservancy*. Last modified 1997. Accessed April 27, 2020. https://conser vancy.umn.edu/handle/11299/46590.

Madison College Libraries. "Information Literacy: Guide for Students: What Is Information Literacy?" Last modified March 25, 2020. Accessed April 26, 2020. https://libguides.madi soncollege.edu/InfoLitStudents.

Mudure-Iacob, Ioana. "Digital Literacy: From Multi-Functional Skills to Overcoming Challenges in Teaching ESP." *Astra Salvansis* 7, no. 14 (2019): 59–70. https://search.eb scohost.com/login.aspx?direct=true&db=aph&AN=138711904&authtype=cookie,cpid& custid=csl&site=ehost-live&scope=site.

Ogden, Jen. "How I Learned to Teach Reading." *Educational Leadership* 77, no. 5 (February 2020): 28–30. https://search.ebscohost.com/login.aspx?direct=true&db=aph&AN=141670215& authtype=cookie,cpid&custid=csl&site=ehost-live&scope=site.

Raphael, T. J. "Your Paper Brain and Your Kindle Brain Aren't the Same Thing." *Technology*. Last modified September 18, 2014. Accessed April 27, 2020. https://www.pri.org/stories /2014-09-18/your-paper-brain-and-your-kindle-brain-arent-same-thing.

Rosenwald, Michael S. "Why Do Digital Natives Prefer Reading in Print?" *Washington Post*, February 23, 2015. Accessed April 27, 2020. https://search.proquest.com/washingtonpost /docview/1657262425/CF8A4AD6B7DB4007PQ/1?accountid=46995.

Sharpened Productions. "Digital Definition." *Tech Terms*. Last modified 2020. Accessed February 25, 2020. https://techterms.com/definition/digital.

Udoewa, Victor. "Helping the Next 4 Billion Go Online Part II: Prototyping Solutions for Digital Literacy Education." *International Journal for Service Learning in Engineering, Humanitarian Engineering, and Social Entrepreneurship* 12, no. 1 (Spring 2017): 13–40. https:// search.ebscohost.com/login.aspx?direct=true&db=aph&AN=123579882&authtype=cook ie,cpid&custid=csl&site=ehost-live&scope=site.

University of Texas, Arlington Online. "A Brief History of Literacy." *Education Archives*. Last modified September 9, 2015. Accessed September 12, 2021. https://academicpartnerships .uta.edu/articles/education/brief-history-of-literacy.aspx.

Utah Education Network. "Digital Literacy." Utah Core. Last modified 2020. Accessed April 26, 2020. https://www.uen.org/core/core.do?courseNum=520420.

Wissinger, Christina L. "Privacy Literacy: From Theory to Practice." *Communications in Information Literacy* 11, no. 2 (2017): 387–89. Accessed September 12, 2021. https://pdxscholar .library.pdx.edu/comminfolit/vol11/iss2/9/.

Zinkhan, Helena. "Reading and Researching Photographs." Prints and Photographs Reading Room. Last modified 2007. Accessed April 28, 2020. https://www.loc.gov/rr/print/resource /researchertool.html.

CHAPTER 2

Subscription Databases

LSS know the role of technology in creating, identifying, retrieving, and accessing information resources and demonstrate facility with appropriate information discovery tools.

Topics Covered in This Chapter

Selection Process
    Collection Analysis
    Needs Assessment
Evaluation Process
    Reliability and Reputation
    Database Reviews
    Trials
    Search Features
    Statistics and Metrics
    PlumX Metrics
Acquisitions Process
    Pricing
    Discount Purchasing
    Statewide Discounts
    License Agreements
    Access
Webinars and Training
Chapter Summary

Key Terms

Collection analysis—This process determines what materials patrons find desirable, what materials are not, and where gaps exist in subjects or content.

Dynamic IP range—Consecutive numbers randomly assigned to library computers speed database searching with devices preregistered on the library network.

Federated search—This type of search cross-indexes multiple databases simultaneously with results viewed in one screen as an efficient way to search many products at once.

License agreement—This contract between the library and the database company provider specifies how long and under what conditions library patrons may use the subscription database or resource.

Needs assessment—This process is used to gather data that will help to determine the strengths and shortcomings of the library collections.

Performance metrics—These are figures and data representative of a library's actions, abilities, and overall quality of materials.

Remote access—This provides a patron the ability to externally access and use a library subscription database from outside of the library.

Simultaneous use—More than one patron may access a subscription database at the same time.

Subscription databases—These are collections of searchable and authoritative documents, articles, images, sound, media, websites, or other information formats clustered around a broad theme or subject.

Trial—This is an agreed-upon length of time when a library can try a database without cost with its patrons to help evaluate whether it meets an information need.

SELECTION PROCESS

Today a significant amount of resources in library collections are digital. In some collections, such as serials, the number of digital titles far exceed a library's print holdings. Except for a few unique titles, such as the *New York Times* or *National Geographic*, most digital serials are acquired as a package with other titles in **subscription databases**. A key difference between free web searching and subscription databases is that libraries carefully select, evaluate, and subscribe, either by purchase or lease, to databases that fulfill the information needs of users. These databases of searchable documents, articles, images, sound, media, websites, or other information formats are bundled around a broad theme, demographic, or subject. LSS support the selection, evaluation, acquisition, and use of subscription databases.

Collection development policies are important guides for libraries that help to coordinate the mission and purpose of the library with its collection of materials. LSS should be aware of their library's collection development policy, not only to make connections with the library mission and its materials, but also to better understand and explain to others why the collection is purposed as it is. It is important for each library to craft a collection development policy that serves its users. LSS who work directly with collections and know the library collection development policy can better understand how to handle gift donations, weeding of materials, and issues that may arise about censorship and intellectual freedom.[1] The American Library Association[2] has many resources available for library staff on collection development policies, including the selection of digital content.

Collection Analysis

Before purchasing databases, staff must know what the library has and how it is used. Data is needed to establish need and predict usage of subscription databases. An analysis of the print collection can help determine what materials patrons find desirable, what materials are not, and where gaps exist in content. Annual usage statistics of subscription databases the library currently owns should be analyzed. Comparisons between the content of the current collection and the content of subscription databases can identify user preferences and needs (see figure 2.1).

Figure 2.1. Collection Data Analysis. *shapecharge/ E+ via Getty Images*

LSS support the **collection analysis** process. It is most helpful to have a systematic approach to collection analysis. The following steps can initiate an analysis of a typical collection.[3]

1. Use integrated library system (ILS) or subscription management software for a usage report.
2. Create a spreadsheet of the data that identifies last accessed, popularity, and other key data about how resources are being used.
3. Use acquisition vendors, book reviews, and so on, to learn about new options.

LSS support acquisitions librarians. Such data would be helpful in determining whether a library should acquire a database that offers research articles, e-books, media, and other information on specific themes or topics. What are the patrons' interests, hobbies, and needs for information?

Needs Assessment

By analyzing and comparing the depth and breadth of content, authorship, and the circulation data, LSS can extrapolate if there is a need by users for a subscription database it does not currently own. How is the current collection being used, and will a new database improve the quantity and quality of information patrons may need? Collection analysis identifies what patrons currently *use*. But collections may not align with what patrons *need*. LSS are in a key position to hear what patrons need because they are the ones who most often interact directly with patrons at checkout or other services. LSS observe what materials patrons use, and often patrons tell them what they seek. The simple question at checkout by the LSS, "Did you find everything you need?" is an important way LSS can gather data to share the shortcomings of the collection and the needs of the patrons with their supervisors.

How do LSS participate in the **needs assessment**? There are several ways. The Online Computer Library Center (OCLC) WebJunction,[4] a site for library staff training and professional learning, offers many ideas and tools to help conduct a library needs assessment. LSS participate in needs assessment by

- understanding and working with documents and suggestions from WebJunction,
- sharing with acquisitions librarians observations of topics that are popular with patrons yet hard to fill,
- asking patrons if they found what they came for, and
- conveying patrons' suggestions to acquisitions librarian.

Online surveys are useful tools for collecting data user information about their current and projected use of databases. A Likert or rating scale of 1 to 5 measures the degree to which a person feels about an issue, identifies a need, or would likely use a product. Survey data from both patrons and staff would be most helpful to acquisition librarians and administration in the selection and purchase of databases. The Digital Library at the University of North Texas[5] provides an example of a thorough needs assessment survey that was designed for students, faculty, and staff about their intended use of its digital collections. Many of its questions, with slight modification, could be adapted for a library survey on subscription databases.

Librarians reach out to peers and other professionals to informally survey their opinions about subscription databases. These suggestions are adapted from a medical school library[6] that wanted evaluative feedback on subscription databases.

1. Find other libraries whose missions are a close match to yours. Ask about the subscription databases they use.
2. Seek information from professional organizations about collection management and databases. For example, does a professional organization offer discounts on certain subscriptions? If so, why were the databases selected and what users do they target?
3. If working in a school or academic library, follow the decisions of curriculum and department committees about new topics or classes to be taught.
4. Schedule a product trial of a subscription database to evaluate whether it is a good fit for the identified needs.

EVALUATION PROCESS

The purpose of obtaining subscription databases is to improve information access for patrons. As with any important acquisition, subscription databases should be evaluated both prior to and after purchase. Prior to purchase, the library staff and, if possible, patrons should have the opportunity to trial its content and their intended use. After purchase, LSS can help evaluate the usefulness of the database by sharing with supervisors their own observations and patron feedback.

Reliability and Reputation

Librarians have well-established policies and procedures for selecting each book, piece of media, and other physical items that are shelved and circulated. However, subscription databases often contain content from hundreds of different companies and publishers. It is impossible to use the same one-on-one selection policy for a subscription database as librarians use to select a specific print magazine. Rather, librarians use multiple means, using factors of reputation and reliability, to evaluate it.

Reliability of a database has many considerations. Professional journals have standards for accepting authors' work and often require an extensive editorial and/or peer review process. Peer review is when a small panel of experts in the same field as the author read and make suggestions to improve the article before it can be considered for publication.

Reputation of database providers and publishers is another important consideration. How often is the database updated? Do searches link to full text or are there only bibliographic citations? Table 2.1 describes key criteria to determine the reliability of a database.

Table 2.1. Reliability of Databases

Authority	What is the reputation of the journals, periodicals, and other resources of the database? If they are of scientific nature, do they require peer review? Use professional library reviewing sources such as *LJ*, *Choice*, *Booklist*, etc. to see how the database is evaluated.
Content	Analyze the subjects or topics presented. Are there topics omitted? Compare to other subscription databases in the same general category. What is the depth and breadth of topics? Does the content address the library needs assessment?
Level	Is the reading and writing level of the database content appropriate for the intended users?
Date	How often is the database updated? Is the information contained in the database date sensitive?
Media and Visuals	Does the database contain media or visuals that help convey information? Who are the producers?
Assistive	Is the database ADA compliant and does it have assistive features and supports? For example, is media close captioned? Is the database offered in multiple languages?
Ease of Use	Is the database easy to use and not confusing? Look for a format that is clean and understandable.
Technical Support	Is technical support robust? Will IT work with your staff to ensure 100 percent reliability?

Database Reviews

Similar to the process of reviewing books, database reviews are now common sources to help influence acquisition decisions. Most the reviews are about recently released products, but at times subscription database reviews may be thematic around a subject area such as literature, science, history, and so on. Reviews in library professional literature are written by librarians who have thoughtfully evaluated the reliability of the databases. Reviews are not marketing materials or advertisements. Librarians are ethically obligated to uncover the strengths and weaknesses of a product. Reviews are essential in the evaluation process.

A review is typically a firsthand experience written in an annotation describing the contents of the database and the opinion about its overall quality, effectiveness, coverage, and sources. The ease of use and depth of searching features, along with any technology requirements of the library are also noted. There are many reviewing sources for databases including *Library Journal, Choice, Booklist, School Library Journal,* and *Resources for College Libraries*. Technical journals and columns, professional organizations, and conferences and workshops are additional sources. Upon the reviews, the acquisition librarian may make the decision to seek a trial.

Trials

A **trial** is a limited amount of time when a library can try a database with its patrons to help evaluate whether it meets the need. Most database vendors offer the library a period of trial use, typically thirty days when staff and users can authentically have full use of the database. This is an opportunity for LSS to introduce a database to patrons and observe its potential value as a new information resource. During the trial, LSS may record both observational and other data about patrons' receptivity and use, such as informal exit surveys that will be later shared with supervisors.

Libraries may arrange for their own trials or may participate in trials through their state library or other state-sponsored purchasing group. The Nebraska Library Commission[7] has a trial site on its webpage where Nebraska libraries can sign up to participate to evaluate new databases. The Connecticut Library Consortium[8] provides for trials of databases that are under their contract for discounts to libraries in Connecticut. LSS can investigate trial opportunities in their states through the state library website or designated discount provider.

Search Features

An important criterion in evaluating a database is its search features. Most scholarly database searching have embedded and robust metadata structures that will cross-reference search queries, providing specific and related results. Search features may vary depending upon the vendor; however, often if the vendor offers multiple products, such as EBSCO or Gale Cengage, its search application is comfortably similar across databases. LSS who become familiar with the databases search features are most helpful to patrons to support the best search practices. LSS can help others conduct searches with advanced search features to ensure the patron's search has an adequate number of hits, produces relevant and legitimate information, and produces results accessible in full text or other media formats.

Searching aggregated or multiple databases at once is called **federated searching**. The database provider sets up a search box that interfaces with some or all of their multiple databases. Textbox 2.1 suggests ways to use federated searching.

In chapter 3 advanced search features will be further discussed as they relate to discovery products.

TEXTBOX 2.1: FEDERATED SEARCHING

One search query simultaneously used for multiple databases.

- Enter search terms in the *basic* search box. Expect many results! If needed, narrow the results by

  - selecting search limiters such as full text or media type;
  - selecting Advanced Search and limit by disciplines;
  - narrowing with field options such as author, journal source, ISBN, etc.; and
  - sorting the results list by relevance, date newest, date oldest.

Statistics and Metrics

Another way to evaluate a database is by its user statistics. Statistics is a branch of mathematics whereby numerical or quantitative data is collected, analyzed, and used to make predictions.

LSS can keep informal statistics of use during the trial period simply by taking random samplings of how often the database is used or through brief exit surveys. Once the library subscribes to the database, statistical data is available to be generated into regular reports. Librarians and others use these reports to monitor not only the amount of usage but how the database is used and shared. These data are invaluable when deciding whether to renew the subscription. They also help library staff understand patrons' usage patterns (anonymously), such as which items in the database are most popular. If staff find database usage is not up to expectations, intervention, such as targeted one-on-one instruction, can be taken.

Metrics are methods of measuring. How we measure will influence the type and number of statistics collected. A more common type of metrics used in business, including libraries and education, are **performance metrics** that include sales, profit, return on investment, customer happiness, customer reviews, personal reviews, overall quality, and reputation in a marketplace. Performance metrics can vary considerably when viewed through different industries.[9]

PlumX Metrics

While not exclusive to libraries, PlumX Metrics is available from EBSCO and other major scholarly databases to help librarians understand how individual content is being used. The performance metrics[10] are divided into five categories: citations, usage, captures, mentions, and social media.

- Citation counts in PlumX Metrics are measures of how many times a research piece has been cited by others.
- Usage is a way to count how many have read an article or otherwise used it for research.
- Captures track when end users bookmark, favorite, become a reader, become a watcher, and so forth.
- Mentions are the blog posts, comments, reviews, and Wikipedia links about an article or piece of research.
- Social media includes the tweets, Facebook likes, and so on, that reference the research.

PlumX Metrics provides data for how journal articles are used. Its metrics for one article showed 459 abstract views, 180 full-text views, and 34 links. In the captures category, there were 25 exports or saves and 1 reading.

While monthly or annual statistics provide an overall assessment of the use of a database, performance metrics tell the story of how specific articles, media, and other formats of information have been used. Both types of data provide librarians insight into the success of the database.

ACQUISITIONS PROCESS

Unlike the purchase of books, the most common method libraries use to acquire access to databases is through subscription leasing. Subscriptions are agreements with vendors to lease or use a product for a specific period in a specific manner. Databases, while occasionally purchased, are more commonly acquired through subscriptions because of their outright expense. Agreements are reached between the library and vendor that include the length of the contract, price, patron privileges, and types of access, vendor support, training materials, and technology requirements.

Pricing

Most providers do not advertise their prices for subscription databases. They negotiate with individual libraries based on formulas that may involve

- type of library,
- number of users or patrons,
- population of the town or college, and
- expected use.

Small- to medium-sized public libraries and large school districts may budget in a range of $5,000–$25,000 or more per year for subscription databases. Academic and special libraries could budget well over $500,000 per year for databases. Unlike the book collections, patrons do not "see" the databases on shelves to browse and make selections. Because databases are not obviously displayed, it is important that LSS become very familiar with all of the library databases so that they can suggest and even demonstrate them to users.

Discount Purchasing

There is power in numbers. Discounts may be offered to libraries through a consortium or a group purchase. It behooves the library to ask vendors if group discounts are available, and if so, to seek partners in purchasing. Discounts may also be given to new users as a means to attract business or to libraries that can pay in advance. A library may be able to negotiate last year's price for early renewal.

Some states or agencies authorized to negotiate contracts on behalf of libraries and schools obtain deep discounts for member libraries. For example, the Washington State Library of the state of Washington[11] negotiates discount pricing for ProQuest and other databases for all libraries in the state. LSS who suspect their library is not subscribing to databases should investigate if their state offers discount purchasing via its state library, state department of education, or other authorized agency. Subscription databases may become affordable to the library through discount purchasing.

Statewide Discounts

Most of the fifty state libraries have contracts with database providers for a selection of databases for their residents. Residents have access to these excellent databases through their public library. For students, the state also contracts for school and university use. These contracts save libraries millions of dollars in subscriptions. The state libraries obtain discount purchasing at much better pricing than any individual library can get. Vendors are agreeable because they have large sales from states. Taxpayers who would be funding the higher cost if libraries purchased alone benefit from the savings. Statewide contracts support lifelong learning and result in a more educated and informed workforce.

LSS have an important responsibility to become familiar with all databases provided by the state and to ensure they are easy to access on computer workstations. LSS share their knowledge of the databases with patrons who seek information. Similarly, statewide college and university systems also obtain discount purchasing for academic databases that are available to higher education users. LSS working in academic libraries should know about these databases and be able to promote them to users and support patrons in their use (see figure 2.2).

Figure 2.2. Promote Databases. *pictafolio/ E+ via Getty Images*

License Agreements

Subscription databases are not for indefinite library ownership. Libraries and providers enter into a **license agreement** that explicitly states a specified period of time and under certain conditions the provider allows the library and its patrons to use the database. Each provider has its own legal licensing agreement. LSS may be helpful by reading agreements and asking questions about such things as patron privileges to ensure the agreement meets the needs of users. The majority of agreements are made for one year because

1. public and school libraries are more often not allowed to enter multiyear contracts because their budgets are based on taxes and set on an annual basis;
2. both parties may want to change the terms of the agreement; and
3. the cost is often determined on town or school population, which may change year to year.

License agreements also specify copyright and ownership of the content. The library does not own subscription databases and typically are not allowed to archive the content. Printing and copying rights are specified in the agreement. The example of EBSCO license agreement with Nebraska Library Commission[12] is helpful for those who are new or want to better understand library subscription database contracts.

Access

Patron access may vary according to the license agreement or contract. Access will always be available within the library or institution. **Remote access**, or access from anywhere outside the library, is important to negotiate for patrons. In order to use a database remotely, the account is set up so that some type of information that authorizes the patron as a user is supplied, such as the library barcode, a password, or a combination of both.

Computers have an IP or internet protocol address that identifies them on the internet network. Somewhat similar to a telephone number that is associated with a phone, the IP is associated with a particular computer. When setting up a new database, the library shares its workstation IP addresses with the vendor so that users at these computers have access to the databases. The same applies to wireless access. The range of IP addresses associated with the wireless access is also shared so that users inside the library can access the database on their own devices using the library Wi-Fi. At larger libraries, universities, and schools, computers have a **dynamic IP range**. Simply put, when a patron logs on to the library computer he or she is assigned the next open IP address that is already authenticated. This efficient process increases access speed for the user and communicates to the database provider that this computer user is cleared to access the database.

Most subscription databases allow **simultaneous use**. Simultaneous use means multiple people can access the database at the same time. Typically simultaneous usage is set to such a high number that it appears unlimited to the patrons because at no time will all accounts be utilized. However, to rein in costs, some subscription databases allow for limited simultaneous use, such as a maximum of five users simultaneously. When the sixth person tries to use the database, she is notified to wait until an opening occurs. Limited simultaneous use is desirable for very expensive databases that will have specialized use by fewer people.

WEBINARS AND TRAINING

Each subscription vendor has its own interface and searching capabilities. In the absence of formal training, LSS can do much to guide their own learning to effectively use subscription databases on the job with patrons. Vendors offer training webinars of their product. A webinar is a real-time shared learning experience with an instructor and others located at different sites. A webinar is scheduled for a specific time, and participants are asked to preregister so that access information is provided beforehand. At the designated time the participant may call in to the instructor and open the training website. The real-time instructor will guide learning of the product using resources on the website. Participants are encouraged to ask questions. Webinars may be repeated and are an excellent way to become familiar with subscription databases.

Another method of training is for LSS to use provider-created tutorials for self-paced learning. It is common for each database to have tutorials or presentations that cover in great detail the functions of the product and how to effectively use its features. Patrons can be directed to provider tutorials. Providers offer many promotion brochures, posters, and even short media clips that can be shared by library staff and patrons. YouTube is another source that is robust with educational tutorials on how to use popular subscription databases.

LSS learn technology from each other. When the library management provides support and encouragement for staff learning, there likely will be a climate that fosters collaboration and peer coaching among LSS.

CHAPTER SUMMARY

Subscription databases are a core information resource in all types of libraries. Users today expect to obtain information digitally and automatically seek the internet for answers. What many of them are unaware of is that libraries invest in subscription databases that provide authoritative and trustworthy published content that has been vetted by scholarly or peer review. The quality of information far surpasses the sporadic and often biased information from the web.

LSS have important roles in the selection, evaluation, and acquisition processes of subscription databases. Working directly with the public and being attentive to their information needs, LSS can introduce, demonstrate, and support patrons' use of high-quality subscription databases on a wide variety of general and subject-specific knowledge.

DISCUSSION QUESTIONS

1. Why are collection analysis and needs assessment important to the selection process?

2. What are performance metrics and how are they used in the evaluation process?
3. What is a subscription trial and how does it work?
4. Where may libraries find discount purchasing for database subscriptions?
5. How can LSS learn to be expert users so that they, in turn, can help others with library subscription databases?

ACTIVITY

Depending upon whether you are a student, library employee, or have the benefit of subscription databases from your state library, select two unfamiliar databases from a library where you have user privileges. For each database do the following:

1. Read the online help and view any tutorial provided by the database provider.
2. Search YouTube for instructional videos on the use of the database.
3. Go to the database provider website and see if they offer instructional materials about the database. Read or view all that is offered. If there is a webinar session available, sign up and take the webinar.
4. Construct three searches of the database. Do each search in the basic search. Then do the search again using the advanced search features. Try different search limiters (e.g., select journals, time periods, etc.)
5. Make a list of features you did not know about this database. Include the strengths or usefulness of the content.
6. With your new knowledge of the database, write a simple, one-page brochure about the database and how to use it. Write the brochure in a helpful way for someone who is unfamiliar with it.

NOTES

1. Helen N. Levenson, "Notes on Operations: Nimble Collection Development Policies: An Achievable Goal," *Library Resources & Technical Services* 63, no. 4 (October 2019): 206–19, https://search.ebscohost.com/login.aspx?direct=true&AuthType=cookie,ip,cpid&custid=csl&db=aph&AN=139888723&site=ehost-live&scope=site.

2. American Library Association, "Collection Development," Tools, Publications and Resources, last modified 2020, accessed June 9, 2020, http://www.ala.org/tools/atoz/Collection%20Development/collectiondevelopment.

3. Sarah Jorgenson and Rene Burress, "Analyzing the Diversity of a High School Library Collection," *Knowledge Quest* 48, no. 5 (May/June 2020): 48–53, https://search.ebscohost.com/login.aspx?direct=true&AuthType=cookie,ip,cpid&custid=csl&db=aph&AN=143267576&site=ehost-live&scope=site.

4. OCLC, "Needs Assessment," *WebJunction*, last modified 2020, accessed June 10, 2020, https://www.webjunction.org/search-results.html#q=Needs%20Assessment.

5. University of North Texas, "Needs Assessment Survey," UNT Digital Library, last modified 2020, accessed June 10, 2020, https://digital.library.unt.edu/ark:/67531/metadc33129/m1/1/.

6. Nadine Dexter, Joanne Muellenbach, and Elizabeth Lorbeer, "Building New Twenty-First Century Medical School Libraries from the Ground Up: Challenges, Experiences, and Lessons Learned," *Journal of the Medical Library Association* 107, no. 1 (January 2019): 6–15, https://search.ebscohost.com/login.aspx?direct=true&AuthType=cookie,ip,cpid&custid=csl&db=aph&AN=134089907&site=ehost-live&scope=site.

7. Nebraska Library Commission, "Database Trials," last modified 2020, accessed June 10, 2020, http://nlc.nebraska.gov/discounts/trial.aspx.

8. Connecticut Library Consortium, "Discounts from Scholastic Digital," last modified 2020, accessed June 11, 2020, https://www.ctlibrarians.org/page/scholasticdigital.

9. American Society for Quality, "What Are Performance Metrics?" *About Performance Metrics*, last modified 2020, accessed June 13, 2020, https://asq.org/quality-resources/metrics.

10. Plum Analytics, "PlumX Metrics," last modified 2020, accessed June 13, 2020, https://plumanalytics.com/learn/about-metrics/.

11. Washington State Library, "Statewide Database Licensing Project," last modified 2020, accessed June 14, 2020, https://www.sos.wa.gov/library/libraries/projects/sdl/.

12. Nebraska Library Commission, "Database Trials."

REFERENCES, SUGGESTED READINGS, AND WEBSITES

American Library Association. "Collection Development." Tools, Publications and Resources. Last modified 2020. Accessed June 9, 2020. http://www.ala.org/tools/atoz/Collection%20 Development/collectiondevelopment.

American Society for Quality. "What Are Performance Metrics?" *About Performance Metrics*. Last modified 2020. Accessed June 13, 2020. https://asq.org/quality-resources/metrics.

Connecticut Library Consortium. "Discounts from Scholastic Digital." Last modified 2020. Accessed June 11, 2020. https://www.ctlibrarians.org/page/scholasticdigital.

Dexter, Nadine, Joanne Muellenbach, and Elizabeth Lorbeer. "Building New Twenty-First Century Medical School Libraries from the Ground Up: Challenges, Experiences, and Lessons Learned." *Journal of the Medical Library Association* 107, no. 1 (January 2019): 6–15. https://search.ebscohost.com/login.aspx?direct=true&AuthType=cookie,ip,cpid& custid=csl&db=aph&AN=134089907&site=ehost-live&scope=site.

Jorgenson, Sarah, and Rene Burress. "Analyzing the Diversity of a High School Library Collection." *Knowledge Quest* 48, no. 5 (May/June 2020): 48–53. https://search.ebsco host.com/login.aspx?direct=true&AuthType=cookie,ip,cpid&custid=csl&db=aph&AN =143267576&site=ehost-live&scope=site.

Levenson, Helen N. "Notes on Operations: Nimble Collection Development Policies: An Achievable Goal." *Library Resources & Technical Services* 63, no. 4 (October 2019): 206–19. https://search.ebscohost.com/login.aspx?direct=true&AuthType=cookie,ip,cpid&cust id=csl&db=aph&AN=139888723&site=ehost-live&scope=site.

Nebraska Library Commission. "Database Trials." Last modified 2020. Accessed June 10, 2020. http://nlc.nebraska.gov/discounts/trial.aspx.

———. "EBSCO License Agreement for Database Licensing." Last modified 2020. Accessed June 14, 2020. http://www.nlc.state.ne.us/discounts/ebscoagreement.aspx.

OCLC. "Needs Assessment." *WebJunction*. Last modified 2020. Accessed June 10, 2020. https://www.webjunction.org/search-results.html#q=Needs%20Assessment.

Plum Analytics. "PlumX Metrics." Last modified 2020. Accessed June 13, 2020. https:// plumanalytics.com/learn/about-metrics/.

University of North Texas. "Needs Assessment Survey." UNT Digital Library. Last modified 2020. Accessed June 10, 2020. https://digital.library.unt.edu/ark:/67531/metadc33129 /m1/1/.

Washington State Library. "Statewide Database Licensing Project." Last modified 2020. Accessed June 14, 2020. https://www.sos.wa.gov/library/libraries/projects/sdl/.

"The Web vs. Library Databases—A Comparison." Unpublished manuscript, Library, Yale University, New Haven, CT, n.d. Accessed June 11, 2020. http://www.library.yale.edu.

CHAPTER 3

Library Discovery Services

LSS know the role of technology in creating, identifying, retrieving, and accessing informa-tion resources and demonstrate facility with appropriate information discovery tools.

Topics Covered in This Chapter
Discovery and Delivery
    Searching
    Procurement
Discovery Libraries
    WorldCat Discovery
    State Digital Libraries
    User-Generated Content
Vendors and Products
    Vendors
    Discovery Search Example
    Training
Chapter Summary

Key Terms

Bundling—Multiple databases, typically all from a single vendor, are sold as a unit to the library customer.

Direct Object Identifier—Commonly referred to as the DOI, this is a set of numbers, letters, and symbols that uniquely and permanently identifies an article or document. The DOI links the item to the web. The DOI may be used in bibliographic citations.

Discovery—This is the ability to search library catalogs, databases, and other resources simultaneously.

Metadata—This includes both basic bibliographic information such as the title, author, publisher, date, etc. and wider and more thorough descriptions and associations about the attributes of library resources.

Open access—These are scholarly articles, commentaries, research reports, etc. that are made free to anyone on the web.

Search entry—Acting like a search engine for a specific discovery service, this is the program used to simultaneously find items in the library ILS, subscription databases, and open-access resources on a subject or keywords.

DISCOVERY AND DELIVERY

Library **discovery** services provide the ability to search multiple sources of information at once. These sources are local library items, online subscription databases, and open-access resources. **Open-access resources** are research materials that have been made available to the general public free of charge by the authors. These include data and datasets, books and articles, including scholarly research articles without copyright infringement.[1] The nature of the content discovered is highly aligned with academic research; thus these systems were primarily created for academic libraries. However, with the explosion of information sources, including local digital collections, the need for a simple entry to search multiple resources simultaneously also exists in school, public, and special libraries. Not a Google search of limitless websites, discovery services focus on more research or scholarly content. However, like search engines, discovery services use indexes. These are tools that search seamlessly across a wide range of indexed local and remote content. Relevance-ranked results provide a single point of entry into many, if not all, of the library's collections.[2] The single point of entry is often the library online public access catalog (OPAC), whereby LSS simultaneously search the library's print, media, and digital collections, subscription databases, and open-access resources. Figure 3.1 is based on a vendor's product[3] and shows a simple representation of how discovery services work.

1. The patron enters a search query into the library OPAC.
2. The search term is compared to the discovery service index. The index contains bibliographic and **metadata,** subjects, full text and abstracts of database articles, URL links, and **direct object identifiers** (DOI).
3. If there is a direct and reliable link to the result, it can move forward to the search interface.
4. If the link is broken or cannot be verified for a potential result for the search, the result is sent to the link resolver. The link resolver finds a workaround such as the DOI as an alternative location source or may find links to the entire e-book or e-journal so that the article can be located and retrieved from its full source.
5. Once a good link is established, the results are screened in the search interface. Acting as filters, the interface works to screen out results that do not meet the user's criteria.

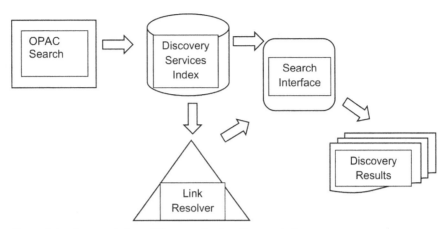

Figure 3.1. Representation of Discovery Services Process. *Author*

Searching

There are three types of searching:

1. *Aggregated searches* yield wide-based results from across the web by using a favorite search engine as the point of entry.
2. *Federated searches* yield specific results from typically a single vendor's full line of databases or products. The user enters a query into the vendor's search box. The documents and all other content files hosted by the vendor are searched in a proprietary index.
3. *Discovery services* offer search access via OPAC to local library collections, the library's online subscription databases that may be from multiple vendors, and open-access documents and files available on the web.

Aggregated search results are presented in rank order. To aggregate means to gather disparate parts or things into one mass or place. This is the type of search that occurs with most internet search engines. Websites from all over the world may be aggregated into one display screen we call our results list. Federated searching is discussed in chapter 2. Because discovery products continue to improve, the differences or gaps between federated searching and discovery services are closing. Until recently, federated searches were limited to the product line of databases and other sources of a single vendor. Today a federated search of EBSCO's databases would not include databases of Gale Cengage. As the field of vendors may change and technologies advance, the line between federated searching and discovery services is narrowing.

Procurement

Patrons who use discovery services expect timely access or delivery of the e-book, full text article, image, or other type of document or file. Delivery services share online catalogs, and member libraries control the parameters of how they will circulate their collections through interlibrary loan. Patrons may be able to place electronic holds on some items without staff intervention, which saves LSS time and expedites the process. If holds are allowed, books and physical items may be delivered through a consortium, institutional, or statewide service. Depending upon the library and situation, they may also be shipped via mail or carrier with responsibility for postage predetermined and return policies clearly stated.

The majority of resources found through delivery services are digital. Subscription databases are clear as to whether they offer full text or abstract only. If they offer full text, most common file types are PDF and HTML that can be downloaded by the user. Subscription databases and open-access materials are typically in full text. For open-access items, Google Scholar is often a reliable way to obtain articles and other research. For some selected items, such as educational documents in ERIC or ProQuest's thesis or dissertations, the user level of subscription database may not offer full text. If this is the case, there are procedures for ordering and purchasing the full document from the vendors. If LSS are unfamiliar with such procedures, let the patron know that another staff member will assist.

Not all government documents are digitized, and the user may need to seek assistance from library staff to have a document photocopied, and so forth. LSS may be asked to help with document delivery. If it is not clear how it can be done, always seek advice from the reference librarians.

DISCOVERY LIBRARIES

Academic libraries have a critical role in research as they supply texts, databases, and other information sources. General web information sources, while often helpful, are not, as a group, peer reviewed and vetted for reliability and validity. Some of the key advantages to databases versus websites are listed below.

- Database content often is peer reviewed or has scholarly filters.
- Results are manageable.
- Articles have been vetted through a publisher.
- The search process provides comprehensive features.[4]

WorldCat Discovery

WorldCat is a global online catalog of mostly academic library collections. Using early machine readable cataloging records (MARC) cataloging and computing technology, the OCLC Online Union Catalog was established in 1971 by librarians at Alden Library at Ohio University. Now known as WorldCat, the online catalog includes approximately five hundred million bibliographic records and more than three trillion holdings.[5] With almost five hundred languages represented, WorldCat is truly an international online catalog.

Discovery services simultaneously search online catalogs, subscription databases, and open-access scholarly material. Being the largest online catalog with so much content, it was logical for WorldCat[6] to partner with database vendors to become a leading comprehensive discovery service. With ten thousand members, most of them academic libraries, WorldCat Discovery offers a **search entry** for not only the rich bibliographic and holding records of members but also for the internal and external databases created or subscribed to by member libraries. WorldCat Discovery connects users to the electronic content of their library by combining data about a library's e-resources with linking features that make collections easier to share, manage, and use across multiple systems. In other words, WorldCat includes records from major vendors such as EBSCO and ProQuest, Gale and Springer, and Wiley and Elsevier, among many other content suppliers.[7]

It is important to note that WorldCat Discovery service is not tied to a single database vendor. Rather, unlike traditional federated searching where only a single vendor's products could be searched, WorldCat libraries obtain discovery access to all of their subscription databases, regardless of vendor, with a single query in the online catalog search box. Free and open-access materials are also simultaneously accessible. WorldCat's members are primarily academic, with a minority of large special and public libraries. It serves as a model for how smaller consortia of public, special, and school libraries can broker with vendors for discovery services when the ILS is linked to subscription databases and local collections.

While WorldCat is a leader in discovery services, many people are using variations of such services through their state libraries. Many state libraries have created union or statewide catalogs and provide a number of subscription databases, as well as local digital collections, to their residents to provide opportunities for resource sharing and higher learning. Relationships between state libraries and state universities are strong, making it logical for them to partner to advance discovery services for state residents.

State Digital Libraries

Many state libraries offer their residents a statewide online catalog of bibliographic records and holdings of the collections of the school, academic, public, and some special libraries located within that state. They may also contract with subscription databases to provide an array of accessible research for patrons. Typically access is acquired by student ID and/or public library cardholders to the state digital library. Some state libraries have contracted with a discovery service for simultaneous searching of its statewide online catalog, local digital collections, subscribed research databases, and free open-access resources. The digital libraries of Kentucky, Alaska, and Oklahoma are examples of how entire populations of states, without restriction through their libraries, have access to discovery services.

Kentucky Department for Libraries and Archives (KDLA)—Kentucky offers comprehensive discovery services to its residents using WorldCat Discovery as its search entry. Kentucky is a WorldCat member that, in addition to sharing its statewide catalog, has also linked its subscription databases, archives, local collections, government, and other digital information through WorldCat Discovery services for comprehensive searching. KDLA WorldCat Discovery provides the following questions and responses about their discovery services.

Q: What types of items does WorldCat Discovery search?
A: WorldCat Discovery allows you to search for all items (books, audiobooks, DVDs, etc.) that are physically located at KDLA, content from research databases, and items from other libraries worldwide.

Q: How do I use WorldCat Discovery?
A: Enter your keywords into the single search box and click on the Search button. Use the options on the left to refine your search.

Q: What if my WorldCat results were not relevant to my search?
A: If you are finding that WorldCat Discovery results do not fit your search, you may need to refine or enhance your search strategies.

Alaska State Library (ASL)—Alaska is an example of the cooperation among multiple agencies to bring EBSCO discovery services to residents in a state less populated yet geographically more expansive than any other. While not a department of the Alaska State Library, the Alaska Library Network (ALN) is a nonprofit consortium that works with the ASL to support libraries by negotiating discounts for materials and databases. The ALN also administers the Alaska Digital Library, which makes subscription databases primarily from EBSCO available to all residents using EBSCO Connect discovery services.

As do most state libraries, the ASL archives and catalogs state documents and other important government materials. The University of Alaska is another important partner whose collections are represented in the statewide catalog. With all institutions working for the common goal and using EBSCO discovery services, through the ASL online catalog, state residents have access in a single search entry to the collections of the State Library, the Alaska university libraries, public libraries, and the Alaska Digital Library. It is important to note that state government documents are cataloged and included as resources in the discovery service.

The Oklahoma Department of Libraries (ODL)—The ODL offers discovery services to its residents through a dual pathway. As a member of WorldCat, it provides access to ODL collections and engages in interlibrary loan from other WorldCat libraries. Users can also reach free open-access resources through WorldCat. ODL uses EBSCO for its subscription and local databases called the Digital Prairie, which serves as the state digital library. Digital Prairie was established prior to discovery services and continues to be separate from WorldCat. Digital Prairie has a search entry for subscription databases and state digital collections. Because the ODL is a member of WorldCat, in the future searching of all discovery services for ODL could be through a combined search box representing WorldCat Discovery and EBSCO.

User-Generated Content

Most discovery services offer content that is user generated through social media or knowledge-sharing tools. A user responds with her own commentary, which is then posted and becomes part of the database. For example, if a library subscribes to EBSCO Novelist, one of its features is to encourage the user to rate and give his own reviews for titles. The educational purpose of social media sites such as YouTube where viewers have the option to generate content can be found via discovery services. User-generated content may also be found from professional and scientific organizations that encourage discourse among viewers on new research and innovation. Many discovery services include social media components that present an opportunity for users to engage in conversation with the library and the community, creating shared knowledge and demonstrating the value of libraries as institutions for information and learning.[8]

Libraries have the choice to turn on or off user-generated content. If it is allowed, the library should adopt policies that define the time, place, and manner in which the user contributes the content to the library's discovery system. Any restrictions must be reasonable and cannot be discriminatory. Libraries should declare user-generated content. If a publicly funded library does choose to allow users to contribute content to the library's discovery system, the commenting system may be considered a limited public forum. Staff and community should be informed of policies and expectations about usage.[9]

Who uses discovery services? The potential is for every library patron in the United States to be a user through their local and state libraries. Academic libraries have accustomed students to the service, and once graduated, they will expect to use discovery services in their home, workplace, and on the go with mobile devices. The market is strong for continued growth. In the next section some of the vendors and products are discussed.

VENDORS AND PRODUCTS

Most LSS will work with discovery services, making it important for them to know the vendors, products, and terminology. While competition exists among vendors to provide unique environments and options, the field of commercial vendors for integrated library systems (ILS) and discovery systems is fairly narrow. Consolidations and buyouts have occurred between and among discovery vendors, leaving just a few major companies dominating the market.

Because libraries have the MARC 21 cataloging standard for records, large statewide and union catalogs can accept and merge bibliographic records from all types of libraries and ILS systems. Some vendors who offer the software, equipment, and support for ILS also offer discovery services that are linked to the online catalog. But discovery vendors do not have to be in the business of managing and hosting libraries' online catalogs. Like WorldCat, where record data is shared via linking and not gathered into one central catalog, so too can discovery vendors such as EBSCO, with its rich subscription databases, link its resources to libraries' catalogs. Figure 3.2 shows this phenomenon.

In option A, the library contracts with the ILS vendor for its system for circulation, cataloging, OPAC, acquisitions, serials, and other functions critical to the library operations. The vendor also offers discovery services, which are searched through the OPAC search feature. In option B, the library contracts its ILS system with another vendor. The discovery services vendor is the same company from which the library obtains the bulk of its subscription databases. This vendor enables links to the ILS, local collections, and open-access resources. Option B discovery services are searched through the subscription database's search entry. More likely than not, libraries that are satisfied with their ILS vendor will stay with the vendor (option A) if it offers quality and cost-effective discovery services.

Option A – ILS vendor is the host

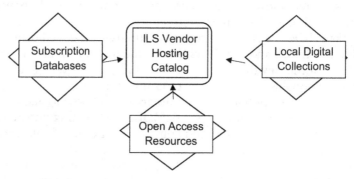

Option B – Discovery vendor is the host

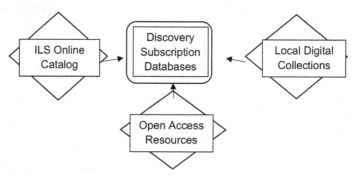

Figure3.2.   Linking Discovery Services. *Author*

Vendors

The discovery vendor field has shrunk, with the largest companies obtaining the greatest market share. One way to think about vendors is in two sizes or tiers. The largest vendors have been most successful with their database products because they have the breadth and depth of information libraries seek. It is inevitable that vendors and products will evolve and change as new ways of linking data become expected and commonplace. Discovery services evolved from single vendors, such as EBSCO or ProQuest, offering federated searching or one-stop searching to a suite or all of their databases. Linking the ILS for record searching and free open-access scholarly materials rounded out discovery services as we currently know them.

Selling a predetermined package of databases is called **bundling**. Bundled databases are most often sold as a unit with little or no choice from the customer to be able to separate them. The vendor may offer choice among bundles, such as a group of databases specific to K–12 schools, but libraries would not be able to select specific databases without getting access to the others. Vendors make bundles cost effective, but perhaps some libraries do not want some of the databases in their collections and would rather purchase à la carte.[10] Some patrons would rather be informed and direct their research by selecting specific topical databases rather than search a bundled package. Some services allow users to select or deselect specific databases in the bundle.

Those vendors that offer ILS are heavily invested in library management systems and can offer sophisticated features for searching and browsing the library collections. However, they fall short on offering content for discovery and must rely on other database vendors.[11] More libraries are seeking alternatives to expensive ILS through open source and make the determination that it is not as critical to have the ILS provider and shop other vendors for their research content. As librarians use professional knowledge and skills to select books to best represent their patrons, so to do librarians need to select databases that offer content that supports the information and research needs of their users (see figure 3.3).

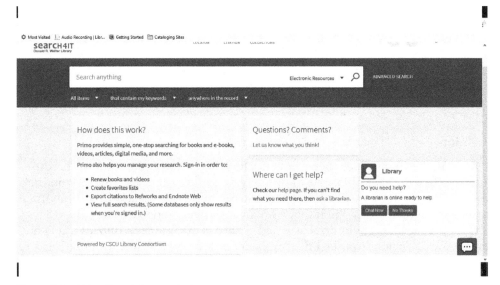

Figure 3.3. Primo Search Screen. *Author*

Discovery Search Example

Using the ExLibris product Primo,

1. In the Search Anything box, enter a search term.
2. Set limiters by material type, keywords, or location in record with drop arrows underneath the search box.
3. The search term "offshore wind farm" yielded more than 66,000 results defaulted by term relevance.
4. Using features on the left side of the screen in figure 3.4, the user can limit results by peer review, resource type, new records, date, author, subject, collections, journal title, and more.
5. Shown are delivery options for materials not available online.

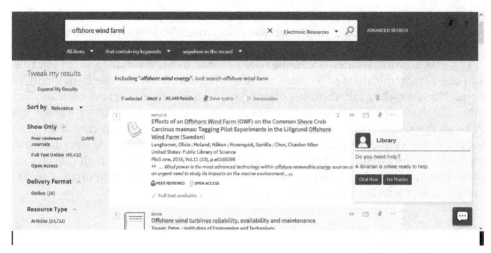

Figure 3.4. Discovery Search Example. *Author*

The amount of content and information from this simple search is astonishing, and it could even be overwhelming to most users. In the next section the need for discovery training and how LSS may obtain it are discussed.

Training

LSS are in the forefront as they work closely with the technology and its products, and are often the staff library customers rely on for help and support. LSS routinely use the ILS to check out books, catalog items, run reports, and other important management operations. But if they work in a discovery services library, the ILS may also be the search entry to databases and scholarly open-access content. If it is not, the library collections may be linked to database searching as it is with ExLibris and OCLC. Regardless of the setup, LSS are expected to help patrons with their information needs. LSS can reinforce instruction by professional librarians by explaining the benefits of the library's chosen system and showing users how to obtain the benefits of the systems functions.

All ILS and discovery content vendors offer instructional and training materials. Many offer online chat help from professional librarians. But patrons often want the support of a staff member with whom they can discuss their search approach and needs. It behooves every LSS to be a user of their library discovery services and to take the training made available to them.

Using EBSCO[12] as an example, training is offered in numerous ways and formats:

- Live classes on a regular basis for staff who work in libraries that are EBSCO customers.
- Recorded sessions of the webinars that are available to anyone at any time with a thorough description of the topic, trainer, and learner expectations.
- Many articles and other documents for downloading.

In addition, via YouTube there is a comprehensive offering of EBSCO training videos and videos made by academic and other librarians. The LibGuides Community,[13] a wealth of information mostly created by academic librarians, leads to an extensive number of LibGuides that support training of discovery products.

Contacting the vendor is always a reasonable way to learn about a product. Marketing and sales often have instructional materials and training options. Sometimes no more than a phone call is needed to get the answer to a question that has stymied staff and users. Vendors appreciate user feedback that can improve their products.

What is the future of discovery services? They are definitely here to stay but will certainly change as technology evolves. In the larger picture, most research begins with web searches and not discovery searches. LSS and librarians can introduce, instruct, and support their patrons in using these remarkable resources. With artificial intelligence systems becoming more commonplace, so may the way users are supported change. It is important for LSS to be users of discovery services and to keep current with advancements and new features as they occur.

CHAPTER SUMMARY

Any database has the potential to be searched by discovery, making it imperative that LSS are knowledgeable of best practices to guide users to searches and to help them select resources from overwhelming numbers of results. LSS who know the role of technology in creating, identifying, retrieving, and accessing information resources and demonstrate facility with appropriate information discovery tools can effectively use discovery services in both their personal lives and in their work with others.

DISCUSSION QUESTIONS

1. What are some of the reasons WorldCat Discovery has a large market share with academic libraries?
2. What role can state libraries have in providing discovery services for their residents?
3. What concerns should libraries have with user-generated content?
4. What should patrons know before they use a discovery service to make their experience more successful?
5. Where can LSS obtain training to be better prepared to help others with discovery services?

ACTIVITY

Select instructional resources to share with other LSS for the discovery service EBSCO Connect (or a discovery service that your library subscribes to). In order to find appropriate content:

1. View and select three training resources from the vendor training site that would be most helpful to LSS who are unfamiliar with the service.
2. View and select three YouTube videos that support the training you recommend LSS receive.
3. View and select three guides from the LibGuides Community about the discovery service that will also be helpful to new users.

Once you have identified the nine resources, create a brochure that describes each resource and what can be learned from viewing them. Trial test the brochure with three other staff members. Provide a means for trial feedback that can be used to help refine the brochure before it is shared with the full staff.

NOTES

1. Central Michigan University Library, "Website Research: Open Access Resources," CMU University Libraries, last modified July 10, 2020, accessed August 8, 2020, https://libguides .cmich.edu/web_research/oa.

2. Marshall Breeding, "Web-Scale Discovery Services: Finding the Right Balance," *American Libraries*, January 14, 2014, accessed August 7, 2020, https://americanlibrariesmagazine .org/2014/01/14/web-scale-discovery-services/.

3. James M. Day, "Discovery Services: Basics and Resources," Library Technology Launchpad: Library Technology for Every Librarian, last modified March 8, 2017, accessed August 8, 2020, https://libtechlaunchpad.com/2017/03/08/discovery-services-basics-and-resources/.

4. "The Web vs. Library Databases—a Comparison," chart, Yale Libraries, n.d., accessed August 10, 2020, http://web.library.yale.edu.

5. OCLC, "Inside WorldCat," WorldCat, last modified 2020, accessed August 10, 2020, https://www.oclc.org/en/worldcat/inside-worldcat.html.

6. OCLC, "WorldCat Discovery," OCLC, last modified 2020, accessed August 10, 2020, https://www.oclc.org/en/worldcat-discovery.html.

7. OCLC, "Inside WorldCat."

8. American Library Association, "User-Generated Content in Library Discovery Systems: An Interpretation of the Library Bill of Rights," Issues & Advocacy, last modified June 24, 2019, accessed August 9, 2020, http://www.ala.org/advocacy/intfreedom/librarybill/interpretations/usergenerated.

9. American Library Association, "User-Generated Content."

10. Marshall Breeding, "Discovery Services: Bundled or Separate?," *American Libraries* 60, no. 1/2 (January/February 2019): 71, https://search.ebscohost.com/login.aspx?direct=true&AuthType=cookie,ip,cpid&custid=csl&db=ulh&AN=133975635&site=eds-live&scope=site.

11. Marshall Breeding, "The Ongoing Challenges of Academic Library Discovery Services," *Computers in Libraries* 40, no. 1 (January/February 2020): 9–11, accessed August 14, 2020, https://search.ebscohost.com/login.aspx?direct=true&AuthType=cookie,ip,cpid&custid=csl&db=aph&AN=141250481&site=ehost-live&scope=site.

12. EBSCO Industries, Inc., "EBSCO Training," EBSCO Connect, last modified April 30, 2020, accessed August 14, 2020, https://connect.ebsco.com/s/article/EBSCO-Training?language=en_US.

13. Springshare, "LibGuides Community," LibGuides Community, last modified 2020, accessed August 14, 2020, https://community.libguides.com/.

REFERENCES, SUGGESTED READINGS, AND WEBSITES

Alaska State Libraries, Archives and Museums. "Alaska State Library." Online Catalog. Last modified 2020. Accessed August 12, 2020. https://jlc-web.uaa.alaska.edu/client/en_US/asl/.

American Library Association. "Library Bill of Rights." Issues & Advocacy. Last modified 2020. Accessed August 12, 2020. http://www.ala.org/advocacy/intfreedom/librarybill.

———. "User-Generated Content in Library Discovery Systems: An Interpretation of the Library Bill of Rights." Issues & Advocacy. Last modified June 24, 2019. Accessed August 9, 2020. http://www.ala.org/advocacy/intfreedom/librarybill/interpretations/usergenerated.

Breeding, Marshall. "Discovery Services: Bundled or Separate?" *American Libraries* 60, no. 1/2 (January/February 2019): 71. https://search.ebscohost.com/login.aspx?direct=true&AuthType=cookie,ip,cpid&custid=csl&db=ulh&AN=133975635&site=eds-live&scope=site.

———. "The Ongoing Challenges of Academic Library Discovery Services." *Computers in Libraries* 40, no. 1 (January/February 2020): 9–11. Accessed August 14, 2020. https://search.ebscohost.com/login.aspx?direct=true&AuthType=cookie,ip,cpid&custid=csl&db=aph&AN=141250481&site=ehost-live&scope=site.

———. "Web-Scale Discovery Services: Finding the Right Balance." *American Libraries*, January 14, 2014. Accessed August 7, 2020. https://americanlibrariesmagazine.org/2014/01/14/web-scale-discovery-services/.

Central Michigan University Library. "Website Research: Open Access Resources." CMU University Libraries. Last modified July 10, 2020. Accessed August 8, 2020. https://libguides.cmich.edu/web_research/oa.

Commonwealth of Kentucky. "KDLA WorldCat Discovery." Kentucky Department for Libraries and Archives. Last modified 2020. Accessed August 12, 2020. https://kdla.ky.gov/common/Pages/WorldCatDiscovery.aspx.

Day, James M. "Discovery Services: Basics and Resources." Library Technology Launchpad: Library Technology for Every Librarian. Last modified March 8, 2017. Accessed August 8, 2020. https://libtechlaunchpad.com/2017/03/08/discovery-services-basics-and-resources/.

EBSCO Industries, Inc. "EBSCO Training." EBSCO Connect. Last modified April 30, 2020. Accessed August 14, 2020. https://connect.ebsco.com/s/article/EBSCO-Training?language=en_US.

OCLC. "Inside WorldCat." WorldCat. Last modified 2020. Accessed August 10, 2020. https://www.oclc.org/en/worldcat/inside-worldcat.html.

———. "WorldCat Discovery." OCLC. Last modified 2020. Accessed August 10, 2020. https://www.oclc.org/en/worldcat-discovery.html.

Oklahoma Department of Libraries. "About Oklahoma Digital Prairie." Oklahoma Digital Prairie. Last modified 2020. Accessed August 10, 2020. https://digitalprairieok.net/about/.

Springshare. "LibGuides Community." LibGuides Community. Last modified 2020. Accessed August 14, 2020. https://community.libguides.com/.

University of Illinois Board of Trustees. "Discovery Services—General Information." Illinois Library. Last modified 2020. Accessed August 7, 2020. https://www.library.illinois.edu/geninfo/discoveryservices/.

"The Web vs. Library Databases—a Comparison." Chart. Yale Libraries. n.d. Accessed August 10, 2020. http://web.library.yale.edu.

"Welcome to the Alaska State Library" [State of Alaska]. Alaska State Libraries, Archives, and Museums. Last modified 2020. Accessed August 12, 2020. https://library.alaska.gov/.

CHAPTER 4

Primary Sources

LSS know the role and responsibility of libraries for introducing relevant applications of technology, including digital literacy, to the public.

Topics Covered in This Chapter

Primary Sources
    Collaboration
    Artifacts
LSS and Primary Sources
    Locating Sources
    Selecting Sources
Digitization
    Planning
    Process
Chapter Summary

Key Terms

Accession—This refers to the act of acquiring and including items in a digital collection according to library policy.

Artifacts—These are two- or three-dimensional objects that have artistic, cultural, personal, or historic value that are preserved for future generations.

Cloud computing—Libraries use this type of storage system for digital collections of remote servers that ensure offsite backup and reliability.

File format—TIFF and JPEG are the commonly used formats for scanned files for library digital collections. The format tells a software program how to display the contents in the file.

OCR—Optical character recognition is the process of scanning an item and turning it into digitized code.

Primary sources—These are artifacts, documents, sound recordings, film, clothing, inventions, and other objects and materials that are authentic and present firsthand accounts or direct evidence.

Secondary sources—These materials interpret and analyze primary sources. They are written by those who have special expertise on topics, providing historical context or critical perspectives.

Tertiary sources—These sources are even more removed from the original than secondary sources as they index, abstract, organize, compile, or digest other sources.

PRIMARY SOURCES

Primary sources present firsthand accounts or direct evidence. They are created by witnesses or recorders who experienced the events or conditions being documented, and may include autobiographies, memoirs, and oral histories. Memoirs share firsthand accounts of significant events and experiences of an author that impacts her attitudes, beliefs, and worldview. Primary sources may be studies, sketches, correspondence, and personal papers[1] that are original to the person, period, or event, such as a personal narrative or legal document. One of the key elements of a primary source is the firsthand relationship to the speaker, author, or creator. Documents, photographs, **artifacts**, letters, plays, and artwork are just a few examples of primary sources. Table 4.1 offers examples of primary sources LSS may encounter that can be considered for digitization commonly found in libraries or shared by library patrons.

Primary sources are associated with history, such as armaments from a battle or an important speech of a world leader. But primary sources are equally found in science, literature, cultural heritage, medicine, mathematics, technology, and the arts. They are not restricted to a certain discipline, time, or place. In some instances, published materials can also be viewed as primary materials for the period in which they were written. The Library of Congress defines primary sources as "the raw mate-

Table 4.1.   Examples of Primary Sources Found in Libraries

Letters and correspondence	Important documents	Film and video of local events
Photographs	Audio narratives	Documentary film
Autobiographies, memoirs	Diaries	Speeches
Artifacts	Oral histories	Original fine art, sculpture, paintings, literature
Music	Government documents	Original manuscripts
Original books, magazines, newspapers, pamphlets	Maps	Dissertations
Genealogy records	Interviews	Civil records
Legal proceedings	Census data	Studies, sketches
Practical arts, furniture, etc.	Clothing	Research notes

rials of history—original documents and objects that were created at the time under study."[2] It further suggests close contact primary sources that are unique and often profoundly personal documents and objects can give others a sense of what it was like to be alive during a long-past era by prompting their curiosity and improving critical thinking and analysis skills.[3] Until the recent onset of digitization, most library users would never be able to view such artifacts and objects unless they had special access or could travel to a museum.

Collaboration

Most towns support a public library and school district libraries. In addition to libraries, located in some towns and cities are historical societies or small museums. The majority of historical societies and small museums in the United States were established by wealthy donors or industrialists in the latter part of the nineteenth century to honor the legacy of ancestors, to commemorate local heroes, or to preserve historic architecture or artifacts. Rapid urbanization in the twentieth century led to another wave of interest in preserving local history with an estimate of more than ten thousand local historical societies and museums existing in the United States today. Rarely are historical societies fully funded by towns, cities, or states. Approximately 15 percent of local historical societies are staffed entirely by volunteers. Only 25 percent have more than one professional staff member, meaning that staff resources are stretched thin and many historical societies are run by people with little formal training in history.[4] These institutions lean heavily on the local public library to be, in situ, an arm of the historical society because of common interests and the fact that they often serve the same population.

Library staff has the knowledge and skills of developing, organizing, and cataloging collections. They have technology expertise and an interest in the community and its history. Historical society volunteers and staff have deep interest in and knowledge of local history. Working together, library and historical society staff have talents and skills to create digital collections from primary sources.

Many a collaboration has been made among schools, public libraries, historical societies, and small museums. They promote local history education through commemorative events and engagement of expert speakers to document, explain, and share the history of the community. They know and interact with key people, such as historians and collectors, and they promote resources and programs among themselves. An example of such cooperation is the town of Groton, Connecticut, which has within its boundaries two historical societies, a historical association, the Friends of Fort Griswold, the Battlefield (state park) of Fort Griswold, two endowed private-public libraries, a university branch, and the municipal Groton Public Library. In a communitywide effort with matching state library funding, the Groton Public Library was designated the central location for the Groton History Room (see figure 4.1) and digital archive to preserve, digitize, and display primary sources from across the town for public access. The cooperation among the aforementioned institutions has strengthened community interest in history, academic, and genealogical research through joint initiatives and programs.

Figure 4.1. Groton Public Library History Room. *Groton Public Library*

Artifacts

Some primary sources found in libraries are artifacts. Artifacts are unique objects that were created by a person from a particular place, event, or time. Artifacts may have artistic, cultural, historic, or other significance and are limited in number. They may be one unique object or thing or one of a set of original duplicates made at the same time that are considered originals. For example, at one library the mysterious mummy's hand brought over from the pyramids of Egypt is a unique artifact, where its dozens of perfectly preserved butterflies from more than one hundred years ago together make it an original collector's set.[5] Libraries house all kinds of unique or special artifacts. Because many need special handling, they are not circulated to the public. Look around your library and identify its artifacts. Many libraries serve the multiple purposes of not only delivering traditional library services, but also curating local artifacts for the community. Does the library have a separate inventory of its artifacts? Surprisingly, many libraries do not. Librarians are very good at cataloging circulating collections, but they are not always as thorough with its artifacts. LSS can volunteer to create such an inventory, collecting any descriptive data or information available about it such as color, size, date, donor, creator, location of origin, and so on. Pictures should be taken as part of the inventory. Meet with library administration to discuss next steps. Are there artifacts and primary sources in disrepair? What needs to be cleaned? Has the library ever had the artifacts appraised? Are they insured? All of these and other questions should be asked and answered to ensure that precious and unique artifacts are being preserved properly and that appropriate security measures are in place. A process should be created with assigned responsibilities of regular inventories to be taken of all inventoried items. Artifacts owned by libraries have great potential to be scanned or photographed to become information sources in digital collections.

LSS AND PRIMARY SOURCES

LSS support locating, selecting, and using[6] primary source items and artifacts for information and research. LSS who understand the unique nature of primary sources and know where to find and select them can support those seeking this type of original research and information.

Locating Sources

Library collections are treasure troves of primary sources! Original writing and spoken words permeate fiction and nonfiction. Libraries circulate unlimited primary sources found in books and media. Photographs taken at the event (see figure 4.2),

Figure 4.2. Day after Lunar Landing, July 21, 1969. *Keystone / The Image Bank via Getty Images*

songs that were written and sung for a cause, and actions that were captured on film are all part of the resources of the library. LSS can find primary sources throughout the book collections. Original novels are primary sources. So are parts of a book such as when the author enhances his or her research with original quotations and photographs. The same primary source may be found in multiple libraries, such as a popular autobiography that has thousands of copies in print that are circulated by many libraries. Original town documents may be preserved and archived solely by the library. Primary sources that are also artifacts should be handled with extreme care and restricted by library staff from circulation or handling by the public.

In addition to LSS helping patrons locate primary sources within the library collections, they assist patrons finding digital collections of primary sources online. Chapter 5 explores exemplary global, national, and state digital information services created by libraries, universities, museums, and governments that share primary resources for educational and research purposes. These digital libraries contain famous, historic, or important images of photographs, newspapers, documents, maps, and manuscripts, as well as audio and video files of original film, music, sound recordings, and interviews. Some of these same forms of primary sources may be found by LSS in their local libraries and could be accessed by the public if converted to a digitalized format.

Many websites can be found with advanced internet searching. When creating a search, add the words "primary source" next to the search topic. Similarly, as shown in figure 4.3, this technique works searching the online catalog as shown with the example of the U.S. Civil War.

Locating primary sources takes time and research. It also takes background knowledge to know how to identify and make appropriate selections.

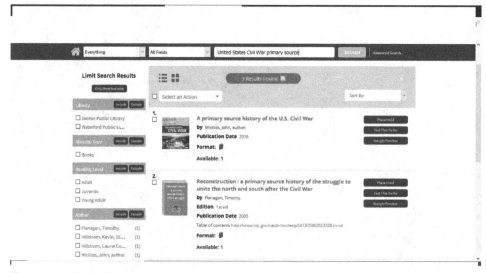

Figure 4.3.   Catalog Search. *Author*

Selecting Sources

There is a distinction between primary and secondary sources. Primary sources are developed during a specific time or event. Think of primary sources as being *firsthand*. **Secondary sources** interpret, paraphrase, or translate information, helping people think about what was said, why an event occurred, or significant influences during a time period. These sources examine critical elements to help those who were not there to form opinions and guide their thinking. Secondary sources involve reading, hearing, viewing, or communicating about the event or notable person. In the course of their daily work, LSS handle materials that are both primary and secondary sources. LSS who can distinguish between the two can support patrons' selection of information.

Most **tertiary** sources are common reference sources. Think of tertiary sources as being at a third level removed from the original primary source. Examples of tertiary sources are indexes, encyclopedias, dictionaries, fact books, guidebooks, manuals, some textbooks, and abstracting services. Many websites, including Wikipedia, are usually considered tertiary sources depending upon the content.

Autobiographies and firsthand historical accounts are primary sources that provide authentic perspectives of a person, place, or event. *Long Walk to Freedom*, the autobiography of Nelson Mandela, provides readers insight into his life commitment to end apartheid in South Africa. Secondary materials, such as nonfiction and textbooks, synthesize and interpret primary materials.[7] Books written about apartheid by scholars who did not live the experience, while factual and accurate, cannot convey the firsthand information and emotion of an autobiography. It is common for many secondary source textbooks to contain some primary source materials such as photographs, speeches, or copies of original degrees or other documents from the event. Table 4.2 provides examples of secondary sources found in libraries.

Table 4.2.   Examples of Secondary Sources

Textbooks	Biographies	Histories
Reference books	News reports	Magazine and journal articles
Chronologies	Maps	Abstracts
Handbooks	Interpretations	Translations

LSS make valid distinctions between a primary and secondary sources and confirm with patrons what type of source is desirable. Similar to frameworks reference librarians use to ensure they are providing accurate and appropriate information to patrons,[8] LSS can take the following steps to help select primary sources:

1. Categorize the request.
2. Visualize how the primary source presents itself.
3. Check to see if you are proceeding in the right direction for the patron.
4. Provide access to the primary source.

First, categorize the request. Is the primary source simple to find or will it take more research to locate it? Is it specific to one discipline or does it cross into multiple disciplines? For example, primary sources on counterculture in the 1960s may be categorized and found with history, music, women's rights, drug culture, civil rights, political assassinations, or the Vietnam War. Listen carefully to and verify the patron's request. Is she asking for multiple primary sources or one specific item? Are the sources appropriate, meaning will they be able to be interpreted and understood by the user or should another search be done?

Second, how the primary source presents itself is important for the ways patrons can use it. Can photos be legally taken of the artifact? Is a photocopy sufficient, or does the patron need a digital image? The format of the primary source is necessary to know in the selection process.

Third, keep the patron engaged in the process to ensure the LSS is on the right track. Offer options at pivotal points to affirm the patron's needs. Often the first request of the patron is not entirely or correctly related to the real information sought. Monitor search progress with the patron.

Fourth, is the source accessible or inaccessible? Potential restrictions and other considerations need to be known early in the **accession** process.

We use primary sources to learn more about ourselves by understanding those who lived before us through reading, touching, viewing, and listening to authentic artifacts, documents, and stories. Students today are required to make meaning from primary sources, drawing conclusions and citing evidence from multiple primary sources. Connecting students with their past prepares them for the present and future. Local sources should be utilized in K–12 curriculum.[9]

At the academic level, primary source research fosters deep learning and student engagement. Professors and academic librarians incorporate primary source research in their instruction, teaching students how to use national and state digital libraries and archives as important information sources. Many library staff benefit from primary source training so that they can effectively guide others.[10] There are tools and services, such as those by the Library of Congress,[11] LSS may access freely.

DIGITIZATION

Using digitization technology, libraries have the potential to share artifacts from special collections that would not normally circulate or be displayed. A digital collection should be born from a well-devised plan that addresses a need. Its objective must be purposeful and enhance library service. For example, if the library has developed genealogical resources, a digitization genealogy project would likely be successful because there would be demand for it by current or potential researchers.

Planning

LSS can help by exploring to ascertain whether other digital collections may exist on the same theme being proposed. Will the project add to research or will it be repetitive of what already is available? Establish at the planning stage that there is a need for this project because it will draw on library staff, time, and resources.

While planned at the local level, ask how the project will "fit" with the regional or state digitization. If the project is to digitize local artifacts associated with the town's role in the Revolutionary War, at the planning stage, the state library and universities should be consulted to ensure that this new collection can be linked to larger digital collections on related themes. For example, the Connecticut Digital Archive Community[12] is an organization that provides its library members persistent storage, including appropriate backup, recovery procedures, audit tracking, replication, and format migration. It also is a portal for members to have their digital collections branded and be participants of the Connecticut Digital Archive and the Digital Public Library of America. Chapter 6 explores these relationships between local libraries and state or historic institutions in detail. Most importantly, standards that are required at the state level for its digital collections are planned for, adopted, and used by the local library.

To create a digital collection, it takes the right technology, including a commitment with a hosting cloud service, legal permissions, much staff and volunteer time and training, as well as partnerships and collaboration with outside agencies.

Every digitization project plan should consider selection, standards, and access.[13] Does the library have legal permissions to digitize each item? What is the physical condition of the primary sources? Are they fragile? Will handling damage them? Do staff have the knowledge and equipment to work with such artifacts? If volumes are bound, how will photos be digitized from them?

As eager LSS may be to begin a digital project, it never should be undertaken until all standards are in place. Standards are around the type of file format, size and color of digital images, quality of pictures, and other guidelines that ensure the local collection can be linked to larger collections. In library cataloging, MARC 21 and BIBFRAME standards ensure local book and media records can be displayed in larger regional and statewide union catalogs. Chapter 8 discusses metadata, the standard for cataloging digital images. The Association for Library Collections and Technical Services (ALCTS) offers extensive guidelines for libraries. Libraries that digitize according to ALCTS specifications create collections that will be accessible well into the future.[14] Table 4.3[15] lists some of the current **file format** standards by material type recommended to libraries considering digitizing projects.

Table 4.3. File Format Standards

Material Type	Resolution	Intensity or Bit Depth	File Type	Minimum Color
Books—text without images	300 dpi	8	JPEG	Grayscale
Books—text with images	400 dpi	8	JPEG	Grayscale
Maps	300 dpi	8/24	JPEG	Grayscale/color
Photographs	400 dpi	8/24	JPEG	Grayscale/color

Today the majority of libraries use cloud or offsite computing services to store digital collections rather than trying to do so on locally owned servers. **Cloud computing** has many benefits including backup, 24/7 technical support, and the capacity to add space as projects increase in size.

Rights management, such as copyright permission for each scanned item, must be ensured. How will the digital item be used? A large maritime history museum requires negotiated contracts for use of its images. For example, the price could be quite high for commercial use compared to a college course where fair use may allow free onetime educational use.

Process

Scanning technology has greatly advanced. Today LSS may use 3D box scanners
and other devices to capture digital images of artifacts clearly and accurately. LSS
scan photographs, personal narratives, maps, letters, and other primary sources into
digital format. Libraries obtain inexpensive **OCR** or optical character recognition
software that enables viewing, reading, and editing scanned content on e-readers
or computing devices. An excellent guide, *Digitization Guidelines for Photographs and
Textual Documents*[16] lists key steps LSS can use to digitize documents, photos, and
artifacts. Adapted from the guide, the major steps of the digitization process are
found in table 4.4.

Table 4.4.   Steps for Digitization

1. *Prepare to scan*—clean glass top of scanner and set lighting appropriately.
2. *Select scanner settings—color mode*
   Bitonal—a simple two-tone black-and-white scan
   Grayscale—choose from a palate of 256 shades of gray
   Color—a palate of 256 to thousands of color tones
3. *Select scanner settings—resolution*
   Bit-depth—refers to how many levels of colors the scan will capture from 256 to 65,000.
   DPI stands for dots per inch and how finely spaced pixels per inch (PPI) will be. The higher the DPI,
      the higher the details of the scan.
4. *Enhance scanned image* with filters or scanning software to sharpen the image, remove the scratches,
   remove "red eye," adjust the size.
5. *The material should be copied "as is"* without alternations to keep the authenticity of the primary
   source.
6. *Scan and save*—Set object on a piece of light-colored paper such as white or gray. Do not crop edges
   of documents.
7. *Scan flat or loose pages*—Scan the front, then the back. Keep scan in the order of the material.
8. *Scan bound materials*—lightly press along the spine to capture all text or writing inside. Use judgment
   about the amount of pressure applied to fragile materials.
9. *Save scanned images* as TIFF files for high-quality master files and JPEG format as the second choice.
10. *Use the nomenclature* that was agreed upon in the planning phase for naming files.

Start the digitization process slowly with one or two items. As the project grows,
expect it will take more time to fully research each item so that it can be classified
and cataloged appropriately before it is uploaded to the library website or database.
Step 4 in table 4.4 is very important in that you review the scanned image to be sure
that it is not blurry and best shows the item or artifact. Do not crop or otherwise
edit the image; that changes its authenticity to the primary source. Practice scanning
and be patient with the results; with each scan, LSS learn much about placement
and settings for the best image.

LSS can monitor new tools and processes to enhance digitalization, such as the
low-cost Shotbox found at https://shotbox.me, which is a tabletop digital studio
with portable lights and better 3D scanning results.

CHAPTER SUMMARY

LSS can support the use of primary sources in many ways. They locate firsthand information for patrons and create scanned images of texts, photographs, and artifacts for local library digital collections. With advancements in scanning technology and the internet, items that were once in reserve collections or not for circulation can now be shared with patrons through the library website. LSS who are knowledgeable in searching and competent in the use of technology can apply their skills to create digital collections of local primary sources.

DISCUSSION QUESTIONS

1. What are primary sources and why are they important to library research?
2. What are some examples of primary sources libraries may typically have in their collections? Secondary sources?
3. How can LSS locate primary sources?
4. How can LSS participate in the planning process of digitizing primary sources?
5. What are key steps in digitizing a primary source for a library collection?

ACTIVITY

Gain practice identifying and locating primary sources in your library that could become a digital collection on a topic or theme.

1. Choose a topic that is well represented in your library such as local history or a historic event or person.
2. Locate a minimum of five primary sources in your library on your topic, looking through books, photographs, and other collections. Talk with the reference librarians to ask if there are artifacts the public does not typically have access to on your topic. Be sure to select at least one three-dimensional artifact.
3. Create a detailed chart of the five primary sources on your topic with the following information: title, source, location, format, description, other relevant information.
4. Digitize two or three items as a prototype. Obtain feedback from others.

NOTES

1. Yale University, "Art History Research at Yale: Primary Sources," Yale University Library, last modified August 13, 2020, accessed September 10, 2020, https://guides.library.yale.edu/arthistoryresearch/primary-sources.

2. Library of Congress, "Getting Started with Primary Sources," Program Teachers, last modified 2020, accessed September 10, 2020, https://www.loc.gov/programs/teachers/getting-started-with-primary-sources/.

3. Library of Congress, "Getting Started with Primary Sources."

4. American Historical Association, "The Future of Local Historical Societies," *Perspectives on History*, last modified 2020, accessed September 10, 2020, https://www.historians.org /publications-and-directories/perspectives-on-history/december-2012/the-future-of-lo cal-historical-societies.

5. The Bill Memorial Library, "Library on Display," last modified 2020, accessed September 10, 2020, https://www.billmemorial.org/library-on-display.

6. American Library Association, "Primary Sources on the Web: Finding, Evaluating, Using," RUSA, last modified 2020, accessed September 8, 2020, http://www.ala.org/rusa /sections/history/resources/primarysources.

7. American Library Association, "Primary Sources on the Web."

8. Kay Ann Cassell and Uma Hiremath, *Reference and Information Services: An Introduction*, fourth ed. (Chicago: ALA Neal-Schuman, 2018), 35–38.

9. Annette Lamb, "A Dozen Ways to Promote Cultural Heritage Through Image Collections," *Teacher Librarian* 47, no. 4 (April 2020): 56–60, http://search.ebscohost.com/login.aspx ?direct=true&AuthType=cookie,ip,cpid&custid=csl&db=aph&AN=143257208&site=ehost -live&scope=site.

10. Brigitte Billeaudeauz and Rachel E. Scott, "Leveraging Existing Frameworks to Support Undergraduate Primary Source Research," *Reference & User Services Quarterly* 58, no. 4 (Summer 2019): 246–55, https://search.ebscohost.com/login.aspx?direct=true&AuthType=cook ie,ip,cpid&custid=csl&db=aph&AN=139336740&site=ehost-live&scope=site.

11. Library of Congress, "Getting Started with Primary Sources."

12. Connecticut Digital Archive, "Join the CTDA," CTDA Reference Center, last modified September 10, 2020, accessed September 13, 2020, https://confluence.uconn.edu/display /CTDA/Join+the+CTDA.

13. Alice L. Scott, "Best Practices and Planning for Digitization Projects," *WebJunction*, last modified May 23, 2018, accessed September 12, 2020, https://www.webjunction.org/news /webjunction/best-practices-and-planning-for-digitization-projects.html.

14. American Library Association, "Minimum Digitization Capture Recommendations," ALCTS, last modified 2020, accessed September 13, 2020, http://www.ala.org/alcts/resources /preserv/minimum-digitization-capture-recommendations.

15. Scott, "Best Practices and Planning."

16. University of Michigan, "Digitization Guidelines for Photographs and Textual Documents," Bentley Historical Library, last modified December 2018, accessed September 13, 2020, https://bentley.umich.edu/.

REFERENCES, SUGGESTED READINGS, AND WEBSITES

American Historical Association. "The Future of Local Historical Societies." *Perspectives on History*. Last modified 2020. Accessed September 10, 2020. https://www.historians .org/publications-and-directories/perspectives-on-history/december-2012/the-future-of-lo cal-historical-societies.

American Library Association. "Minimum Digitization Capture Recommendations." ALCTS. Last modified 2020. Accessed September 13, 2020. http://www.ala.org/alcts/resources /preserv/minimum-digitization-capture-recommendations.

———. "Primary Sources on the Web: Finding, Evaluating, Using." RUSA. Last modified 2020. Accessed September 8, 2020. http://www.ala.org/rusa/sections/history/resources /primarysources.

Billeaudeauz, Brigitte, and Rachel E. Scott. "Leveraging Existing Frameworks to Support Undergraduate Primary Source Research." *Reference & User Services Quarterly* 58, no. 4 (Summer 2019): 246–55. https://search.ebscohost.com/login.aspx?direct=true&AuthType=cook ie,ip,cpid&custid=csl&db=aph&AN=139336740&site=ehost-live&scope=site.

The Bill Memorial Library. "Library on Display." Last modified 2020. Accessed September 10, 2020. https://www.billmemorial.org/library-on-display.

Cassell, Kay Ann, and Uma Hiremath. *Reference and Information Services: An Introduction.* Fourth ed. Chicago: ALA Neal-Schuman, 2018.

Connecticut Digital Archive. "Join the CTDA." CTDA Reference Center. Last modified September 10, 2020. Accessed September 13, 2020. https://confluence.uconn.edu/display/CTDA /Join+the+CTDA.

Lamb, Annette. "A Dozen Ways to Promote Cultural Heritage through Image Collections." *Teacher Librarian* 47, no. 4 (April 2020): 56–60. http://search.ebscohost.com/login.aspx ?direct=true&AuthType=cookie,ip,cpid&custid=csl&db=aph&AN=143257208&site=ehost -live&scope=site.

Library Connection, and Connecticut State Library, comps. *Digitization Project: Easy as 1, 2, 3.* Accessed September 13, 2020. http://www.libraryconnection.info/pdfs/digitization123 Aug2009.pdf.

Library of Congress. "Getting Started with Primary Sources." Program Teachers. Last modified 2020. Accessed September 10, 2020. https://www.loc.gov/programs/teachers/getting-start ed-with-primary-sources/.

"Library of Congress Offers Free Primary Sources and Teacher Guides." *Curriculum Review* 58, no. 7 (March 2019): 5. http://search.ebscohost.com/login.aspx?direct=true&AuthType =cookie,ip,cpid&custid=csl&db=aph&AN=134875983&site=ehost-live&scope=site.

Princeton University. "Primary Sources: A Guide for Historians." Princeton University Library. Last modified August 27, 2020. Accessed September 10, 2020. https://libguides.princeton .edu/history/primarysources.

Scott, Alice L. "Best Practices and Planning for Digitization Projects." *WebJunction*. Last modified May 23, 2018. Accessed September 12, 2020. https://www.webjunction.org/news /webjunction/best-practices-and-planning-for-digitization-projects.html.

University of Michigan. "Digitization Guidelines for Photographs and Textual Documents." Bentley Historical Library. Last modified December 2018. Accessed September 13, 2020. https://bentley.umich.edu/.

CHAPTER 5

Digital Collections and Libraries

LSS know the general trends and developments in technology applications for library functions and services.

LSS know the role and responsibility of libraries for introducing relevant applications of technology, including digital literacy, to the public.

Topics Covered in This Chapter
Digital Content
   Assets
   Collections
Digital Libraries
   Description
   Collaboration
National Libraries and Museums
   Library of Congress
   Museums
Research Institutes and Academic Libraries
Consortia
Chapter Summary

Key Terms
Assets—These objects include digital photos, videos, and song files that reside on computing storage devices or cloud networks for fast access and reliability.
Consortium—Multiple libraries, museums, or other institutions create a formal and legal partnership to fund, staff, and accomplish the mission and goals.

Curation—This is the process of selecting and caring for important artifacts and objects so that they can be displayed, grouped, or digitized as part of a specific collection or around a theme.

Digital collections—These are clusters of digital assets that are commonly grouped and linked around a topic or theme for improved organization and access for users.

Digital library—This is a specialized form of library that encompasses electronic collections of visual, text, audio, or film digital assets that are accessed by users over a computer network.

Digitization—This is the process of transforming physical material into a digital (electronic) form by scanning or imaging.

Portal—This is a website designed to be a starting point or opening to information on the web because it simplifies searching by consolidating and organizing links from different digital libraries and other sources.

DIGITAL CONTENT

During the pandemic of 2020–2022, when much of the world economy was shuttered or furloughed, libraries provided key services online with internet and mobile technologies. People participated in library programs, exhibits, meetings, and book discussions online. **Digitization** provided sources of text, pictures, and sound. E-books, e-journals, and streaming video enabled users to read, listen to, and view quality digitized books, sound recordings, and film. While the buildings may have been closed, library access was open to digital materials, staff, and programs through technology.

Assets

Assets, including the internet, are textual, audio, and visual modalities encoded in searchable digital formats. Examples of such assets include digital text, images, videos, and sound recordings. Digital assets can be scanned versions of physical resources such as books, photographs, and maps or materials. They can also be databases, websites, online reports, email, and forms. Patrons have remote access to digital assets on a wide range of topics downloadable to their devices.

From their inception, libraries have selectively collected and preserved physical artifacts of local interest and history. Today libraries use digitization to make accessible artifacts in various file formats of JPEG, PDF, MP3, MP4, and others. Digital assets reside on storage devices, such as a local server or a cloud network. Much like our physical artifacts, digital assets can hold valuable and meaningful content worth preserving that requires special considerations and legal agreements to make them accessible to the public. Textbox 5.1[1] lists types of personal digital assets people are archiving today.

Digital assets, similar to any property, are subject to federal and state laws of ownership and copyright. See chapter 11 for discussion on copyright and digital assets.

Digital assets need equipment having electrical, digital magnetic, wireless, optical, electromagnet, or similar capabilities.[2] Considerations for selecting file types that will work with future equipment are discussed in chapter 6.

TEXTBOX 5.1: PERSONAL DIGITAL ASSETS

- Emails / email correspondence
- Photographs (saved on mobile devices, desktop computers, or in social media)
- Social media such as Tweets, Instagram posts, or Facebook pages
- Digital receipts
- Tax returns (digital)
- Scanned family photos
- Medical records
- Contracts or lease agreements
- Personal websites or online portfolios

Collections

Libraries group digital assets into **digital collections**. Digital collections are clusters of digital assets that have a relationship that makes sense for them to be grouped. These assets are stored in folders that provide organization and speedy searching. The groupings may be made around a time period, topic, place, or even format.

Most digital collections are classified into one of the four types: themes, places, time periods, or digital format. Each type is then subdivided more specifically. A digital collection of fifty image assets of existing pre-1800 local houses has a thematic grouping. A digital collection of local historic maps is an example of format.

The Institute of Museum and Library Services (IMLS) is a federal agency whose mission is to advance, support, and empower America's museums, libraries, and related organizations through grant-making, research, and policy development.[3] Digital collections created by libraries and museums use standards established by IMLS. By having common standards and practices, similar to cataloging books, digital collections maximize access and searching capabilities. IMLS has nine principles that are explained here. Strategies are suggested for LSS who plan, create, use, manage, or help others with library digital collections.

1. *A good digital collection is created according to an explicit collection development policy.* Libraries have collection policies to best serve their community of users. Digital collections, like print collections, should be guided by the library collection policy.

   Strategy: LSS understand library digital collection policy. Discuss ideas with supervisor and other staff to clarify how a new digital collection will complement the other collections of the library.

   Strategy: LSS know areas of traditional collections in high demand and brainstorms with others ideas for new digital collections that would serve community needs. For example, if crafts are popular, LSS may propose a digital collection of local crafts and craft making.

2. *Collections should be described so that a user can discover characteristics of the collection, including scope, format, restrictions on access, ownership, and any information*

significant for determining the collection's authenticity, integrity, and interpretation. Forms of metadata or descriptive elements about each digital asset are used to provide better access and searching.

Strategy: LSS who catalog already are using a form of descriptive metadata in MARC. They can seek training in PastPerfect or Dublin Core (or whatever metadata system supervisors chose) so that they can support cataloging of the digital assets.

Strategy: LSS may serve as active members who manage the library digital collections, making recommendations for new collections, being responsible for the quality of content, and other tasks that ensure digital collections as a viable library resource.

3. *A good collection is curated, which is to say, the resources are actively managed during the entire lifecycle.* Digital curation is the process of monitoring and making decisions about a collection from the time it is proposed until the time it is no longer useful and taken offline.

Strategy: LSS can recommend and offer to be a member of a small user group that drafts a manual of operating procedures or guidelines for future staff.

Strategy: LSS can be a user of the library's digital collections. Just as LSS observe damage or other issues around books, as users, they can also identify things that need correction such as spelling, confusing metadata, or broken links.

4. *A good collection is broadly available and avoids unnecessary impediments to use.* Collections should be accessible to persons with disabilities and usable effectively in conjunction with adaptive technologies. Digital collections are accessible 24/7.

Strategy: LSS ensure elements of website design, such as user-friendly links, size of font, and clear instructions that are built into the operation.

Strategy: LSS tests the library digital collections on numerous platforms and operating systems to ensure that the digital assets work and show as expected regardless of computing device or app for maximum ease of use and display on mobile devices.

5. *A good collection respects intellectual property rights.* Similar to books and other physical library resources, digital assets are intellectual property, subject to federal and state laws and acts. LSS should have a working understanding of basic copyright and intellectual property law when working with any library item.

Strategy: If items to be digitized are not property of the library, LSS can participate in researching ownership and in the process of obtaining permissions and copyrights.

Strategy: Rights management requires detailed and thorough recordkeeping. LSS can volunteer to set up a database of the intellectual property rights for assets in the library collections.

6. *A good collection has mechanisms to supply usage data and other data that allows standardized measures of usefulness to be recorded.* Decisions about whether to add to or otherwise modify digital collections should be data driven.

Strategy: LSS may be in a position to observe who are using them, how, and why. This qualitative data would be helpful to administration evaluating the use of the collections.

Strategy: Quantitative data can also be obtained from ILS or other management systems that provide access to the library digital collections. LSS can offer to compile monthly statistics on the use of each collection for administration to evaluate usefulness.

7. *A good collection is interoperable.* Digital collections should be designed not only to operate within the parameters of the library, but also to be able to be accessed, linked, or used by any person with web access (unless permission is restricted under copyright).

   Strategy: When cataloging digital assets, LSS should advocate for the highest level of standards so that the digital collection may become part of a larger digital library. In order to do this, metadata cataloging should be used that meets state and national standards of IMLS.

   Strategy: If LSS are catalogers, they should consult with regional or state catalogers of metadata to ensure that the level of cataloging is appropriate, is in step with other institutions, and will meet future searching needs.

8. *A good collection integrates into the user's own workflow.* LSS should be aware of how patrons will find and use the digital collections.

   Strategy: LSS can be part of a marketing team to make potential users aware of the library digital collections and what value they will bring them. Just as we set up displays of new books, digital collections need to be brought to the attention of potential users even more.

   Strategy: LSS know their customers and, by word of mouth, can introduce people to new digital collections. Similar to sharing a good book, when LSS are familiar with the content of a digital collection, he is in a key position to talk about it to others.

9. *A good collection is sustainable over time.* Much work and effort go into creating digital collections. Collections should be planned for and expected to be used for many years.

   Strategy: LSS can ask to be mentored by those currently responsible for planning, creating, and maintaining collections.

   Strategy: LSS who have common interests with other outside agencies or institutions, such as the local historical society, can promote the library digital collections. Having outside sponsors and users will help to sustain collections.

LSS can greatly contribute to the success of library digital collections. At every juncture there is need for skilled staff to work to promote these new library resources.

LSS learn about the exemplar digital collections and libraries available via the internet so that they, in turn, can help patrons navigate through these excellent information sources.

DIGITAL LIBRARIES

Just as a traditional library organizes its resources into collections, so does a digital library. A **digital library** is made up of numerous strategic and specific collections that address a particular area of interest or research. These specialized forms of libraries encompass collections of visual, text, audio, or film digital assets that are accessed by users over a computer network or internet. Librarians set policy, organize, and maintain processes to retrieve media or files that make up the collections. As do traditional libraries, digital libraries differ in terms of size, scope, and purpose. Assets may exist only in digital format, or many may have been converted into digital from another form, such as traditional photograph to a digitized image. Digital libraries can be updated daily and accessed 24/7 by users. Without boundaries, they can store more information than physical libraries, and offer access to multiple resources simultaneously.[4]

Description

Digital libraries, also called electronic or virtual libraries, may be local and regional, statewide, national, or international in scope. The Council on Library Resources[5] provided several descriptions of a digital library, including

- a collection of materials digitized or encoded for electronic transmission;
- an institution that possesses or an organization that controls such materials;
- an agency that links existing institutions for providing access to electronic information, establishing prices, providing finding aids, and protecting copyright restrictions;
- a consortium of collecting institutions; and
- a library that scans, keyboards, and encodes all its materials to make the entirety of its holdings electronically accessible from anywhere.

In addition, a digital library may contain or be linked to

- resources that are located both locally and remotely;
- a complex of digital assets that are bibliographic, numeric, text, sound, visual, and spatial;
- a single point of entry to several hundred scholarly resources;
- navigational assistance and transparent connections to any resource selected by the user, and high-quality user support and instructional services.

Collaboration

Whether the goal is to establish a unique digital library or to create multiple digital collections, achievement is enhanced in collaboration or partnership with others. Libraries seek technical expertise, legal advice, and other supports that they do not have on staff. They may also seek sources of content from universities, historical societies, and other institutions who will grant rights to digitize artifacts and/or share digital assets. In collaborative partnerships, there is the potential to better leverage resources, including access to critical hardware and software products. The development and implementation of digital libraries are enhanced when librarians and LSS can collaborate with others to formulate ideas, designs, and pilot prototypes, and evaluate and make improvements. Collaboration also spurs innovative thinking, sharing of expertise, and improved productivity.

A common model of collaborate stakeholders in the planning and implementation of a digital library is

- library administration to set policy, establish external relationships, acquire resources and funding, and ensure all legal and other processes are adhered to;
- project leadership to guide the day-to-day activities and report to library administration and to solve problems as they occur;
- LSS contribute ideas, help research artifacts, and assist with implementing the plan to create the digital library;
- representatives of library users help generate ideas and offer expertise;
- volunteers help with creating digital objects and cataloging in metadata; and
- technical and vendor support help with the design, testing, implementation, and management of the new digital library.

An essential advantage in partnering is the ability to cut costs and improve outcomes for each organization by allowing broader (aggregated) resource inputs in the design through implementation stages of a project. The collaborative model is prevalent in the development of digital library resources.[6]

LSS can enhance their reference and information skills by learning about what type of institutions sponsor digital libraries and then by "visiting" them often to learn about each library's collections. Just as we would with any physical library, LSS can draw such a comparison between how they become familiar with the content of a traditional library and how they can gain specific knowledge about an online digital library. Table 5.1 is an example of such an analogy.

Table 5.1. Comparative Strategies with Libraries

Traditional Library	Digital Library
Determine the type of library (public, academic, school, special) and sponsors (municipality, university, K–12, etc.).	Read introduction or description of the digital library and learn about its sponsorship.
Tour the library and learn where materials are located.	Are the digital collections grouped by place, topic, format, or other arrangement? Are they freely available or password protected?
Learn how the library categorizes and classifies materials (i.e., Dewey Decimal or Library of Congress classifications).	Is there a classification, accession, or other type of organizational system used so that similar items are near each other?
Search the online catalog for specific items and locate them on the shelves.	Are the digital assets integrated into the library online catalog or are they searched through a collection management program?
Determine scope and range of the collections as well as target audience.	Spend time to view, listen, or read digital artifacts so that you are able to refer others to the digital library as an appropriate reference or information source.
What are the rules or parameters for use and circulation?	Are there restrictions on the use of the digital assets?

NATIONAL LIBRARIES AND MUSEUMS

Countries take pride in their history, culture, discoveries, inventions, and unique environmental resources. In 1990s the Library of Congress (LOC) began what was to be a five-year pilot, the National Digital Library Program (NDLP) of digitizing selected collections that chronicled the nation's rich cultural heritage. It has not stopped.

Library of Congress

The vision of the NDL program in part, says, "A digital library is more than a database, and the future National Digital Library will be much more than a universal union catalog. Some interfaces may offer comprehensive access to the entire resource, while others will be specialized by content, by intended audience, or by primary purpose."[7]

At the time of this writing, the LOC has 445 digital collections containing approximately three million digital assets or artifacts. Each asset is classified and categorized with extensive metadata. The NDL will continue to expand each year. The LOC has the largest amount of digital content in the world. To search all 445 as well as more than one hundred new collections[8] in various stages of development, visit https://loc.gov/collections. A few of the prominent NDL collections are

American Memory—written and spoken words, sound recordings, still and moving images, prints, maps, and sheet music documenting the American experience.
Chronicling America—searchable database of U.S. newspapers and historic pages.
Prints and Photographs—over one million digital images of photographs, fine and popular prints, drawings, posters, and architectural and engineering designs.
Maps—largest and most comprehensive cartographic collection in the world.
Performing Arts Encyclopedia—searchable music, theater, and dance resources.
Songs of America—Special collections of recorded sound, such as National Jukebox and Songs of America—audio sound recordings of American Memory and Performing Arts and other digital collections.
Films—LOC began collecting descriptive material related to motion pictures in 1893.
Manuscripts—millions of manuscripts in eleven thousand separate collections of American history and culture.

The LOC has hundreds of other collections that are all free. The American Folklife Center fosters Americans telling short, interesting, and meaningful stories that are digitally recorded as part of the most popular StoryCorps broadcast on National Public Radio.

The IMLS supports and guides digitalization projects for both libraries and museums. Museums, centers of preserving art and artifacts, are also doing much work to digitize important assets of their collections.

Museums

Many countries support and take pride in their national museums. The Louvre in Paris, the National Museum of China, the British Museum in London, and the

National Museum of India in New Delhi are a few of the most visited museums in the world. The Metropolitan Museum of Art and the Morgan Library and Museum in New York, as well as the Art Institute and the Field Museum in Chicago and Colonial Williamsburg are just a few of the top museums among the 35,000 in the United States. Washington, DC, is the home to many other national museums and galleries. The Smithsonian and its eighteen museums and National Zoo, including the National Air and Space Museum, National Museum of Natural History, National Museum of American History, National Museum of African American History and Culture, and the National Museum of the American Indian are treasures of artifacts.

Museums and libraries both collect, preserve, and share informational, historical, and cultural resources. A major difference between their collections is that libraries have a primary focus on textual literacy while museums primarily focus on visual literacy. LSS may not immediately think of a museum as an information source. However, many museums are leaders in creating digital libraries and collections as a means to share with the public some of the important artifacts in the collections.

The Smithsonian has combined its collective libraries and archives into one entity called the Smithsonian Libraries and Archives. The digital collections of all nineteen Smithsonian museums and zoo are consolidated into its Digital Library, which is divided into three sections:

Books Online—The libraries have over seven thousand rare books, journals, and manuscripts online with focus on History and Culture, Art and Design, and Science and Technology.

Collections—Selected images from illustrated books, digitized drawings and photos, as well as indexes to some of its special collections such as art and artist vertical files, trade catalogs, postal history ephemera, and more.

Exhibitions—The libraries produce both physical and online exhibitions that use its vast collections to delight and educate.

LSS enhance research and reference skills and can support others with the dynamic digital libraries of the Smithsonian and other world museums. Treat yourself to these most interesting and free visual experiences with museum artifacts that have been professionally digitized.

RESEARCH INSTITUTES AND ACADEMIC LIBRARIES

Other sources of exemplary digital collections can be found at research institutions, universities, and academic libraries. Many research institutes are associated with universities, but they can also be privately endowed; LSS are encouraged to explore the digital collections of exemplar institutions such as the following:

J. P. Getty Institute is located in Los Angeles; its mission is the presentation, conservation, and interpretation of the world's artistic legacy. The Getty's focus of research is around the **curation** of Greek, Roman, and European art and artifacts. More than one hundred thousand artwork digital images are free and available to the public.

The Brookings Institution conducts research and education in the social sciences, primarily in economics, metropolitan policy, governance, foreign policy, and global economy.

NASA Space Technology Institutes conducts research and technology development critical to NASA's future. Its digital images and video galleries are an excellent resource for students studying earth science and astronomy.

Purdue University Libraries: Neil Armstrong, a 1955 Purdue graduate, began donating personal papers to its Division of Archives and Special Collections in 2008 after carefully considering other repository options. Following his death in 2012, Purdue became the recipient of the bulk of Armstrong's papers and continues the process of digitizing its content.

The Center for Research Libraries (CRL)[9] is an international consortium of more than two hundred university, college, and independent research libraries. CRL supports research and teaching and makes available to scholars a wealth of primary source materials in the areas of humanities, sciences, and social sciences from all world regions. With collections of more than five million newspapers, journals, books, pamphlets, dissertations, archives, government publications, and other resources, CRL digitizes documents, newspapers, books, and journals.

CONSORTIA

A **consortium** is a partnership of multiple libraries, museums, or institutions bound by a formal agreement to undertake a large project, service, or even a way of conducting and improving business that is beyond the resources of any one member. Libraries often enter consortium partnerships in order to gain access to others' collections and to share the expense of an ILS or library service platform that they could otherwise not afford on their own. They also gain technical and other staff training and support from each other or from outside experts. The following are examples of consortia digital libraries:

Digital Library Federation (DLF)—DLF's 170 members adhere to its mission *to advance research, learning, social justice, and the public good through the creative design and wise application of digital library technologies.* Some of the key work of the DLF has to do with ensuring

- open digital library standards, software, interfaces, infrastructure, and best practice;
- digital stewardship and curation, including research data management and aggregation and preservation services for digital collections;
- digital humanities and other practices and services that expand access to resources and open new opportunities for research, teaching, and learning;
- education, professional development, lifelong learning, and the growth of the field; and
- community-driven frameworks for policy advocacy, professional standards, ethics, issues of representation and diversity, labor, inclusion, and other matters of concern to digital library practitioners and the people and publics we serve.

While members are largely academic libraries, others are research institutions, state and large public libraries, and international institutions. Users search individual members' catalogs. It is engaging and interesting to browse individual members' collections, such as Cornell University's digital collections, which include its witchcraft collection.

- Click Cornell University Library Digital Library Collections: https://newcatalog .library.cornell.edu/digitalcollections
- Scroll the alphabetical list and click Cornell University Library Witchcraft Collection.
- Click "Search/Browse" to search more than 23,000 digital assets.
- Enter a search term, such as "black art," to find images and texts on witchcraft and magic (see figure 5.1).

Figure 5.1. Black Magick. *Division of Rare and Manuscript Collections, Cornell University Library*

Digital Public Library of America (DPLA)—DPLA is a **portal** that locates and links files to the actual library collection. The portal points to the digital collection that contains the item. DPLA does not have its own collection of items; LSS can click the option "View Full Item" from the results list to connect to the item in the owning member's collection. Searches can be limited by date, format, and other options. When searching an ancestor using the DPLA portal, several results with links to the National Archives catalog provided full images of original census forms. From the National Archives items can be downloaded and printed.

DPLA has the goal of being the portal to all digital collections in the United States. It collaborates with partners to accelerate innovative tools and ideas to equip libraries to make information more accessible. Specifically, its goals are to work with a national network of partners to

- make millions of materials from libraries, archives, museums, and other cultural institutions across the country available to all in a one-stop discovery experience;
- provide a library-controlled marketplace and platform for libraries to purchase, organize, and deliver e-books and other e-content to their patrons; and
- convene library leaders and practitioners to explore and advance technologies that serve, inform, and empower their communities.[10]

The *World Digital Library*'s (WDL's) mission is to share significant, multilingual primary sources of approximately 193 global countries and their cultures by

- preserving and sharing some of the world's most important cultural objects; and
- increasing access to cultural treasures and significant historical documents to enable discovery, scholarship, and use.[11]

Books, manuscripts, maps, and other primary materials are presented in their original languages. More than one hundred languages are represented in the WDL collection, including many lesser-known and endangered languages (see figure 5.2).

WDL has some of the same members of the Digital Library Federation and the Digital Public Library of America. It is a bit confusing to have so many key groups leading the way for digitalization. Here is how their missions vary:

- *DLF* establishes *standards and policies* for creating digital resource collections,
- *DPLA* is the portal interface to *view and use American* digital resources, and
- *WDL* is the portal interface to *view and use international* digital resources.

Europeana—The European Union sponsors a consortium of archives, libraries, and museums of its member countries called Europeana.[12] A primary goal of Europeana is to share cultural heritage for enjoyment, education, and research through access to millions of books, music, artwork, and other documents. Millions of cultural heritage items from around four thousand institutions across Europe are available online via the Europeana collections website. Searching is somewhat complicated by different copyright laws and permissions; the digital catalog users can filter their search by such parameters as type of media, providing EU country, and language.

Figure 5.2. 100 Poems by 100 Poets. *World Digital Library*

Europeana has many thematic digital collections, including a World War I collection. The various search parameters are helpful not only in limiting selection but also in finding items that have a differing point of view or perspective from the many European countries that fought with and against each other in this war. An associate organization, Europeana Pro, is a network of professionals who develop expertise, tools, and policies to embrace digital change and encourage partnerships that foster innovation. Pro helps people to use cultural heritage for education, research, creation, and recreation dedicated to an open, knowledgeable, and creative society.

CHAPTER SUMMARY

Digital libraries are an ever-growing important information source in library information services that are not necessarily found through a typical internet search. LSS who become users of digital collections can apply their knowledge and experience to helping others locate digital assets for research, education, and enjoyment. LSS who are knowledgeable of how to locate and are experienced users of digital collections support their role and responsibility for introducing relevant applications of technology, including digital literacy, to the public.

DISCUSSION QUESTIONS

1. What are key differences among digital assets, digital collections, and digital libraries?
2. How has the Library of Congress demonstrated leadership in digitization of our country's resources?
3. What is the purpose of the Digital Library Federation (DLF) and how does it work?
4. How do the missions of the Digital Federation Library, the Digital Library of America, and the World Digital Library differ?
5. Why are university libraries important places to find digital collections?

ACTIVITY

LSS were introduced to many different sources of digital collections. For an upcoming national holiday or commemoration of a world event, create a webpage for the library website of digital collections from sources discussed in this chapter that would be research based, educational, and interesting to patrons of a particular age group or the general public.

Cite all sources and provide hyperlinks to each source. Add digital images to the webpage and write a brief annotation about each digital collection to spur readers' interest on the topic and encourage them to explore further.

NOTES

1. State Library of North Carolina, "Personal Digital Archiving," last modified 2020, accessed December 5, 2020, https://statelibrary.ncdcr.gov/research/digital-information-man agement/personal-digital-archiving.

2. NYCourts.gov, "What Are Digital Assets?" Ask a Law Librarian: Legal Research, last modified 2020, accessed December 6, 2020, https://askalawlibrarian.nycourts.gov/legalresearch /faq/274963.

3. Institute of Museum and Library Services, "Mission," last modified 2020, accessed December 6, 2020, https://www.imls.gov/about/mission.

4. Techopedia, Inc., "Digital Library," last modified 2020, accessed November 30, 2020, https://www.techopedia.com/definition/14337/digital-library.

5. John McGinty, "Developing a Digital Library: Scale Requires Partnership," ACRL, last modified 2020, accessed November 30, 2020, http://www.ala.org/acrl/publications/whitepa pers/nashville/mcginty.

6. McGinty, "Developing a Digital Library."

7. Library of Congress, "National Digital Library Program," Digital Library Initiatives, last modified 2020, accessed December 10, 2020, https://memory.loc.gov/ammem/dli2/html /lcndlp.html.

8. Congress.gov, "Part OFS for 'American Memory,'" Library of Congress, last modified 2020, accessed December 10, 2020, https://www.loc.gov/search/index/partof/?q=ameri can+memory&sp=1.

9. CRL, "About CRL," Center for Research Libraries—Global Resources Network, last modified 2020, accessed December 13, 2020, https://www.crl.edu/.

10. DPLA, "About Us," Digital Public Library of America, last modified 2020, accessed December 12, 2020, https://dp.la/about.

11. World Digital Library, "Home Page," last modified 2020, accessed December 12, 2020, https://www.wdl.org/en/.

12. European Union, "About Us," Europeana, last modified 2020, accessed December 13, 2020, https://www.europeana.eu/en/about-us.

REFERENCES, SUGGESTED READINGS, AND WEBSITES

Congress.gov. "Part OFS for 'American Memory.'" Library of Congress. Last modified 2020. Accessed December 10, 2020. https://www.loc.gov/search/index/partof/?q=american+memory&sp=1.

Cornell University Library. "Cornell University Witchcraft Collection." Digital Collections. Last modified 2020. Accessed December 12, 2020. https://newcatalog.library.cornell.edu/digitalcollections.

CRL. "About CRL." Center for Research Libraries—Global Resources Network. Last modified 2020. Accessed December 13, 2020. https://www.crl.edu/.

DPLA. "About Us." Digital Public Library of America. Last modified 2020. Accessed December 12, 2020. https://dp.la/about.

European Union. "About Us." Europeana. Last modified 2020. Accessed December 13, 2020. https://www.europeana.eu/en/about-us.

Institute of Museum and Library Services. "Framework of Guidance for Building Good Digital Collections." Publications. Last modified 2020. Accessed December 6, 2020. https://www.imls.gov/publications/framework-guidance-building-good-digital-collections.

———. "Mission." Institute of Museum and Library Services. Last modified 2020. Accessed December 6, 2020. https://www.imls.gov/about/mission.

Lamb, Annette. "A Dozen Ways to Promote Cultural Heritage through Image Collections." *Teacher Librarian* 47, no. 4 (April 2020): 56–60. https://search.ebscohost.com/login.aspx?direct=true&AuthType=cookie,ip,cpid&custid=csl&db=aph&AN=143257208&site=ehost-live&scope=site.

Library of Congress. "Challenges to Building an Effective Digital Library." Digital Library Initiative. Last modified 2020. Accessed December 2, 2020. https://memory.loc.gov/ammem/dli2/html/cbedl.html.

———. "National Digital Library Program." Digital Library Initiatives. Last modified 2020. Accessed December 10, 2020. https://memory.loc.gov/ammem/dli2/html/lcndlp.html.

McGinty, John. "Developing a Digital Library: Scale Requires Partnership." ACRL. Last modified 2020. Accessed November 30, 2020. http://www.ala.org/acrl/publications/whitepapers/nashville/mcginty.

NYCourts.gov. "What Are Digital Assets?" Ask a Law Librarian: Legal Research. Last modified 2020. Accessed December 6, 2020. https://askalawlibrarian.nycourts.gov/legalresearch/faq/274963.

Paneck, Bruce. "Historical Primary Sources Online: Theme-based Digital Archives." University Libraries. Last modified December 4, 2020. Accessed December 5, 2020. https://guides.lib.vt.edu/c.php?g=895000.

Regents of the University of California. "Digital Library Development Program." The Library U C San Diego. Last modified 2020. Accessed December 2, 2020. https://library.ucsd.edu/research-and-collections/collections/digital-collections/index.html.

Roncevic, Mirela. "One Country One Library: The Model for an Open National Digital Library That Serves the Changing Needs of Twenty-First-Century Users, Publishers, and Libraries." *Library Technology Reports* 56, no. 7 (October 2020): 1–32. https://search.ebsco

host.com/login.aspx?direct=true&AuthType=cookie,ip,cpid&custid=csl&db=aph&AN
=146355747&site=ehost-live&scope=site.

Sharpened Productions. "Digital Asset." *Tech Terms*. Last modified 2020. Accessed November 30, 2020. https://techterms.com/definition/digital_asset.

State Library of North Carolina. "Personal Digital Archiving." Last modified 2020. Accessed December 5, 2020. https://statelibrary.ncdcr.gov/research/digital-information-manage ment/personal-digital-archiving.

Techopedia, Inc. "Digital Library." Last modified 2020. Accessed November 30, 2020. https:// www.techopedia.com/definition/14337/digital-library.

Uzwyshyn, Ray. "Open Digital Research Ecosystems: How to Build Them and Why." *Computers in Libraries* 40, no. 8 (November/December 2020): 4–8. https://search.ebscohost.com/login .aspx?direct=true&AuthType=cookie,ip,cpid&custid=csl&db=aph&AN=147057444&site=e host-live&scope=site.

World Digital Library. "Home Page." Last modified 2020. Accessed December 12, 2020. https://www.wdl.org/en/.

CHAPTER 6

Archives and Preservation

LSS know the role and responsibility of libraries for introducing relevant applications of technology, including digital literacy, to the public.

LSS know role of technology in creating, identifying, retrieving, and accessing information resources and demonstrate facility with appropriate information discovery tools.

Topics Covered in This Chapter
Preservation
   Paper
   Expertise from Museums
Archives
   Similarities and Differences
   Interview with an Archivist
National Archives
   U.S. Census
State Digital Libraries and Archives
   Historical Digital Collections
Local Digital Collections and Archives
Digitization Grants
Chapter Summary

Key Terms
Archives—Highly organized and selective places of storage, archives are often associated with museums and libraries, for records, media, and artifacts of significant importance.
Archivists—These people are specially trained to identify documents, texts, media, and artifacts of lasting value and preserve, store, and provide access to records and artifacts of importance.

Census—In the United States, this is the official ten-year count or survey of its population that records various details of individuals and establishes the number of congressional districts.

Enumeration Districts—A term also referred to as "EDs" by the Bureau of the U.S. Census, these are the areas that could be covered by a single census taker or enumerator in one census period.

In-kind—These are the staff, equipment, and other resources the library already has in place that, if a grant is funded, will help make the project successful.

Paper deterioration—This refers to the crumbling and degradation of paper, an essential material for library collections, which is exacerbated by environmental, mechanical, and chemical processes.

Preservation Librarians and archivists use methods to restore artifacts to as close to the original state as possible and share with the public images through digitization.

Videography documentation—Documentation is an ongoing process of community filming; LSS support the documentation and preservation of local heritage by helping to create a local film archive.

PRESERVATION

Preservation, in relation to digitization, is to perpetuate history by constructing authentic images, sounds, or video of the past. Through the use of photography and other digital formats, images and sounds of artifacts that are vulnerable to decay preserve their historic meaning and enhance our knowledge of the past. In the course of daily life, individuals and organizations create and keep information about their personal and business activities.

There are many reasons why we preserve. Preservation helps organizations maintain continuity between past work and actions and the decisions they must make for today and the future. We preserve family memorabilia to help us better understand who we are by linking ourselves to photographs and objects once owned by our ancestors. By viewing intact artifacts, reading primary source documents, and scanning information from records, we step back into history and gain a better sense of cultural change and why societies made decisions that in both large and small ways contributed to the events of history. Digitization allows many forms of preservation. One method that is gaining prominence is **videography documentation**, an ongoing process of videoing and creating an archive of videos of key events, people, and other aspects of the community. Akin to a video yearbook but with a focus on culture, environment, buildings, and other local customs and norms, videography documentation can be readily done with library equipment of camera, sound equipment, tripod, and editing software. LSS may become involved in this work to help to expand preservation to include videography for future generations.

It is important that LSS who work with digitizing artifacts know how to handle and care for them. Never should the process of digitization cause damage or harm to the object. The next section, using nationally accepted standards, will discuss how LSS can best handle artifacts to be digitized.

Look around your library to identify items that are not stored safely. Are there artifacts too close to heating or water sources? Papers, journals, documents, or texts not stored properly can grow mold or otherwise be damaged. Climate control is often mixed in library buildings that are decades or centuries old.

Paper

Paper is one of the most fundamental materials found in libraries, essential to collections of books, magazines, and other circulating content. For the last two centuries, paper was made from the cellulose of wood, an array of botanical cells and fibers, varying its quality and durability. Paper of the past fifty years is more vulnerable to decay than paper that was created five hundred years ago due to environmental and chemical factors. The Library of Congress has the following advice about paper.

1. Prior to the mid-nineteenth century, paper made from long cotton fibers and linen rags was especially durable. We see "rag" content in specialty papers today.
2. Wood then replaced rags around the 1860s with shorter and less durable fibers processed by mechanical or chemical pulping.
3. Mechanical pulping is weaker and deteriorates more quickly than chemically pulped paper.
4. Moisture, acids from air pollution, poor air and storage quality, and other environmental insults accelerate deterioration.
5. Pulp, the fibrous parts of trees and plants, is the main ingredient in the papermaking process. Paper made before the 1980s tends to break down more quickly because alum-rosin sizing was added to the paper to help the inking process. This added compound, when combined with moisture, turned to sulfuric acid that makes this paper more acidic and less durable.
6. Acids, sulfur, and nitrogen oxides form in paper by the absorption of pollutants.[1]

Book leaves that are more brown and brittle along the edges than in the center clearly illustrate this absorption of pollutants from the air. Paper today is sensitive to humidity and sunlight. Stored in cooler temperatures, it is able to last hundreds of years. Unfortunately, it was not until relatively recently that librarians and others recognized how severe the problem of **paper deterioration** was and remedies were sought.

There is now much science around preserving paper. For example, mass deacidification is a process whereby a large number of volumes that were created with acidic paper are neutralized with alkaline treatments in a specialized cylinder or chamber. Hardbound volumes generally treat better than softbound and bindings and should be in good condition with attached covers. The LOC has successfully embarked on a mass deacidification process for millions of its volumes.[2]

Expertise from Museums

In addition to the LOC, many museums and historical societies share expertise for archiving and digitizing artifacts. One example of such is the Henry Ford.[3] Not only does the Henry Ford encourage onsite visitors to tour its collections; it also has robust digital collections available for anyone to view online. In addition, it offers digital resources and educational support for museums, libraries, and individuals who would like to preserve and archive artifacts properly.

The Henry Ford suggests ways to preserve objects made of different materials such as metal, wood, or glass. It also offers advice on the preservation of textiles, paintings, photographs, furniture, and other items. The museum offers material fact sheets, videos, and instructions on how to care for, preserve, archive, and store artifacts.

For example, the Henry Ford factsheet states that photographic materials are the most unstable and difficult collectibles to preserve, yet they are the most common to own.[4] The first step is to eliminate causes of deterioration. Table 6.1 suggests how to prevent photograph deterioration.

Table 6.1.   Prevent Deterioration

Light	Display color photographs under low levels (50 Lux), black-and-white photos under slightly higher levels.
Humidity	Use inexpensive temperature and humidity sensors to prevent curling.
Mold	Use 30–50 percent relative humidity at temperatures of 58–68°F.
Framing	Use acid-free mat board and window mat to avoid sticking to glass.
Pollution	Avoid ozone, sulfur, and peroxides, leather and rubber bands.
Contaminants	Silver particles in black-and-white photographs corrode with metallic substances. Chemical pollutants damage color photographs.
Mishandling	Store in clear mylar envelopes. For extra protection use acid-free envelopes.
Pests	Store in uncoated mylar or polyethylene.
Repairs	Use professioal conservators for extensive cleaning and repair.
Cleaning	Clear surface dirt with a soft brush.
Removal	Remove any metal staples and paper clips and replace with inert plastic paper clips.

Library companies sell archival supplies such as paper, tissue, storage boxes, plastic bags, fasteners, cleaning materials, archival identification tags and pens (see figure 6.1). LSS can seek training from experts in local museums or historical societies to learn how to handle and best preserve integrity and original characteristics of an item. Often state libraries will either provide training workshops or have an expert on staff who can provide guidance on how to

1. handle archival documents and books;
2. avoid factors that cause damage;
3. store, exhibit, and frame items; and
4. lightly repair and clean (especially mold).

LSS can use the Directory of Preservation Organizations and Resources[5] to locate approximately five thousand historical societies and seven thousand museums by state, region, or keywords. Many of these institutions share free information about preservation. Once an item has been preserved or repaired properly, it may be digitized for online access by the public. In the next section archives are introduced.

Figure 6.1. Archival and Preservation Supplies. *uschools/ E+ via Getty Images*

ARCHIVES

Archives are highly organized and selective places of storage for records of significant importance. Archival records take many forms, including correspondence, diaries, financial and legal documents, photographs, and moving image and sound recordings. All state governments as well as many local governments, universities, businesses, libraries, and historical societies maintain archives[6] of records that document people, places, activities, and actions relevant to core purposes and goals. Archival records are kept also as a means to maintain history. Without archives, critical data that document everyday life of the past may be lost.

Archivists are professionals specially trained to identify documents, texts, media, and artifacts of lasting value. They have the knowledge and skills to preserve, store, manage, and share archival items and materials. LSS support the work of archivists when they know and use established standards of preservation, access, and storage. While the work of librarians and archivists have many similarities, there are also differences. A librarian, with training, can also be an archivist.

Similarities and Differences

Librarians and archivists both require strong sets of organizational skills to ensure materials are readily accessible to the public. They both preserve and maintain information databases so future generations can access, select, and use information remotely. Librarianship requires strong interpersonal skills as most librarians work directly with the public, helping them find information and conduct research.

Archivists are in charge of appraising, processing, and cataloging important documents and records. They rarely work with the public. While they share common skill sets, librarians and archivists approach their work quite differently. Archivists

- work with historical records and documents, often with a small team of specialized researchers;
- appraise and determine the value of each piece or record;
- use a system to document new arrivals;
- determine the best way to organize the document or artifact within the institution;
- use innovative methods to help the institution become more efficient with storage;
- apply standards for preservation for each material type;
- have limited direct interaction with patrons if the institution is strictly an archive;
- respond to outside inquiries and requests; and
- work with permanent records and historically valuable documents such as photographs, prints, and maps.

LSS may support the work of the archivist. In many small libraries, LSS, with training, often assume the role of local or town archivist. LSS who support archives may work, in addition to libraries, in government offices, museums, universities, or even hospitals.

Interview with an Archivist

The following questions were asked of an expert archivist, Dr. Anastasia Weigle.[7] Below are her responses regarding how LSS can prepare to work in archives:

1. *Why it is important LSS learn about and are able to do the work of preservation and archives?*

   I believe it is essential for LSS to understand the differences between library collections and archival collections. The work required to maintain archives and special collections is very different from traditional library work. In libraries, books are organized by author or subject, but archival collections are organized by provenance and original order. That is very different. While books and journals are cataloged using DDC or LOC and contain subject headings, archival collections have "finding aids" containing multiple access points— subject, the creator's name, and geographic headings. Preservation of archives requires stricter environmental conditions. Library materials circulate while archival materials do not. Library materials are open to the public for browsing. Archival materials are in closed stacks with supervision. LSS must understand these differences to protect and preserve historical records for future generations while making them accessible for research.

2. *What should LSS know and be able to do to support these areas now and in the future?*

   Library support staff should be able to differentiate the theoretical foundation of library information science and archival science. While LIS [Library and Information Science] focuses on the organization of resources and how users seek, find, retrieve, and use these resources, archival science places its foundation on provenance (ownership of records) and original order. Library support staff should know how to read and use finding aids. Library support staff should be competent in technology, particularly digital preservation, as they may be involved in digitizing historical documents. Library support staff should be able to assist researchers in finding archival materials via the finding aid—digital or in print. Library support staff should understand how to handle historical records and monitor environmental conditions.

3. *What work experiences or other training besides LSS education would be helpful?*

There are a number of wonderful organizations that offer workshops, including opportunities for volunteer work in archives. For example, those who work in the New England area may be interested in joining New England Archives. Those in the Mid-Atlantic States should find out about MARAC—Mid-Atlantic Regional Archive Conference. Talking to a trained archivist is also helpful as they can provide guidance and advice. The Society of American Archivists offers two certificate programs—"Digital Archives Specialists" and "Arrangement and Description." The latter is key to archival work.

4. *What advice can you give a new LSS who is interested in pursuing archival work?*

In addition to my previous answer, I think LSS interested in archival work should seek out archive and records management courses, material preservation, and even digital curation. Also, studies in the humanities are helpful, in particular, U.S. History. There are plenty of reading materials about this field, so I encourage LSS to read and learn as much as they can to build their knowledge. I also encourage LSS to find volunteer work at museums, historical societies, and public library archives. If one is so inclined and has a great love for history, an MLS degree in archive management is a plus and can open up doors to excellent opportunities in the archival world.

5. *Is there anything else you would like to say or add?*

There are so many hidden collections in archives waiting to be found. We need more LSS knowledgeable in maintaining library and archival collections. Understanding how to care for and preserve historical records will open up dynamic working opportunities for LSS not only in public and academic libraries but in historical societies and museums. We have a moral obligation—to preserve, organize, and make available historical documents that can educate, inspire, and teach us about our past that help us understand our current events, which in turn can lead us into a future of wisdom and knowledge.

The job outlook for those who work in both libraries and archives is strong. The need to manage archives spurs the demand for both professional and support archivists, curators, and museum technicians.

NATIONAL ARCHIVES

We begin the discussion of archives by introducing America's federal archive, the National Archives and Records Administration (NARA)[8] that serves as the nation's record keeper of approximately 1–3 percent of all federal documents and materials.

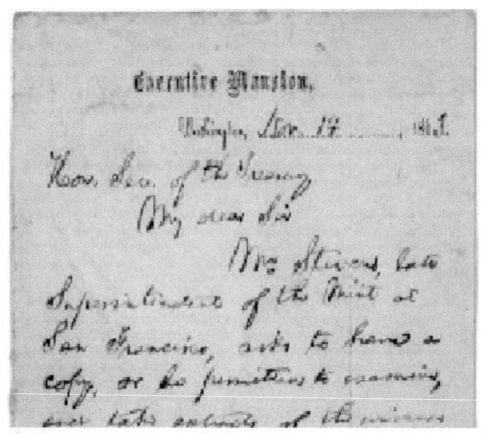

Figure 6.2.   Letter from Abraham Lincoln. *National Archives*

LSS use NARA to search U.S. veterans' records, visit a presidential library, or delve into genealogy. The majority of NARA's records have been digitized and are available freely online. Just one example of historic significance from the wealth of correspondence by and to President Abraham Lincoln is his letter to Salmon P. Chase, his secretary of the treasury (see figure 6.2).

While the Library of Congress is the library of the House of Representatives and Senate, NARA is the archive of important federal documents and items that need to be preserved, accessed, and available to future generations.

U.S. Census

NARA also maintains and digitizes U.S. Census records. NARA has digitized census schedules from 1790 to 1940. The 1950 Census is digitized and released in 2022.

The 1940 **census** occurred at the end of the Great Depression and many people were put to work gathering significantly more data than any previous census. The first step is to identify the appropriate **enumeration district** or geographic location where a person lived. A large city may have many enumeration districts, narrowed by street-level information.[9] Table 6.2 lists steps to search the 1940 Census online.

Table 6.2.   How to Search the Online 1940 Census

1	Access the National Archives U.S. 1940 Census at http://1940census.archives.gov/
2	Search by the enumeration number if you know the page EN. If you do not know the enumeration number, search by location, filling in menu for state, country, town, and street (if street is not available, searching the census sheets of the town will be more laborious).
3	Select either map, descriptions, or census schedules.
4	Provided will be maps of the town specific to the street area.
6	Census schedules are located by EN or enumeration number. The EN references the actual page in the census book or schedule.

The 1940 census provided more comprehensive data than had been collected by the federal government before. Many libraries subscribe to the library edition of Ancestry. Ancestry includes many other sources of genealogical records, including the federal census. Enumeration numbers are easy to find using a library edition of Ancestry. FamilySearch is another helpful genealogy source. FamilySearch is a nonprofit organization and website offering genealogical records, education, and software. It is operated by the Church of Jesus Christ of Latter-Day Saints and is closely connected with the church's Family History department. Both sites provide access to national archives of digitized family records. LSS search the 1940 census and the other genealogical sites as a rewarding personal experience as well as to be able to help others search family history.

STATE DIGITAL LIBRARIES AND ARCHIVES

State libraries primarily support the research of the state legislature and preserve and archive important records and documents. Responsibilities of state libraries vary but often include leadership, materials, programming, education, and funding supports for academic, public, and school libraries.

The majority of state libraries offer digital libraries, offering subscription databases to their residents. Every state varies in the titles, providers, and quantity. Indiana offers a virtual library called Inspire.[10] In addition to subscription databases, it has a searchable archive of digitized Indiana newspapers and digital collections of Indiana history and genealogy. The New York State Archives is a department within the New York State Department of Education. It offers abundant digital collections about New York, its history, genealogy, and the people who made it the Empire State. Archives support academic research. A useful site compiled by NARA is an alphabetical listing of the fifty State Archives with active links to each archive website as well as email and phone contact information.[11]

Historical Digital Collections

In addition to archives, there are state historical societies. Libraries, archives, universities, and museums share common interest in the preservation, organization, and access of records, books, media, and artifacts. These institutions often work together, both formally and informally, to ensure the history of the states be preserved and shared with future generations.

An example of collaboration is the Connecticut Digital Collections, which provide free access to digital records and artifacts from the State Library, the State Archives, and the University of Connecticut, among other places.[12] As one of the original thirteen colonies, Connecticut has extensive primary source materials on colonial history, the American Revolution, the War of 1812, the Civil War, and other eras and events that shaped the nation.

LSS can explore and use state digital archives and collections to research American history. Encourage patrons to use their state library and historical society databases to locate primary sources and other information.

LOCAL DIGITAL COLLECTIONS AND ARCHIVES

Uncountable artifacts, texts, manuscripts, and images of important historic and cultural heritage exist in local libraries, historical societies, and museums. Across the country, local library collections are the foundation to larger state resources. The State Library of Ohio offers grants to local Ohio libraries and institutions to build the Ohio Memory, which includes collections from more than 360 cultural heritage institutions from all of Ohio's eighty-eight counties. The Online Archive of California provides free public access to primary source collections created and maintained by more than two hundred libraries and other institutions. These are just a few examples of how state libraries are collaborating and supporting the local digitization efforts of local libraries. LSS can explore their state libraries and the state historical societies to find opportunities for financial and other guidance to digitize local libraries' treasures.

Digital collections and archive projects do not have to expensive, nor do the artifacts always have to be housed in the library. An example is the Groton History Online project.[13] The library asked the community to share with them original postcards of historic scenes or past events that occurred in Groton, home of submarine building and a Revolutionary War battlefield. Over a thousand postcards were offered. Staff scanned each postcard, entered simple metadata about the creator, location, date, event, and related terms for the database. The postcards were returned to owners. LSS may use this model to suggest a digitized archive of local postcards around themes of historic or other importance in their local town or city.

DIGITIZATION GRANTS

The Institute of Museum and Library Services (IMLS) is a federal agency that supports more than 123,000 libraries and 35,000 museums in the United States. The IMLS Grants to States program is a major source of federal funding that distributes well over $1 million per year. The grants are distributed to the fifty state libraries and agencies of U.S. territories that develop library services as mandated by the Library Services and Technology Act (LSTA). LSTA grants have many purposes, including support of digitization of special collections and access to electronic databases and e-books. State libraries disburse LSTA grants to local libraries that apply for competitive funds.

The National Endowment for the Humanities (NEH) has a program for the preservation of and access to collections of cultural value. Applicants must be small to mid-sized libraries, historical societies, museums, or like institutions that have never received any type of NEH grant. About one-third of the applicants who apply are successfully awarded grants for their projects. The NEH website has extensive resources and examples on how to apply for their grants.

Public and school libraries may consider town and regional funding sources. For example, the newspaper, *The Day*,[14] in New London, Connecticut, is a nonprofit entity. Twice a year after operating and capital expenses are met, the newspaper disperses any profit to other nonprofit organizations, including libraries. Its foundation has funded local library digitization projects.

LSS can familiarize themselves with the Bank of America (BoA) Philanthropic Solutions page.[15] BoA compiles numerous grants for libraries, education, and nonprofits. To search,

1. go to https://www.bankofamerica.com/philanthropic/search-for-grants/;
2. select a foundation (repeat this step for each search);
3. narrow search by category (optional);
4. narrow search by state (optional); and
5. keep trying any combination of the above steps.

Not only will LSS find grant descriptions, but on each grant site is the online application with instructions. BoA coordinates and supports grant opportunities for nonprofits across the country from its Philanthropic Solutions website.

LSS work with library patrons and materials and often have excellent ideas of what new services the public wants and would use. A grant has a much better chance of being funded when there are **"in-kind"** contributions. In-kind contributions are what the library already has in place to help the project. In-kind may be funding, staffing, materials, or other expertise. LSS can be contributors to digitization projects and identified on the grant application to help with the selection, scanning, and metadata creation. Their time and expertise have in-kind value. LSS who are familiar with BoA and other funding institutions may research and share funding opportunities with supervisors. LSS can help locate grants and become a skilled resource for digitizing local primary sources and artifacts.

CHAPTER SUMMARY

LSS who understand the importance of archiving and preserving important records and artifacts and are able to perform the work of digitization support the role and responsibility of libraries for introducing relevant applications of technology to find, select, and make digital collections and archives available to the public. LSS who have digital and archive training are able to create, identify, retrieve, and help others access information resources from national, state, and local archives and digital libraries.

DISCUSSION QUESTIONS

1. Why is it important for LSS to learn about and be able to work in preservation and archives?
2. What are some of the key differences between the types of work LSS perform in libraries rather than in archives? What are similarities?
3. What suggestions can LSS make to prevent paper deterioration?
4. Why should LSS know about and use national and state archives? What can they tell patrons about them?
5. Why should LSS know about grants and how can LSS be part of the grant-seeking process?

ACTIVITY: CREATE A LOCAL DIGITAL ARCHIVE

This activity is to gain initial practice in creating an archive.

1. Look around your local library and discuss with librarians and others what artifacts they may have that could be an important archive or digital collection for patrons to access online.
2. Develop a theme or purpose for the collection, such as historic postcards, a community event, an important industry, and so forth.
3. Gather five to ten items. Scan or take digital pictures of them.
4. Insert each image on a PowerPoint or other presentation slide and describe its importance.
5. Present your collection to stakeholders (i.e., library staff and administrators) for feedback.

NOTES

1. Library of Congress, "The Deterioration and Preservation of Paper: Some Essential Facts," *Preservation*, last modified 2021, accessed January 11, 2021, https://www.loc.gov/preservation/care/deterioratebrochure.html.

2. Library of Congress, "Mass Deacidification," *Preservation*, last modified 2021, accessed January 12, 2021, https://www.loc.gov/preservation/about/deacid/index.html.

3. The Henry Ford, "Mission, Vision, and Board of Trustees," last modified 2021, accessed January 12, 2021, https://www.thehenryford.org/about/mission-and-board-of-trustees/.

4. The Henry Ford, "The Care, Storage, and Handling of Artifacts," last modified 2021, accessed January 11, 2021, https://www.thehenryford.org/collections-and-research/digital-resources/caring-for-artifacts/.

5. PreservationDirectory.com, "Preservation Organizations and Resources," Preservation Directory, last modified 2021, accessed January 13, 2021, https://www.preservationdirectory.com/preservationorganizationsresources/OrganizationListings.aspx?catid=3.

6. Smithsonian, "What Are Archives?" National Museum of American History, last modified 2021, accessed January 9, 2021, https://americanhistory.si.edu/archives/about/what-are-archives.

7. Anastasia S. Weigle, interview, University of Maine–Augusta, December 30, 2020.

8. National Archives and Records Administration, "National Archives," last modified 2021, accessed January 14, 2021, https://www.archives.gov/.

9. U.S. National Archives and Records Administration, "Getting Started—1940 Census," 1940 Census—National Archives, last modified 2021, accessed January 14, 2021, https://1940census.archives.gov/getting-started.asp?.

10. Indiana State Library, "Inspire," Inspire: A Service of the Indiana State Library, last modified 2021, accessed January 14, 2021, https://inspire.in.gov/.

11. U.S. National Archives and Records Administration, "State Archives," Archives Library Information Center (ALIC), last modified 2021, accessed January 14, 2021, https://www.archives.gov/research/alic/reference/state-archives.html.

12. Connecticut State Library, "Connecticut Digital Collections," last modified 2021, accessed January 14, 2021, https://libguides.ctstatelibrary.org/dld/CT_Digital_Collections.

13. Groton Public Library, "Archives," last modified 2021, accessed January 14, 2021, https://grotonct.pastperfectonline.com/archive.

14. *The Day*, last modified 2021, accessed January 14, 2021, https://www.theday.com/.

15. Bank of America, "Find a Foundation," Philanthropic Solutions, last modified 2021, accessed January 14, 2021, https://www.bankofamerica.com/philanthropic/search-for-grants/.

REFERENCES, SUGGESTED READINGS, AND WEBSITES

Bank of America. "Find a Foundation." Philanthropic Solutions. Last modified 2021. Accessed January 14, 2021. https://www.bankofamerica.com/philanthropic/search-for-grants/.

Connecticut State Library. "Connecticut Digital Collections." Last modified 2021. Accessed January 14, 2021. https://libguides.ctstatelibrary.org/dld/CT_Digital_Collections.

The Day. Last modified 2021. Accessed January 14, 2021. https://www.theday.com/.

Groton Public Library. "Archives." Last modified 2021. Accessed January 14, 2021. https://grotonct.pastperfectonline.com/archive.

The Henry Ford. "The Care, Storage, and Handling of Artifacts." Last modified 2021. Accessed January 11, 2021. https://www.thehenryford.org/collections-and-research/digital-resources/caring-for-artifacts/.

———. "Mission, Vision, and Board of Trustees." Last modified 2021. Accessed January 12, 2021. https://www.thehenryford.org/about/mission-and-board-of-trustees/.

Indiana State Library. "Inspire." Inspire: A Service of the Indiana State Library. Last modified 2021. Accessed January 14, 2021. https://inspire.in.gov/.

Library of Congress. "Mass Deacidification." *Preservation*. Last modified 2021. Accessed January 12, 2021. https://www.loc.gov/preservation/about/deacid/index.html.

National Archives and Records Administration. "National Archives." Last modified 2021. Accessed January 14, 2021. https://www.archives.gov/.

———. "Preservation as a Treatment." Technical Preservation Services. Last modified 2021. Accessed January 9, 2021. https://www.nps.gov/tps/standards/four-treatments/treatment-preservation.htm.

PreservationDirectory.com. "Preservation Organizations and Resources." Preservation Directory. Last modified 2021. Accessed January 13, 2021. https://www.preservationdirectory.com/preservationorganizationsresources/OrganizationListings.aspx?catid=3.

Smithsonian. "What Are Archives?" National Museum of American History. Last modified 2021. Accessed January 9, 2021. https://americanhistory.si.edu/archives/about/what-are-archives.

The U.S. National Archives and Records Administration. "Census Records." Resources for Genealogists. Last modified 2021. Accessed January 14, 2021. https://www.archives.gov/research/genealogy/census.

———. "National Archives Grants—November 2020." National Historical Publications and Records Commission. Last modified 2021. Accessed January 14, 2021. https://www.archives .gov/nhprc/awards/awards-11-20.

U.S. National Archives and Records Administration. "State Archives." Archives Library Information Center (ALIC). Last modified 2021. Accessed January 14, 2021. https://www .archives.gov/research/alic/reference/state-archives.html.

Weigle, Anastasia S. Interview. University of Maine–Augusta. December 30, 2020.

PART II

Web Services, E-Books, Responsibilities, and Media

CHAPTER 7

Searching the Internet

LSS know concepts and issues concerning the appropriate use of technology by different user groups.

LSS are able to assist and train users to operate public equipment, connect to the internet, use library software applications, and access library services from remote locations.

Topics Covered in This Chapter
Web Directories
   Academic and Professional Directories
   Business Directories
   Google My Business—Google Analytics
Search Engines
   Web Browsers
   Fundamentals
   Voice Assistants
Search Strategies
   Advanced Shortcuts
   Using Critical Thinking
   International Searching
Internet Archive
   Distributed Web
Chapter Summary

Key Terms
Algorithm—This is a set of rules that a computer needs to complete a task. Search engine software is embedded with such rules and procedures in order to index sites from the web.

Distributed web—As opposed to a centralized, top-down internet, this configuration is a peer-to-peer network where users' computers can be accessed to speed up searching.

Graphical User Interfaces—More commonly known as GUIs, this is a component of a web browser that enables images, video, and other media to be viewed from websites.

Index—Search engines compile an index of websites and URLs that, in turn, are where the results of a search derive.

Link rot—This is a slang term for hypertext links or URLs that are broken and thus websites or pages cannot be found.

Spiders—This is search engine software that crawls through the internet to build its indexes based on algorithms and other criteria.

Uniform Resource Locator—More commonly referred to as the URL, this is the internet address of a webpage.

Web browser—A key component of the search process that enables users to retrieve and view the websites once they are located.

Web directories—Similar to LSS creating library bibliographies, directories are databases of preselected websites on a theme or subject that serve to provide quick access to informative websites.

WEB DIRECTORIES

There are two fundamental tools or approaches to search websites: web directories and search engines. **Web directories** are databases of preselected lists of linked websites on a theme or subject that serve to provide quick access to informative websites. Unlike search engines that generate lists of websites by computers, the sites listed in web directories are selected and organized by humans into subject categories. For example, in the broad category of health, there may be subcategories such as medicine, fitness, surgery, men's health, or alternative medicines. Directory databases are smaller than search engine databases.[1] Here are two of the most comprehensive general topic directories[2] that LSS may find useful:

Open Directory Project—The ODP (also known as DMOZ) is an open categorized list of sources that are unranked and carefully reviewed before inclusion in the directory. See http://odp.org/.

Aviva Directory—Aviva Directory is a general web directory that organizes the internet's best websites by topic and, when appropriate, by region. See https://www.avivadirectory.com/.

Web directories aim to provide quick access to quality websites and to build a user base that will rely on the directory to support their searching. Keeping a directory current is a tremendous task as websites and their links often change. People will not use a directory that has an abundance of **link rot** or broken links, nor would library staff recommend such a delinquent directory to patrons. Link rot is created when a webpage is moved, taken down, or reorganized. Clicking on a rotten link usually results in a 404 error, with a message that the page cannot be found.

Directory searching begins with determining the subject category that best matches the information sought. Directory editors decide which sites will be included into each subject category. Because web directories are built and maintained by people, they contain far fewer websites than the indexes of search engines. Web directories may potentially deliver higher quality, less irrelevant returns than search engines. Conversely, web directories may point to URLs that have had content changes, have moved, or no longer exist.[3]

Today there are few general topic web directories. Search engines have improved as people have become more proficient users who no longer feel the need to rely on directories for everyday searches. The more successful web directories are related to the academic and business world where there is a need to be able to quickly find vetted websites.

Academic and Professional Directories

Academic and professional organizations selectively create directories in order to provide quick access to websites on topics of importance or interest to their members. LSS can rely on academic and professional web directories:

- These directories are authoritative, created by librarians or other specialists for educational and/or professional purposes.
- There is a focused purpose that aligns with the core values of the organization.
- Subject classifications found in these directories align with professional practices, education, and other categories.
- Directories are updated regularly by subject matter experts.
- These directories offer sites with new research.

Academic and school LSS may be familiar with a library product service called LibGuides, a directory-like approach to organizing research and information websites around a subject, project, or class. Public libraries are also using LibGuides to organize reference and information services. Because of the many additional robust features of LibGuides, this product will be discussed in chapter 9.

Business Directories

Subscription business directories are aimed for certain interest groups and provide research and other information about businesses that may not be available to the public elsewhere. Business directories may also provide services to customers, such as financial guidance or planning. The Dunn & Bradstreet B2B (business to business) database contains more than 150 million companies and 130 million people searchable by name, location, or industry. Users can build targeted sales lists, read reports of competitive information, access financial information, and use research that provides insights to thousands of industries. Depending upon the library mission and users' needs, a library may subscribe to several business directories.

There are also free and available online directories that, while not offering as many services, are strong contenders for providing basic company information. Yelp for Business provides free web pages for companies to market themselves. Thomas, a well-known company directory, has a free online directory searchable

Table 7.1. Business Directories

Best of the Web	https://botw.org/	With more than 400,000 unique categories to choose from, each website listed is hand-reviewed by expert editors.
Jasmine	https://www.jasminedirectory.com/	Websites and businesses categorized topically and regionally.
Kompass	https://us.kompass.com/	Search by product and/or company. Locally based teams update information regularly.
Manta	https://www.manta.com/	Offers free listings for small businesses looking to get their name featured across the web.
Thomas	https://www.thomasnet.com/	Since 1898 Thomas specialists have vetted and provided up-to-date company information.

by category, company, or brand. Table 7.1 describes just a few of the many useful and free online business web directories LSS can share with patrons who seek company or product information.

Google My Business—Google Analytics

As a segue to search engines, LSS should know about two Google products, Google My Business and Google Analytics, that support a greater web presence for libraries, nonprofits, and businesses by providing statistical feedback about how websites are used. Important ways for libraries to connect with current and potential users is through websites and social media. Library administrators, boards, and others need to know to what extent the website is serving its community.

For example, each month a library director in a large Connecticut public library informs the board of trustees about the library web services and how they are being used with Google My Business and Google Analytics data. Google My Business is a free and easy-to-use tool for businesses and organizations to manage their online presence across Google, including Search and Maps. When people find a library on Google Maps and Search, they can also find information about its hours, website, and address. Library administration can read and respond to reviews from customers and learn how customers search for the library and if they are local. Librarians can also learn how many people call the library directly from the phone number displayed on local search results in Search and Maps.[4]

Google Analytics compiles the keywords people use to find the library website. Using this information, library web staff can adjust the website to ensure these most popular keywords are optimally scripted into the site. It also reports which pages and links are most accessed from the website. For example, if the library produces online children's story hours and programs, Google Analytics can report how many clicks they receive, the users' locations, whether these are first time or repeat users, and other helpful statistics and data to be used to optimize or tune the library website.

Library staff and others can draw conclusions about the success of the library website through both of these products. Rather than assuming that the library website is successful, each month via the Google reports staff can track how people find the site and which web pages or links had the most traffic. In turn, staff can use this data to make improvements to the design and information of the library website to increase its usefulness to the community it serves.

While directories continue to have validity as a means to search the internet, the most popular and expansive way to search takes place using search engines. LSS who understand the underlying structures of search engines can effectively use them to quickly obtain high-quality information for patrons.

SEARCH ENGINES

No doubt, searching the internet has become easier. Where once only the exact words that appeared in a few tags of code in order to "hit" a website, today we are in an incredible transition where search engines are beginning to use the tools of algorithms, artificial intelligence (AI) and machine learning to intuitively augment the process of searching the internet. Google sets a high bar for searching, with its massive content indexes, ranking algorithms, AI, and other content and technology components. However, search engines are subject to manipulation and bias. They are not transparent about the sources they index or how they rank results. They operate primarily as advertising platforms and are optimized to maximize revenue.

The remainder of this chapter focuses on the basics of search engines and how to structure searching. Rather than relying solely on the mechanisms of the computers that primarily serve the needs of commercial enterprises, LSS are able to construct searches that are meaningful, informative, trustworthy, and embedded with human thought and purpose.

Web Browsers

Searching the internet is a two-application process. First, users must open a browser to access a search engine program. Second, the search engine finds and locates websites through its proprietary indexed databases. After the user clicks on the link to a website, the **web browser** enables retrieval and viewing of the website. A search engine must be accessed in a browser. The web browser is a program developed to retrieve and view the information from web pages. We have choice in the browsers and search engines we use. Some people have multiple browsers and search engines on a single computing device and mix and match as they choose (see figure 7.1).

When an LSS turns on his computer, the first thing he may do is click on the icon to start up the Chrome browser. A rather bland site opens that is waiting for an URL to be typed or a bookmark to be opened. Some libraries set a search engine as a default "home" page (meaning the browser's first instructions are to automatically open a browser and then the search engine). Once in the Chrome browser, this LSS who likes to use a variety of search engines decides to begin searching with Microsoft Bing. He may then close out Bing and select Google while leaving Chrome as the browser.

Web browsers use the search engine to retrieve and view web pages present on web servers. Web browsers are intended to display the webpage of the current URL accessed. There is no database of websites stored in a browser other than a cache memory for cookies that will make repeated openings of previously used websites move more quickly. Browsers consist of **Graphical User Interfaces** (GUIs) that enable images, video, and other media to be viewed. They contain a search box for URL addresses. The style of the browser page can be rather bland or dynamic—

Figure 7.1. Searching the Web. *grinvals/ iStock via Getty images*

depending upon the company. The protocols for moving data from web servers to computing devices called TCP/IP and HTTP are used by web browsers.[5]

Listed are the more common web browsers. Remember, people have a choice in browsers and may download multiple ones on the same computing device.

- *Google Chrome*—An Alphabet product, Chrome is used on approximately 75 percent of computing devices.
- *Apple Safari*—Safari web browser is the default for the iPhone, iPad, and macOS. The popularity of the Safari browser exploded with the iPhone and the iPad, and currently has half the market share of mobile browser usage in the United States.
- *Microsoft Edge*—Edge replaced the old workhorse Internet Explorer (IE) and is trying to grow market share.
- *Mozilla Firefox*—Firefox share is shrinking from a once-high percentage of users.

Fundamentals

The purpose of a search engine is to find information on the internet. It has its own indexes of webpages where it gathers information of sites and their **Uniform Resource Locators (URLs)**.

Unlike directories that are human-made lists, search engines are software programs that use computer instructions to find best matches to keywords. These programs use **algorithms**. Algorithms are formulas created by search engine companies that determine how certain web pages show up in the results list. All search engine programs are not the same. Depending upon the search engine you choose, you will obtain different results because of the algorithms they use to find and prioritize websites. Google's search engine has a significantly higher market share than any other. Alternatives to Google to consider are as follows:

- *Bing*—Launched in 2009 to replace Microsoft's MSN Search.
- *BASE*—Especially for academic web resources providing more than 240 million documents from more than eight thousand content providers.
- *DuckDuckGo*—A non-tracking and metasearch engine. It gets its results from many sources, including Bing, WolframAlpha, and its own web crawler.
- DogPile—A metasearch engine that searches Google, Yahoo!, and Bing simultaneously.
- *WolframAlpha*—A free online computational knowledge engine that generates answers to questions in real time.
- *Yippy*—Clusters results by topic, source, time, and site.

LSS who understand the workings behind search engines are more confident in their use. Regardless of the company, search engines are built around some simple principles. We have heard the term web crawlers or **spiders**. These terms refer to the ongoing process of the search engine company to search methodically and continually for quality websites across the internet. Depending upon the search engine formula or algorithm, websites are compiled with addresses. The spider "crawls" through millions of servers of the World Wide Web to gather up all websites as directed by the search engine algorithm.

Similar to an **index** for a book, the search engine now stores keywords and website data into a filing system of indexes to be readily selected by users and retrieved by web browsers. Users actually search the search engine indexes, not the entire internet. The best matches to our search query immediately appear in a ranked result list from the search engine. In addition to finding keywords in indexes, each search engine has other criteria for formulating results, such as the number of hyperlinks within a site, the popularity or past usage of the site, and even sites related to the user's past searches or online purchases. The search process takes the following steps:

1. Spider or web crawler computer programs examine keywords on millions of web pages located on servers over the globe.
2. Information about selected web pages is added to the search engine's comprehensive indexes.
3. User's keywords are matched to webpage information found in the indexes.
4. The algorithm of the search engine helps to construct a result list the user will review in the web browser.

As the dominant search engine, Google's search index contains hundreds of billions of webpages and the sheer breadth of users it has amassed is difficult if not impossible to replicate.[6]

Google has segmented its indexes into a variety of Google products. In addition to Google Search, there is Google Scholar, Google Images, Google Books, and Google News. Google also offers numerous products that LSS may use or encounter in their daily work such as Gmail, YouTube, Google Classroom, Google Docs, Google Meet, Google Maps, and numerous other applications.

Voice Assistants

We command computing devices when we drive, select music, or search the web with voice assistants. The majority of mobile computing devices have the option of voice commands. Apple users have Siri make a phone call, Amazon users ask Alexa to help them shop, Microsoft product users talk to Cortana, and Google Home Assist is waiting and able to help with most, if not all, Google applications.

More than 75 percent of households have at least one voice-activated device and approximately 25 percent of Google searches are spoken. These numbers will grow. There are many benefits to being hands-free while we operate devices. Voice assistants may provide speed, safety, and the comfort of hearing a "human" voice that would like to help us.

Websites are designed for keyboard searching and access. Spoken phrases tend to be wordy and not as direct or clear as typed keywords. We speak extemporaneously, and search engines are challenged to figure out what the topic of the search really is. Voice search engine optimization (V-SEO) is a process that, if used in web design, gives the sites a better chance to be accurately read aloud by a voice search device. V-SEO works to filter out duplication and odd word usage, and concentrates on patterns of spoken words that have yielded successful results from past searches. LSS who work with or contribute to the library website can help the site be receptive to voice assist searches using the following suggestions.[7]

- *Optimize website speed.* Quick loading of the library website is critical for successful voice searching.
- *Use schema markup.* Incorporating schema markup (see https://schema.org/) on your website provides the search engine bots with specific semantic information in the exact language they understand.
- *Use Google My Business, Google Map,* and other Google applications to have the library website found more quickly by search engines.
- Make sure the library directory listings used by the voice search industry are completely accurate.
- *Answer Questions on the Library Website.* Websites should use longer questions that match natural language when using a voice search feature.

By preparing the library website for voice assist queries, libraries can ensure that users with assistive technologies find the library website and its invaluable resources.

SEARCH STRATEGIES

A search query consists of words typed into the blank box of a search engine to match and locate websites on the same topic. How the query is constructed determines the results. A keyword search looks for matching documents that contain the words that are specified by the user. But often the results do not obtain the desired match of the keywords. There are many reasons why this happens, including choice of words and misspellings. LSS can suggest synonyms as other vocabulary to improve a patron's search. LSS can demonstrate how different combinations of words and using advanced shortcuts can improve results.

Advanced Shortcuts

Search engines offer advanced shortcuts to improve the searching performance. LSS who use advanced shortcuts will obtain better results more efficiently. Each search engine has its own advanced search features and shortcuts. Table 7.2 describes some of the most effective Boolean and Google search shortcuts.[8] Boolean is a type of advanced shortcut that either expands or limits the results of a search. Common Boolean operators are the words *and, or,* and *not.* Boolean operators are universal to search engines. They connect keyword search terms to help specify the user's intent for the search by adding or excluding multiple search terms. When LSS use a search engine other than Google, they should learn the advanced shortcuts by reading help screens offered by the search engine.

Table 7.2. Advanced Shortcuts

Exact match	Use quotations. Results will have these quoted words together. *"Mystic Seaport"*
To exclude words	Use a minus sign in front of the word(s) you wish to exclude. Do not leave a space between the minus sign and the word. *breakfast menus–eggs*
Either one or the other	This is a most inclusive search. Type the word OR between keywords. Results will yield sites on both or either of these sports. *swimming OR kayaking*
Must have both terms	This is a more exclusive search. Type the word AND between keywords. Results will yield sties with only both sports. *swimming AND kayaking*
To select a domain	Type the word *site:* and the domain such as edu, org, gov, etc. followed by a space before the keywords. The results will only come from the domain specified. *site:gov pandemic*
To retrieve a certain file type such as PPT, PDF, XLS, DOC, etc.	Type the file type extension after the keywords preceded by a period. Results for this example yield only menus in PowerPoint. *Breakfast menus.ppt*

Search by domain is one of the most effective ways to obtain quality results. The searcher is in control of what domain source they wish to search. If a patron seeks to find research and information on biodiversity from only higher education sites, she types *site:edu biodiversity.*

- Do not add any spaces between the operator, colon, or domain (site:edu).
- Do leave one space before the search term (biodiversity).
- No other domains (such as the commercial .com) will be included.

Searching by the site domain is very powerful. Simply by substituting "edu" with "gov" one can flip the search immediately to search only U.S. government sites with the search term. Or by substituting "gov" with "org," one can now look at results for nonprofit organizations. Top-level domains are established by the Internet Corporation for Assigned Names (ICANN).[9] LSS can greatly enhance their searching proficiency by becoming familiar with *"site."* This one advanced shortcut can do much to obtain quality results.

Using Critical Thinking

A second successful keyword search strategy is to include a word that describes the level of critical thinking desired. Should the results contain mostly facts like almanacs or should results provide evaluative or opinionated pages? The work of an educational theorist, Benjamin Bloom,[10] is particularly helpful to select keywords that will yield websites on scaled levels of critical thinking.

LSS who regularly combine levels and words from Bloom's Taxonomy found in table 7.3 with their search topics are able to obtain quality results for themselves and others. For example, a search *site:edu predict biodiversity* will obtain research at the highest level 6 from academic websites. Change the search to *site:gov define biodiversity* for results at basic knowledge level 1 from U.S. government sites. Control your searches using Bloom's words, domains, and Boolean or Google search operators, and LSS searching ability soars! Try it!

Table 7.3. Words for Levels of Searches

Level 1 Knowledge	Level 2 Understanding	Level 3 Application	Level 4 Analysis	Level 5 Synthesis	Level 6 Evaluation/ Creativity
list	classify	apply	compare	compose	evaluate
identify	summarize	show	contrast	develop	predict
name	describe	change	analyze	assemble	judge
define	explain	discover	differentiate	design	defend
facts	review	illustrate	experiment	revise	value

International Searching

The internet is global, and LSS should be aware that searching in the United States does not always reflect a valid international perspective. A way to gain an international perspective is add Google international country codes to the Google URL. For example, to search websites hosted in France, modify the U.S. Google URL from http://www.google.com to https://www.google.fr. Likewise, the Google search engine in China can be accessed by adding .cn to the URL. LSS can help patrons gain different global perspectives on controversial topics by adding country codes to the

Google URL. Lists of all Google international country codes can be found simply by Googling "list Google international country codes."

A directory of international search engines is Search Engine Colossus,[11] an alphabetical listing of countries. Click each country for search engines either in the native language of the country or in English. Colossus provides the country flag as well as some information. Colossus and Google international search enhance users' perspectives about the world as they obtain information that is not necessarily sourced from the United States.

When assisting with an international site, there is a computer translation taking place from the native language into English (or other preferences if there is a choice). Even if the international search engine is in English, a straight translation could derail the search.

INTERNET ARCHIVE

Looking for a website that was accessible on the internet five years ago but is not available now? Is there a version of a book that is out of copyright that you would like to find? The Internet Archive is a nonprofit library with free access to billions of webpages, millions of e-books and digital sound and video recordings, and thousands of software programs that were once current on the internet.[12] These resources are no longer searchable on the internet through regular search engines.

In 1996 it was recognized that there was no process for saving ephemeral web content. The Internet Archive or library was established with a free search engine called the Wayback Machine. One can search more than a quarter century of web history contributed by hundreds of libraries and other institutions using the Wayback Machine.

Anyone with a free account can upload files and media to the Internet Archive. Thousands of partners globally save copies of their work into special Internet Archive collections. Archive-It is used by academic, federal, state, or local libraries, archives, and other cultural heritage institutions to create, store, and provide access to collections of web content.

While not all websites and pages have been preserved in the Internet Archive, it holds a rich amount of content. There is no other service that provides access to the volume of past web content than the Internet Archive. It is a fun and important search tool for LSS to become familiar with to be able to retrieve former content of the internet.

Distributed Web

The internet is in its infancy with continued improvements and enhancements. The internet currently has a centralized network infrastructure whereby websites and tools such as blogs and email are hosted on a designated servers using common or standard protocols such as HTTP (hypertext transfer protocol) for web browsing and SMTP (simple mail transfer protocol) to obtain email. Forthcoming will be a **distributed web** with new peer-to-peer networks that do not rely on centralization or standard protocols. Distributed systems include various possible configurations, such as personal computers, mainframes, minicomputers, workstations, and so on, and have several benefits compared to centralized systems. These include the following:

- Scalability: The distributed system can easily be extended.
- Redundancy: Many machines can offer the same services. Therefore, even if one web host is unavailable, users may be able to access the site from another source.
- Distributed computing systems: A distributed web could operate on hardware provided by multiple vendors, enhancing the capacity of the internet. It could make use of different standards-based software components that use a variety of communications protocols as well as operate on multiple operating systems.[13]

LSS are urged to keep abreast of changes to the internet that will enhance how people search and use information.

CHAPTER SUMMARY

Search engines are tools for locating information on the web. Like any tool, knowledge of its capabilities and practice using it improves work performance. LSS who know the concepts and issues concerning the use of search engines and web browsers support searching by different user groups. LSS are able to assist and train users to connect to the internet to find quality web pages that meet their needs by using a variety of search strategies and techniques.

DISCUSSION QUESTIONS

1. How are directories and search engines similar? How are they different?
2. What is a web browser and what is its function to searching the internet?
3. How would you set up a domain Google search in order to obtain results from only higher education websites?
4. What words from Bloom's list would you use to help a patron construct a search to determine if wind power will replace gas and oil to heat homes in the New York area?
5. When would you recommend an alternate search engine to Google? Give two examples.

ACTIVITY: USING BLOOM'S TAXONOMY FOR SEARCHING

Complete the chart below with your searches on genetically modified foods. Be sure to use the term "genetically modified foods" for each search. Change the "Blooms" verb but keep the search topic consistent.

Bloom's Level	Search Query (Bloom's verb + your search term).	To what extent did the results change, and what kind of information was offered at each level?	Was this level effective? Did you get the results that you hoped?
1—Knowledge			
2—Comprehension			
3—Application			
4—Analysis			
5—Synthesis			
6—Evaluation			

NOTES

1. Moorpark College, "Evaluating Search Engines and Web Directories," Library, last modified 2021, accessed January 1, 2021, https://www.moorparkcollege.edu/departments/student-services/library/evaluating-search-engines.

2. Growmap Centric Mobile Responsive Theme by StudioPress, "What Are the Most Relevant and Valuable Web Directories for 2020?" Growmap, last modified 2021, accessed January 2, 2021, https://growmap.com/valuable-web-directories/.

3. Moorpark College, "Evaluating Search Engines."

4. Google, "About Google My Business," Google My Business Help Center, last modified 2021, accessed January 3, 2021, https://support.google.com/business/answer/3038063?co=GENIE.Platform%3DAndroid&hl=en.

5. Geeks for Geeks, "Difference between Search Engine and Web Browser," last modified January 17, 2020, accessed January 3, 2021, https://www.geeksforgeeks.org/difference-between-search-engine-and-web-browser/.

6. Rishi Iyengar, "Why It's So Hard to Dethrone Google," *CNN Wire*, October 22, 2020, https://search.ebscohost.com/login.aspx?direct=true&AuthType=cookie,ip,cpid&custid=csl&db=n5h&AN=BAQ4h_5f81db4dc2ecf1575c9178cc45224026&site=eds-live&scope=site.

7. Mark Homer, "Find Your Voice: Can Siri, Alexa and Google Assistant Find You?," *Law Practice: The Business of Practicing Law* 46, no. 2 (March 2020): 1–5, https://search.ebscohost.com/login.aspx?direct=true&AuthType=cookie,ip,cpid&custid=csl&db=aph&AN=142052995&site=ehost-live&scope=site.

8. Google, "Refine Web Searches," Google Search Help, last modified 2021, accessed January 4, 2021, https://support.google.com/websearch/answer/2466433?hl=en.

9. ICANN, "Version 2021010400," List of Top-Level Domains, last modified 2021, accessed January 4, 2021, https://data.iana.org/TLD/tlds-alpha-by-domain.txt.

10. Patricia Armstrong, "Bloom's Taxonomy," Center for Teaching, last modified 2021, accessed January 4, 2021, https://cft.vanderbilt.edu/guides-sub-pages/blooms-taxonomy/.

11. Bryon Strome, "Search Engine Colossus," International Directory of Search Engines, last modified 2020, accessed January 4, 2021, https://www.searchenginecolossus.com/.

12. Internet Archive, "Internet Archive," Wayback Machine, last modified 2021, accessed January 7, 2021, https://archive.org/.

13. Techopedia, Inc., "Distributed Computing (DCI)," *Techopedia*, last modified 2021, accessed January 8, 2021, https://www.techopedia.com/definition/27502/distributed-computing-dci.

REFERENCES, SUGGESTED READINGS, AND WEBSITES

Armstrong, Patricia. "Bloom's Taxonomy." Center for Teaching. Last modified 2021. Accessed January 4, 2021. https://cft.vanderbilt.edu/guides-sub-pages/blooms-taxonomy/.

Badke, William E. "Search Tips from a Seasoned Searcher." *Online Searcher* 42, no. 1 (January/February 2018): 59–61. https://search.ebscohost.com/login.aspx?direct=true&AuthType=cookie,ip,cpid&custid=csl&db=aph&AN=127421725&site=ehost-live&scope=site.

Bryon Strome. "Search Engine Colossus." International Directory of Search Engines. Last modified 2020. Accessed January 4, 2021. https://www.searchenginecolossus.com/.

Geeks for Geeks. "Difference between Search Engine and Web Browser." Last modified January 17, 2020. Accessed January 3, 2021. https://www.geeksforgeeks.org/difference-between-search-engine-and-web-browser/.

Growmap Centric Mobile Responsive Theme by StudioPress. "What Are the Most Relevant and Valuable Web Directories for 2020?" *Growmap*. Last modified 2021. Accessed January 2, 2021. https://growmap.com/valuable-web-directories/.

Homer, Mark. "Find Your Voice: Can Siri, Alexa and Google Assistant Find You?" *Law Practice: The Business of Practicing Law* 46, no. 2 (March 2020): 1–5. https://search.ebscohost.com/login.aspx?direct=true&AuthType=cookie,ip,cpid&custid=csl&db=aph&AN=142052995&site=ehost-live&scope=site.

ICANN. "Version 2021010400." List of Top-Level Domains. Last modified 2021. Accessed January 4, 2021. https://data.iana.org/TLD/tlds-alpha-by-domain.txt.

Internet Archive. "Internet Archive." Wayback Machine. Last modified 2021. Accessed January 7, 2021. https://archive.org/.

Iyengar, Rishi. "Why It's So Hard to Dethrone Google." *CNN Wire*, October 22, 2020. https://search.ebscohost.com/login.aspx?direct=true&AuthType=cookie,ip,cpid&custid=csl&db=n5h&AN=BAQ4h_5f81db4dc2ecf1575c9178cc45224026&site=eds-live&scope=site.

Moorpark College. "Evaluating Search Engines and Web Directories." Library. Last modified 2021. Accessed January 1, 2021. https://www.moorparkcollege.edu/departments/student-services/library/evaluating-search-engines.

SEOYV. "5 Benefits of Using Google Analytics in Your SEO Campaign." Last modified 2021. Accessed January 3, 2021. https://seoyv.com/5-benefits-using-google-analytics-seo-campaign/.

Stern, David. "Don't Dis Google: Seamless Resolver Enhancement Beyond Subscriptions." *Online Searcher* 44, no. 6 (November 2020): 24–27. https://search.ebscohost.com/login.aspx?direct=true&AuthType=cookie,ip,cpid&custid=csl&db=aph&AN=147015919&site=ehost-live&scope=site.

Techopedia, Inc. "Distributed Computing (DCI)." *Techopedia*. Last modified 2021. Accessed January 8, 2021. https://www.techopedia.com/definition/27502/distributed-computing-dci.

University of San Francisco. "Search Engines—A Sampling of Alternatives to Google." School of Law. Last modified 2021. Accessed January 3, 2021. https://legalresearch.usfca.edu/SearchEngineAlternatives.

Willson, Amelia. "21 Web Directories That Still Have Value." *Search Engine Journal*. Last modified July 20, 2020. Accessed January 2, 2021. https://www.searchenginejournal.com/web-directories-list/287799/#close.

CHAPTER 8

Metadata and Searching

LSS demonstrate flexibility in adapting to new technology.

LSS are able to assist and train users to operate public equipment, connect to the internet, use library software applications, and access library services from remote locations.

Topics Covered in This Chapter
Protocols
    Cataloging
    Searching
Metadata Management Systems
    Dublin Core
    PastPerfect
    Greenstone
Semantic Web
Linked Data
LSS and Metadata
Chapter Summary

Key Terms
BIBFRAME—These are the new and emerging standards for cataloging library items established in the United States by the Library of Congress that expand the use of metadata.
Element—This is an identifying term or phrase that describes a point of information about an artifact, document, image, or media.
Linked data—With one search, connections will be made to other databases that are associated with a topic. No longer will the internet be a collection of documents, but rather it will be based on relationships among data.

MARC 21—These are the current cataloging standards established by the Library of Congress.

Metadata—This includes both basic bibliographic information such as the title, author, publisher, date, and so on, and wider and more thorough descriptions and associations about the attributes of library resources.

Metatag—This is a top line of computer code on a webpage for inputting searchable subjects that will enhance the ranking of the page. These lines of code influence search engine results by matching the user's search terms with the subjects found in these lines of code. Library programmers can influence the ranking of their websites using metatags.

Semantic web—Also referred to as Web 3.0 or the web of data, this is a framework that allows different applications and programs to share data such as dates, numbers, formulas, and more.

PROTOCOLS

LSS use **metadata** in the processes of searching the internet and cataloging items to be found online. The chapter begins with an explanation of the term *metadata* by discussing first the word *data*, then *meta*.

Data supports decision making in everyday life. *Data*, a word frequently used, are found throughout libraries in materials collections, reports, references, and in every service and process that requires information. Data are

- facts,
- statistics, and
- information sources.

Library boards regularly discuss circulation and usage data to compare and analyze library usage by examining current and past statistics. Data permeates our world, and it is used to support decision making and predictions, and to evaluate new ideas.

The word *meta* has several meanings, but the one that best applies to library materials is the English origin of *beyond* or *going beyond*. Metadata is *going beyond data*.

Cataloging

Catalogers who create metadata records for digital items *go beyond the data that is obvious and straightforward*, conducting research to find internal and external relationships to objects. By doing so, catalogers expand searchable fields, offering more opportunities for the digital asset to be searched, located, and used by patrons. The information explosion is real, and people are confounded by too much data. The cataloger selects or creates metadata—clear and targeted descriptions, subjects, annotations, relationships, and so forth that will lead patrons on the right path to finding exactly what they need.

MARC 21 and **BIBFRAME** are the standards for cataloging library items established in the United States by the Library of Congress. A record is created for a library item or asset using these standards. MARC 21 and BIBFRAME records consist of tags and fields of data. Data are embedded in a programmable way into the templates so that items can be searched on computers. Each tag and its field identify unique data about the library item. Two of the most common MARC 21 tags and fields are the data for author and title.

Tag: 100; Field: Author Personal Name
Tag: 245; Field: Title Statement

LSS also include in a MARC 21 book record the publisher and location, copyright date, size, pages, edition, and other descriptive information. However, the standard MARC 21 record used for physical library items does not provide adequate search fields for items in digitized collections. Today catalogers work with both MARC 21 bibliographic data and metadata.

Creating metadata—going beyond the basic facts of the object—requires the cataloger to research the digital object. Basic data about the object is needed as well as information about important relationships to the object. Three elementary questions LSS ask to help initiate metadata are as follows.

- What is it?
- How is it made?
- What is it used for?

The first question addresses the content or purpose of the object. The second question is about its substance, form, and physical features. The third question seeks relationships the object has to people, events, time periods, places, or other things. Not all metadata is obvious by holding or touching the object. LSS who create metadata are detectives, historians, archaeologists, or even forensic investigators!

Where once cataloging was primarily an inventory process that kept tabs of items within the library building, today establishing useful metadata is essential to users being able to search and use both physical and digitized resources.

Searching

Internet search engines and digitization have changed how users find information. Metadata are the searchable descriptions of specific information in websites, databases, documents, and digital collections. Museums, libraries, and other institutions create metadata when cataloging their objects, documents, and artifacts so that they can be located and used.

Discovery services depend on catalogers applying robust and comprehensive metadata. Think of the enormity of metadata for each item in the OPAC, each record created for local collections, each keyword in every article in every database the library subscribes to, and descriptors of every academic open-access journal, e-book, report, conference, and so forth found on the web. All of this metadata are compiled in discovery services indexes. Millions, if not billions or even trillions, of pieces of data are indexed and searched to obtain results that are then filtered through the user's parameters to obtain desired content.

People use search engines by typing or saying words. The search engine takes these words and matches them as closely as possible in its indexes to the metadata that was created for each website and database. Searching is the process of matching the users' search terms to the descriptive metadata of internet resources. However, many internet resources lack effective metadata. It is essential that catalogers and web designers consistently create detailed metadata or search terms of unique and specific keywords to help searchers locate resources and information. Textbox 8.1 suggests best metadata practices.[1]

TEXTBOX 8.1: BEST METADATA PRACTICES

- Title should be clear and concise.
- Author should be the person or organization that created the file.
- Subject should provide a brief description of the document.
- Record should contain at least six specific and unique keywords.

In the reverse of cataloging, LSS can use these suggestions for themselves and others when searching. Before conducting a search with patrons, if not using author and title, be clear about the users' needs by taking a few moments to create a written list of words that are relevant to the topic. In doing this the users have the opportunity to better articulate what they seek while LSS can create a working list of potential search terms that, during the search, will be matched with keyword metadata.

Unlike cataloging MARC 21, where there are strict Library of Congress rules and identified specific words to use in creating subjects, most programmers and catalogers do not have to use specific words when they create keyword metadata. Metadata guidelines will be discussed later in the chapter, but there is no listing of the actual words or search terms for metadata that must be used. Narrowing the topic with the user prior to searching and using search strategies discussed in chapter 7 greatly enhance the chances of finding online information resources that meet the users' requirements.

Another way to effectively search metadata is to ensure that all information objects, regardless of the physical or intellectual form they take, have three features—content, context, and structure—which can and should be reflected through metadata:[2]

- *Content* relates to what the object contains or is about and is intrinsic to an information object.
- *Context* indicates the "who, what, why, where, and how" aspects associated with the object's creation and subsequent life and is extrinsic to an information object.
- *Structure* relates to the formal set of associations within or among individual information objects and can be intrinsic, extrinsic, or both.

LSS can develop strategies as a framework for when considering content, context, and structure when discussing a search request with others.

Content

- Is the content about the topic of the information, such as a person, event, or thing?
- Is the content classified in an area of history, literature, science, or other subject?
- What else does the content deal with? In other words, break down the topic to manageable and searchable ideas.

Context

- How does the item relate to other people, places, or things around it?
- How does the content relate to other topics? A person wanting information about Eugene O'Neill's play *Long Day's Journey into Night* may also find relevant information about Monte Cristo, Eugene O'Neill boyhood home, which is the contextual setting for several of the playwright's works.

Structure

- What are the formal associations that may impact the search topic?
- Does the topic result from work of an association or an institution?
- Could the topic be between two large concepts that may influence each other, such as politics and global climate?

A record with six or more metadata focused on the content, context, and structure of the item can be located by a search engine with keywords focused in these areas.

Metatags are lines of computer code on a webpage the programmer or cataloger embeds with searchable keywords to enhance the ranking of the page. These lines of code influence search engine results by matching the user's search terms with the keywords found in these lines of code. Library programmers can influence the ranking of their websites and databases using multiple metadata that they anticipate people will use as search terms in the website's metatags.

METADATA MANAGEMENT SYSTEMS

As libraries use either closed (e.g., Sierra, Follett, SirsiDynix) or open (e.g., Evergreen, Koha) source ILS, they may also use a metadata management system for cataloging and access of digital collections. Similar to a field in MARC 21 cataloging, metadata management systems call the data **elements**. An element is an identifying term or phrase that describes a point of information about an artifact, document, image, or media. Elements are metadata created in anticipation of leading a searcher to the item. Metadata management systems provide templates of required and elective elements. The more useful and appropriate elements a cataloger can provide, the more likely the item will be successfully located and used. Metadata elements may be used multiple times for each object. The Smithsonian has digital images of the tires from the plane, the *Spirit of St. Louis*. The element *materials* is used several times, once each for rubber, metal, and fabric.[3] Two closed (Dublin Core and PastPerfect) as well as one open-source system (Greenstone) will next be discussed.

Dublin Core

Dublin Core, first developed in Dublin, Ohio, in association with OCLC, is used by most large digital libraries and museums in English-speaking countries. Dublin Core element metadata is inputted in XML computer code, making it accessible and readable from the web. A few of its elements are also in MARC 21, but even with new BIBFRAME RDA descriptive and relationship requirements, not enough cataloging fields libraries use for traditional collections are available for in-depth metadata searching. There are currently fifteen elements, also called attributes,[4] of metadata that describe a digital object or resource in Dublin Core as shown in table 8.1.

Table 8.1.   Dublin Core Metadata Elements

Contributor	A person, an organization, or a service that contributes to the resource.
Coverage	A named place, location, period, date, or jurisdiction that applies to the resource.
Creator	Responsible for creating the resource.
Date	Point or period of time associated with the resource.
Description	Descriptive information about the resource or primary source.
Format	The file format, physical medium, or dimensions of the resource.
Identifier	Classification or other information that formally identifies the resource.
Language	Language of the resource.
Publisher	Responsible for making the resource available.
Relation	Related resource to this object.
Rights	Information about rights held in and over the resource.
Source	May be derived from the related resource in whole or in part.
Subject	The topic of the resource.
Title	Name given to the resource.
Type	Nature or genre of the resource.

Each element may be used more than once, and some elements may not be used at all. Dublin Core elements may be separated into two categories: mandatory elements and recommended elements. A basic record uses the mandatory elements of title, creator, subject, description, date, format, identifier, and rights management. Rights management is important because it describes copyright, property rights, and how the digital item may or may not be reproduced or used. Recommended elements are the remaining publisher, contributor, type, source, language, relation, and coverage.[5]

PastPerfect

A second closed management system is PastPerfect, a Windows-based, affordable system that is attractive for small to medium-sized museums and libraries (see figure 8.1).[6] With user-friendly templates, PastPerfect metadata can be created for both artifacts and their digital representations. PastPerfect can also manage metadata for scanned journals, letters, and diaries. Data from Excel can be uploaded into Past-Perfect. PastPerfect is an excellent choice for any library or museum to manage and display metadata of digital objects.

Figure 8.1. Example of Past Perfect. *Ledyard Historical Society, Ledyard, CT*

Greenstone

Greenstone Digital Library Software is a suite of open-source, multilingual software for building and distributing digital library collections.[7] It is produced by the New Zealand Digital Library Project and developed in cooperation with the United Nations Educational, Scientific and Cultural Organization (UNESCO) and the nongovernmental organization Human Info. The aim of the Greenstone software is to empower users, particularly in universities, libraries, and other public service institutions, to build their own digital libraries. Creating and sharing of digital resources, particularly among third-world and developing countries, is a way for UNESCO to use technology to support educational standards and goals by

- finding new ways for education dissemination,
- assisting developing countries in the fight against poverty, and
- providing solutions for current global issues.

Library staff who may work with organizations that aim to increase awareness of and help people of developing countries may be interested in digital collection projects that could be shared using open-source Greenstone Digital Library software. The software is compatible with Windows, MAC, and Linux platforms and much documentation is provided on the Greenstone website on how to download and get started.

SEMANTIC WEB

The **semantic web**, which is sometimes called Web 3.0 or the web of data, is a framework that allows different applications and programs to share data such as dates, numbers, formulas, and more. Most of the data on the web today is to be read, but the data on the semantic web will be primarily for computers and humans to link to, use, and categorize. The goals of the semantic web are to

- make data easy to access;
- increase data sharing to make it possible for people and technology to find relationships among data;
- make data available so it can be used to create models of problems in everyday life and try to help solve them;
- make as much data as possible accessible using architecture that is similar to the World Wide Web architecture (e.g., uniform resource identifiers—URIs— and URLs); and
- build machines that are able to "think."[8]

The semantic web, when fully available, will provide an easier way to find, share, reuse, and combine information through customized tagging schemes and common formats for the interchange of data. With the semantic web, search programs will use natural language searches and find context and structures in metadata. Users' searches will be automatically tailored to their needs, location, and identity. There will be a common language for how data relates to real-world objects, allowing a searcher to begin at one database and then move through an unending set of databases that are connected not by wires but by being about the same thing. The new Web 3.0 will have deeper and more extensive links to and among related ideas, concepts, and data. Thus searching will no longer depend on the user coming up with keywords, but rather she will be able to find information through semantics with search engines applying the meanings, words, or associations to concepts.

LINKED DATA

Librarians have linked data long before there were computers. Some recall the library traditional card catalogs where "see" and "see also" cards were interspersed among author, title, and subject cards as ways to link items and alert patrons that there was something else that could be of interest (see figure 8.2).

Linked data makes connections, and in the future will work together with the semantic web to have both human searchers and more advanced computers use structures of metadata to find associations related to other sites and resources. With one search, connections will be made to other databases that are associated with a topic. For example, a search on an author may also result in links to information about other authors who were writing in a similar style or period. Through linking data, the web will no longer be a collection of documents but a global data space where people and machines can not only discover data and its associated relationships.[9] Linked data will continue to use

- URLs to name and identify sites,
- HTTP so that sites can be searched and located,
- standards to enhance linking of web resources, and
- designed systems to enhance searching and deliver optimum service.

LSS are aware of copyright and licensing (see chapter 11). Copyright protects authors from unauthorized use of their work. Data licensing provides libraries contractual rights for their users for specified access to databases and other online resources. The concept and practice of linked data must adhere to copyright and data licensing. One way that libraries and other institutions are moving forward with the semantic web and linked data is using open-source or open-use licenses. The Getty and some academic libraries and museums have made free access to digital collections through open-use licenses. These arrangements, while targeted and specific, are in the forefront of open-lined data that uses the metadata of cataloged records. LSS cannot assume that all data on the internet will be open-accessed and linked. LSS can keep informed and be prepared for the linked data future by

- offering to be involved with acquisition and training of new databases to learn about their potential to be linked to both inside and outside sources;
- volunteering to be on search teams for new or upgraded ILS or discovery systems the library may be considering; and
- being interested in new standards of cataloging, especially with metadata.[10]

With linking data, the semantic web and linked data has the potential to change the way people will use and search metadata and the internet in the future.

Figure 8.2. Library Card Catalog. *Nikada / E+ via Getty Images*

LSS AND METADATA

An archivist and professor of Library Information Science was asked for this book, "Should LSS learn to catalog in metadata, and if so, why?" Here is her response:[11]

> I am going to give two answers to this question. First, standard MARC record cataloging is the use of metadata. And although much of our cataloging is automated via copy cataloging, LSS must learn the basic foundation of cataloging as it is the cornerstone of our profession—information organization. I also believe LSS should expand into other forms of metadata that follow different protocols, such as Dublin Core and EAD [encoded archival description]. Why? Well, not all metadata fields in standard library catalog are searchable, whereas all metadata fields created through Dublin Core or Encoded Archival Description is searchable. As digital collections grow, learning to use this unique markup language is advantageous, opening up exciting work opportunities in digital initiatives.

CHAPTER SUMMARY

Metadata is the foundation of aggregated searching, federated searching, and discovery services. LSS catalogers are already familiar with metadata when they catalog items for library collections in MARC 21 using basic bibliographic information such as the title, author, publisher, date, and so on. However, metadata are also elements of detail descriptions and associations. LSS demonstrate flexibility when they adapt to using metadata management systems and are able to help others with their searches. LSS support users to better search the internet and use databases and library digital collections for specific requests and information needs.

DISCUSSION QUESTIONS

1. What is metadata and how is it used in searching the internet and other library collections?
2. What are some of the key ways LSS can use metadata to enhance searching?
3. How is the semantic web different from the web we currently use?
4. How can LSS prepare to use linked data?
5. What are some of the benefits of metadata management systems?

ACTIVITY

This assignment is meant to sharpen our eyes to metadata elements and how they are applied in digital collections.

- Access the New York Public Library Digital Collections found at https://digital collections.nypl.org/.
- Select a digitized image and click on it.
- Find as many elements on this screen.
- Click "More Details" toward the bottom of the screen to find additional elements.

- Using table 8.1, copy and paste the metadata elements next to appropriate identifying attributes.

NOTES

1. "Metadata Best Practices and Internet Search Tip Practices," *EPA Office of Ground Water and Drinking Water*, 1–3, accessed March 1, 2021, https://www.epa.gov/sites/default/files/2020-06/documents/metadata_best_practices_and_internet_factsheet.pdf.

2. Murtha Baca, "Introduction to Metadata," Paul Getty Trust, last modified 2016, accessed March 1, 2021, https://www.getty.edu/publications/intrometadata/.

3. Smithsonian, "Tires and Wheels, 'Spirit of St. Louis,' Charles A. Lindbergh," Smithsonian National Air and Space Museum, accessed March 1, 2021, https://airandspace.si.edu/collection-object/nasm_A19360007000.

4. Minnesota Government, "15 Dublin Core Element Attributes," *Bridges*, accessed March 1, 2021, https://mn.gov/bridges/dcore.html.

5. University of Mississippi, "Digital Accounting Collection," University of Mississippi Libraries, last modified 2018, accessed March 1, 2021, https://olemiss.edu/depts/general_library/dac/files/user_guide.html.

6. PastPerfect Software, Inc., "PastPerfect Museum Software," last modified 2021, accessed March 1, 2021, https://museumsoftware.com/.

7. New Zealand Digital Library Project, "About Greenstone," Greenstone Digital Library Software, last modified 2021, accessed March 1, 2021, https://www.greenstone.org/.

8. Elizabeth Mohn, "Semantic Web," *Salem Press Encyclopedia of Science* (Salem Press), 1–2, last modified 2019, https://search.ebscohost.com/login.aspx?direct=true&AuthType=cookie,ip,cpid&custid=csl&db=ers&AN=87323271&site=eds-live&scope=site.

9. Educause, "Using Linked Data for Discovery and Preservation," *Educause Review*, last modified 2021, accessed March 1, 2021, https://er.educause.edu/articles/2019/3/using-linked-data-for-discovery-and-preservation.

10. Erik Mitchell, "Technology: Dispatches from the Field. A Linked Data Landscape.," *American Libraries* 47, no. 1/2 (January/February 2016): 30, https://search.ebscohost.com/login.aspx?direct=true&AuthType=cookie,ip,cpid&custid=csl&db=ulh&AN=111971447&site=ehost-live&scope=site.

11. Anastasia S. Weigle, interview, University of Maine–Augusta, December 30, 2020.

REFERENCES, SUGGESTED READINGS, AND WEBSITES

Baca, Murtha. "Introduction to Metadata." Paul Getty Trust. Last modified 2016. Accessed March 1, 2021. https://www.getty.edu/publications/intrometadata/.

Educause. "Using Linked Data for Discovery and Preservation." *Educause Review*. Last modified 2021. Accessed March 1, 2021. https://er.educause.edu/articles/2019/3/using-linked-data-for-discovery-and-preservation.

"Metadata Best Practices and Internet Search Tips Practices." *EPA Office of Ground Water and Drinking Water*, 1–3. Accessed March 1, 2021. https://www.epa.gov/sites/default/files/2020-06/documents/metadata_best_practices_and_internet_factsheet.pdf.

Minnesota Government. "15 Dublin Core Element Attributes." *Bridges*. Accessed March 1, 2021. https://mn.gov/bridges/dcore.html.

Mitchell, Erik. "Technology: Dispatches from the Field. A Linked Data Landscape." *American Libraries* 47, no. 1/2 (January/February 2016): 30. https://search.ebscohost.com/login.aspx

?direct=true&AuthType=cookie,ip,cpid&custid=csl&db=ulh&AN=111971447&site=ehost
-live&scope=site.

Mohn, Elizabeth. "Semantic Web." *Salem Press Encyclopedia of Science*, 1–2. Salem Press.
Last modified 2019. https://search.ebscohost.com/login.aspx?direct=true&AuthType=cook
ie,ip,cpid&custid=csl&db=ers&AN=87323271&site=eds-live&scope=site.

New Zealand Digital Library Project. "About Greenstone." Greenstone Digital Library Software. Last modified 2021. Accessed March 1, 2021. https://www.greenstone.org/.

PastPerfect Software, Inc. "PastPerfect Museum Software." Last modified 2021. Accessed
March 1, 2021. https://museumsoftware.com/.

Smithsonian. "Tires and Wheels, 'Spirit of St. Louis,' Charles A. Lindbergh." Smithsonian
National Air and Space Museum. Accessed March 1, 2021. https://airandspace.si.edu/col
lection-object/nasm_A19360007000.

University of Mississippi. "Digital Accounting Collection." University of Mississippi Libraries.
Last modified 2018. Accessed March 1, 2021. https://olemiss.edu/depts/general_library
/dac/files/user_guide.html.

Weigle, Anastasia S. Interview. University of Maine, Augusta, ME. December 30, 2020.

CHAPTER 9

Website Services

LSS know the role and responsibility of libraries for introducing relevant applications of technology, including digital literacy, to the public.

LSS access and use basic assistive technologies, where appropriate, to ensure that all users have equitable access to technology.

Topics Covered in This Chapter

Library Website Services
    Parent Institutions
    Planning
Web Design
    Organization
    Design Elements
Web Accessibility
    Guidelines
Content Management Systems
    WordPress
    CONTENTdm
    LibGuides
Chapter Summary

Key Terms

Content Management Systems—Also known as CMS, these are tools that provide patrons better access to library digital information services. CMS are used to create, edit, manage, and host websites.
Navigation—This refers to the connecting links within a website that allow users to move from one webpage to another.

Portal—This is a website designed to be a starting point or opening to information on the web because it simplifies searching by consolidating and organizing links from different digital libraries and other sources.

Silo—Communication within an information silo is self-contained and always vertical, making it difficult or impossible for the system to branch out horizontally and work with unrelated systems.

UX—Meaning user experience, in a library these are the interactions a user has to accomplish a task with its products and services, including the library website. UX takes into account how successful the interactions were and how the user felt about them.

Web accessibility—This occurs when there are websites, tools, and technologies that provide equal opportunity for everyone to interact with and contribute to the web.

LIBRARY WEBSITE SERVICES

This chapter is about library website planning, design, accessibility, and content management systems. The library website is a dynamic **portal** to library information and its services. An important distinction can be made between the library website and its social media, which has to do with promotion and access. Social media, discussed in chapter 13, is used to market, advertise, publicize, and bolster promotion of library events, programs, and materials. The library website provides important access to the digital services of the library. In addition to providing access to its social media, examples of other website services are

- online catalog;
- digital collections;
- subscription databases;
- e-book and audiobook services;
- e-magazines services;
- digital media services;
- online library programs;
- online learning and instruction;
- links to exemplary sites, such as the state library digital resources;
- local history and genealogy;
- live librarian chat; and
- reservations, bookings.

The website is the digital branch of the library, providing access to e-books, databases, online research, and so much more. Patrons' first impressions of the website should be that the library is a modern, relevant institution.[1] Many LSS share responsibility for maintaining the library website and understand its primary purpose is to provide access to the digital services of the library; therefore, it should be easy to use and functional. Today it is a rare library that does not have a website; however, how effective the site is in providing access to digital services varies. Often library administrators inherit a website they would like to significantly change but are limited by institutional or cost constraints.

Parent Institutions

Few libraries are autonomous, meaning they are independent of any other institution. Those that are autonomous are likely to be small endowed libraries that serve a town or constituency. Over the years many of the autonomous libraries that were begun in the late nineteenth or early twentieth century could no longer operate solely on endowments or fundraising and became absorbed by the municipality. As expectations of library services have grown, so have expenses.

A parent institution is the organization that sponsors the library. K–12 and academic libraries are a department or unit within the larger school, college, or university. Special libraries are often a division of a company, museum, or other nonprofit. The majority of public libraries are departments of the municipality and mostly funded through taxes. Parent institutions have an overarching website, whether it be a school, university, city, or corporation. The library often is required to use the parent institution's web hosting service. These services are not created specifically for libraries and lack desirable features and templates. Another potential problem is the limited ability the library web staff may have to make changes to its website. The parent institution may restrict or limit how much content can be added or modified by the library. It is not uncommon to hear that librarians do not have authorization to make improvements to the website.

Planning

A planning committee should be formed to recommend change to the library website. The planning process has multiple phases: content analysis, needs analysis, peer analysis, evaluating platforms, and budget. Textbox 9.1 provides a brief description of each phase.[2] LSS are important members of the planning committee and participate in all phases.

TEXTBOX 9.1: PLANNING PROCESS

Content analysis—Test and review all content of the current website. Inherited content may no longer be relevant, redundant, or unnecessary. Links may lead to out-of-date information. **Navigation** may be cumbersome. Make detailed notes of what to keep and what to change.

Needs analysis—Survey all user groups to learn what they would like to see added, changed, or improved upon. Surveys can be conducted both in traditonal methods and informally in focus groups. Another way to get user input is analyze questions on the library chat to determine where people request help so that these areas can be improved upon through the website. All input from surveys, chat, and other sources should be correlated and considered.

Peer analysis—Analyze websites of libraries of similar type, size, and purpose to gain insight into the access services, content, and tools they provide. Borrow ideas about organization and navigation.

(continued)

TEXTBOX 9.1: *CONTINUED*

Evaluating platforms—Can the current website vendor meet the new needs? Does the library ILS or Discovery services offer the right alternative? If these options are feasible, a request for information (RIF) that delineates desired features and functionality can be created and sent to vendors. To be considered, the vendor must be able to integrate its web hosting services with the library's current ILS, subscription and discovery-layer services.

Budget—Determine both onetime and annual licensing and other costs of website software and hosting services. Consider both open and closed sources options as well as consultant or developer fees.

With the results of the planning committee, if the library has a parent institution, administrators work to ensure committee recommendations are within institutional policy and budget. Once agreement is in place, the next steps are to propose design and functionality (see figure 9.1).

Figure 9.1.   Planning the Library Website. *PeopleImages / E+ via Getty Images*

WEB DESIGN

Often the process of elimination helps determine what works and what does not. Poor design frustrates users, such as navigation that does not circle back to the home page from a webpage. Getting lost in a **silo** of information, such as accessing a catalog but being unable to move back to another digital resource, is both time consuming and frustrating. A website that relies too much on color to impart important information at minimum can cause confusion and critically is a problem for colorblind users. Navigation must be clear, consistent, and functional. Use of library jargon or terms that may not be in the vocabulary of users should be avoided. Consistency in terminology is most helpful.

A term common to web design is user experience or **UX**. In a library these are the interactions a user has to accomplish a task with its products and services, including the library website. UX takes into account how successful the interactions were and how the user felt about them. LSS who work with the library website can learn much through UX; they often are in the position to help users or to hear about their experiences. LSS who practice active listening can provide valuable feedback to supervisors about UX with the library website. It is the user who will spot a problem or offer suggestions for improvement.

Organization

Once the content that needs to be accessed via the website is identified, how the site will be organized should be considered. There is much research on organizational schemes as people approach their thinking in many different ways. Embedded in website design should be a clearly mapped organization scheme that is user friendly, accessible, and readable. Some key elements of and understandable organization structure to be considered are as follows.

Hierarchical arrangement—Main and most-used categories of digital services should be clearly accessible on the home page. For example, the online catalog may appear first in order as it is the service most used. Depending upon the library and its purpose, key services that patrons use should be in the top hierarchy.

Logical organization—What makes sense for one library may not for another. Circulation and reference librarians should converse about which services are most sought by users. One library may rank local history digital resources higher than another based on its collections and users' needs. Go back to the needs and peer assessments for help here.

Information arrangement and categorization—Just like arranging a closet, it makes sense to put like or similar information together. Look again at the results of the committee's peer analysis. Be critical of other sites and learn from their successes and mistakes.

Consistency—Once an organizational scheme has been determined, stay the course. Nothing is more frustrating than taking time to look for an item only to discover it was moved or placed in an illogical place. As a result of the pandemic where even going to the grocery store took more time and energy, users may be less patient if they are forced to refine searches several times in order to find the information they seek.[3]

Meaningful headings—Along with consistency, use clear, everyday terms to create headings and labels. For example, while LSS may think of magazines as serials or periodicals, most people do not use these terms. In addition to the organization of the library website, there are specific design elements that should be considered (see figure 9.2).

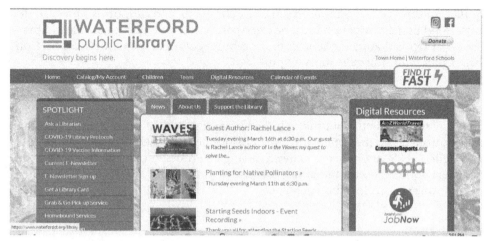

Figure 9.2.   Example of Accessbile Library Website. *Waterford Public Library, Waterford, CT*

Design Elements

Constructing a library website is not a casual task. There are many elements that are required to be in place for the library website to achieve a high level of accessibility and functionality. Table 9.1 contains many of these elements.[4]

Table 9.1.   Key Design Elements

Purpose	• Provides access to digital information services • States intended purpose and UX expectations • Provides library contact and access information
Readability	• Well written • Grammatically correct • Understandable • Appropriate amount of content on each page/readable blocks • Reading-level-appropriate content
Simplicity	• Simple subject headings • Website design optimized for computer screens • Uncluttered layout • Consistency in design throughout the website • Minimized redundant features • Easily understandable features/functions
Navigation	• Menu/navigation bar consistency • Easy access to web pages (e.g., no excessive backtracking/clicks) • Enhanced search features
Images	• Size, color, and resolution of images • Multimedia content (e.g., animation or audio) • Color, font, and size of text • Use of logos/icons • Visual attractiveness/layout • Effective use of white space/avoid visual overload • Minimal loading time for visual elements
Content	• Quality information • Current/up-to-date information • Relevant to the purpose of the website • Provides links to social media—Facebook, Twitter, etc.

LSS may use table 9.1 as a checklist and suggest changes to their library website such as the following:

- LSS suggests website be available in languages of user populations where English is not the first language.
- LSS identifies library jargon and recommends alternate words or clear explanations.
- LSS shares with supervisors and web designer their observations of how people react to the website navigation. Are they able to move into webpages or links quickly or do many seek help?
- LSS identifies images in the website that take longer to load and suggests the images either be modified or replaced.
- LSS monitors links to social media and other resources to ensure they are functioning.
- LSS looks daily to identify out-of-date content.

LSS can compare key design elements with peer websites to identify areas where improvement can be made to support the UX of patrons. Tools such as Google My Business and Google Analytics, as well as subscription reports can be used to determine whether changes to the website result in increased use of the library digital information services.

Access is more than being able to click a link. Accessibility ensures that the information of the library website is both usable and available to all.

WEB ACCESSIBILITY

Accessibility makes digital information services usable, reachable, or obtainable. Up to this point in the chapter, accessibility has been described in terms of website functionality. With thoughtful modifications, people with disabilities have **web accessibility** when there are websites, tools, and technologies designed and developed that provide equal opportunity for everyone to interact with and contribute to the web. The W3C is a nonprofit organization that works with industry, disability organizations, government, and research organizations to ensure accessibility of the web through such initiatives as

- developing accessibility guidelines for web content and applications, browsers, and authoring tools;
- developing resources to improve web accessibility evaluation processes and tools; and
- supporting education and outreach on web accessibility.

Access to the web can be affected by auditory, cognitive, neurological, physical, speech, and visual disabilities.[5] Librarians can modify public access technology to be web accessible regardless of the user's disability. It is best to address web accessibility issues at the initial phase of planning and designing a website. A combination of evaluation tools and human testing help determine if a website meets accessibility guidelines.

Guidelines

W3C summarizes its guidelines for web accessibility.[6] Under the W3C guidelines, categories of perception (seeing and hearing), operation, and understanding are strategies LSS can take to support ADA compliance and web accessibility.

LSS can use the following strategies to make the library website easier to view and listen to.

- Use alternatives to text such as large print, braille, speech, symbols, or simpler language.
- Make captions and prerecorded audio available for multimedia.
- Make content available in different ways, such as simpler layouts without losing meaning.
- Do not rely on color only to convey information.
- Provide a mechanism to pause or stop the audio.
- Visually separate foreground from background.

LSS can use the following strategies to make library website easier to operate.

- Make all functionality available from a keyboard.
- Give users enough time to read and use content.
- Ensure that web pages do not contain anything that flashes more than three times in any one-second period to avoid possible seizures or physical reactions.
- Ensure that motion animation triggered by interaction can be disabled, unless the animation is essential to the functionality or the information being conveyed.
- Make more than one way available to locate a webpage within a set of web pages.
- Create headings and labels that describe the topic or purpose.
- Make it easier to use inputs other than keyboard, such as targets for pointers.

LSS can use the following strategies to make library website easier to understand.

- Make each webpage have a default human language.
- Have a mechanism available for identifying specific definitions of words or phrases.
- Identify and give meaning of abbreviations.
- Offer some of the more difficult content at different reading levels.
- Make web pages appear and operate in predictable ways.
- Help users avoid and correct mistakes with help menus and error messages that offer suggestions for correction.

The American Foundation for the Blind says accessibility is how easily a website can be used, understood, and accessed by people with disabilities. A recent study of home page accessibility at the Ivy League libraries[7] found the following:

- University libraries' homepages all exhibited some issues with accessibility for people with disabilities.

- Users with visual impairments can navigate a website only when it is designed to be accessible with other assistive technologies.
- Links to services for the disabled should be posted on the homepage.
- Expertise and training are needed for people to be skilled in providing web accessibility.
- The design of the library website matters for people with disabilities just as it does in the physical environment.
- Most problems can be fixed. An annual review of the website for accessibility compliance is critical.

Everyone has the potential to become disabled or encounter situational limitations. Temporary disabilities or situational limitations can be such things as broken bones, changes due to aging, lost glasses, bright sunlight, or even having to use small mobile screens. LSS can advocate for better web accessibility for everyone, including those with both permanent and temporary disabilities.

CONTENT MANAGEMENT SYSTEMS

Content Management Systems, or CMS, are tools that provide patrons better access to library digital information services. CMS are used to create, edit, manage, and host websites. CMS customers focus on creating, organizing, and delivering web content instead of dealing with programming and technical aspects of maintaining a website. CMS requires only basic computing skills as templates and other tools are customized for the library. Once the website is in place, CMS enables the user to make changes such as LSS may be asked to keep events calendars up to date.

Libraries can choose between commercial or open-sourced CMS. While open source is less expensive, there likely are costs associated with development and customization. Content management systems are usually priced based on the number of users, volume of content, range of features, and whether it's a subscription service or a lifetime license.

Libraries use CMS to expedite and deliver high-quality digital information services to their users. Without reliable CMS, it would be difficult and expensive for libraries to develop their own software and to manage servers to host its digital services. Next are examples of three different types of the many CMS used by libraries today.

WordPress

An open-source CMS primarily for creating websites and blogs, WordPress.org[8] powers approximately one-third of all websites on the internet. It's free, easy to download and use, and works with all search engines. Thousands of themes and plugins make it one of the most customizable platforms. WordPress recommends hosting services that provide unlimited monthly data transfers, email, storage, and 24/7 support.[9] LSS who work with WordPress.org can join user forums and groups as well as find other useful information on its support website. Libraries that choose WordPress.org as the CMS for their websites will find a large community of other library users who can provide guidance and support as well.

CONTENTdm

CONTENTdm[10] is a CMS used by many libraries and institutions that provides templates, working structures, and hosting services for their digital collections. The state libraries of Illinois and Alaska are just two that use CONTENTdm to power their state digital collections. A service of OCLC, CONTENTdm is designed to work with library online catalogs, ILS, and discovery systems. It is designed to be used by any computer workstation or mobile device. CONTENTdm also works on library and personalized websites, making them more discoverable to people around the world. One of its many features that support library digital collections is that digital originals are preserved in a cloud-based archive so they remain safe for the future.

LibGuides

LibGuides[11] is a web-based CMS popular with many libraries worldwide. A library subscribes to a guide that can contain many pages. Pages provide structure to the library guide and the content within it in boxes. A page can contain many boxes, and a box can contain many pieces of content. Content items vary from box to box. Content could be text, links, databases, books, videos, widgets, RSS feeds, polls, and so on. There are four types of boxes: general, tabbed, gallery, and user profile.

- *General*: used most of the time, general boxes can contain text, links, databases, books, and so on.
- *Tabbed*: similar to General, except you can create multiple tabs within the box, each of which can house its own content items.
- *Gallery*: displays images, which rotate within the box.
- *User Profile*: displays any user's profile in your system. This is the only type of content this box type displays.

LibGuides is an excellent option for academic, school, and medium- to large-sized libraries that need to share resources and instruction in themed, organized webpages. For example, a professor of children's literature may wish to have an online library resource of award-winning books and media for students to explore during the semester. The LSS can create a page from its LibGuide dedicated to the professor's course. On the page can be active links to books and resources, uploaded documents or articles, as well as widgets to media and other sources. Both the professor and LSS could have editing rights to make adjustments to the page as needed. The page would be accessible for the semester and could be easily modified for future classes. LibGuides allow library staff to create professional webpages efficiently with a variety of easy tools for uploading, editing, and sharing.

CHAPTER SUMMARY

This chapter explores relevant applications of technology that enable libraries to offer patrons access to digital information services. LSS are often responsible for aspects of the library website that is a portal to its online resources. LSS support digital literacy when they apply assistive technology guidelines and strategies that ensure equitable web accessibility for all users.

DISCUSSION QUESTIONS

1. What is the fundamental difference between the purpose of the library website and library social media?
2. What limitations and supports for the library website may LSS find who work within a parent institution?
3. What are five of the key design elements of library websites and why are they important?
4. What is web accessibility and how does it differ from web access?
5. Why are content management systems (CMS) important for libraries to use?

ACTIVITY

Conduct an assessment of your library website using the guidelines of the W3C discussed in this chapter. Create a checklist of the guidelines and note how and where the library may be compliant. If they are compliant with a guideline, could it be improved upon? If a guideline is not being followed, how could the library include it its website design? Report your findings and suggestions to the library supervisor and/or website librarian. Consider asking for a role in monitoring the website to improve its accessibility.

NOTES

1. South Dakota State Library Services, "Websites for Libraries," South Dakota Library Resource Guides, last modified 2021, accessed March 7, 2021, https://libguides.library.sd.gov /services/websites.

2. Jesi Buell and Mark Sanford, "From Dreamweaver to Drupal: A University Library Website Case Study," *Information Technology & Libraries* 37, no. 2 (June 2018): 118–26, https:// search.ebscohost.com/login.aspx?direct=true&AuthType=cookie,ip,cpid&custid=csl&db =aph&AN=130397496&site=ehost-live&scope=site.

3. Greg Landgraf, "How User-Friendly Is Your Website? Usability Lessons for Libraries in a Remote World," *American Libraries* 52, no. 3/4 (March/April 2021): 30–33, https:// search.ebscohost.com/login.aspx?direct=true&AuthType=cookie,ip,cpid&custid=csl&db =aph&AN=149005478&site=ehost-live&scope=site.

4. Renee Garett and Jason Chiu, "A Literature Review: Website Design and User Engagement," HSS Author Manuscripts, last modified July 2016, accessed March 8, 2021, https:// www.ncbi.nlm.nih.gov/pmc/articles/PMC4974011/.

5. W3C, "Introduction to Web Accessibility," Web Accessibility Initiative, last modified June 5, 2019, accessed March 8, 2021, https://www.w3.org/WAI/fundamentals/accessibility -intro/.

6. W3C, "WCAG 2.1 at a Glance," W3C Web Accessibility Initiative, last modified 2021, accessed March 9, 2021, https://www.w3.org/WAI/standards-guidelines/wcag/glance/.

7. Wenfan Yang, Bin Zhao, Yan Quan Liu, and Arlene Bielefield, "Are Ivy League Library Website Homepages Accessible?" *Information Technology & Libraries* 39, no. 2 (2020): 1–18, https://search.ebscohost.com/login.aspx?direct=true&AuthType=cookie,ip,cpid&custid=csl&db=aph&AN=143882437&site=ehost-live&scope=site.

8. WordPress.org, "Support," last modified 2021, accessed March 10, 2021, https://wordpress.org/support/forums/.

9. Jeffrey Wilson and Mike Williams, "The Best WordPress Web Hosting Services for 2021," *PC Magazine*, March 10, 2021, accessed March 10, 2021, https://www.pcmag.com/picks/the-best-wordpress-web-hosting-services.

10. CONTENTdm, "Build, Showcase, and Preserve Your Digital Collections," Overview, last modified 2021, accessed March 10, 2021, https://www.oclc.org/en/contentdm.html.

11. Springshare, "LibGuides," last modified 2021, accessed March 10, 2021, https://springshare.com/libguides/.

REFERENCES, SUGGESTED READINGS, AND WEBSITES

Buell, Jesi, and Mark Sanford. "From Dreamweaver to Drupal: A University Library Website Case Study." *Information Technology & Libraries* 37, no. 2 (June 2018): 118–26. https://search.ebscohost.com/login.aspx?direct=true&AuthType=cookie,ip,cpid&custid=csl&db=aph&AN=130397496&site=ehost-live&scope=site.

Clobridge, Abby. "WordPress: The Most Popular (Open) Web Content Management System." *Online Searcher* 40, no. 5 (September/October 2016): 60–62. https://search.ebscohost.com/login.aspx?direct=true&AuthType=cookie,ip,cpid&custid=csl&db=.

Cohen, Sarah, and Rebecca Hyams. "Making Room for TBD: Adapting Library Websites during a Pandemic." *Computers in Libraries* 41, no. 2 (March 2021): 18–21. https://search.ebscohost.com/login.aspx?direct=true&AuthType=cookie,ip,cpid&custid=csl&db=aph&AN=149037123&site=ehost-live&scope=site.

CONTENTdm. "Build, Showcase, and Preserve Your Digital Collections." Overview. Last modified 2021. Accessed March 10, 2021. https://www.oclc.org/en/contentdm.html.

EBSCO. "7 Best Practices for Creating a User Friendly Library Website." EBSCOPost. Last modified 2021. Accessed March 7, 2021. https://www.ebsco.com/blogs/ebscopost/7-best-practices-creating-user-friendly-library-website.

Garett, Renee, and Jason Chiu. "A Literature Review: Website Design and User Engagement." HSS Author Manuscripts. Last modified July 2016. Accessed March 8, 2021. https://www.ncbi.nlm.nih.gov/pmc/articles/PMC4974011/.

Kachel, Debra E. "The Library Website as an Advocacy Tool." *Teacher Librarian* 47, no. 4 (April 2020): 61–63. https://search.ebscohost.com/login.aspx?direct=true&AuthType=cookie,ip,cpid&custid=csl&db=aph&AN=143257209&site=ehost-live&scope=site.

Landgraf, Greg. "How User-Friendly Is Your Website? Usability Lessons for Libraries in a Remote World." *American Libraries* 52, no. 3/4 (March/April 2021): 30–33. https://search.ebscohost.com/login.aspx?direct=true&AuthType=cookie,ip,cpid&custid=csl&db=aph&AN=149005478&site=ehost-live&scope=site.

South Dakota State Library Services. "Websites for Libraries." South Dakota Library Resource Guides. Last modified 2021. Accessed March 7, 2021. https://libguides.library.sd.gov/services/websites.

Springshare. "LibGuides." Last modified 2021. Accessed March 10, 2021. https://springshare.com/libguides/.

W3C. "Introduction to Web Accessibility." Web Accessibility Initiative. Last modified June 5, 2019. Accessed March 8, 2021. https://www.w3.org/WAI/fundamentals/accessibility-intro/.

———. "WCAG 2.1 at a Glance." W3C Web Accessibility Initiative. Last modified 2021. Accessed March 9, 2021. https://www.w3.org/WAI/standards-guidelines/wcag/glance/.

Wilson, Jeffrey, and Mike Williams. "The Best WordPress Web Hosting Services for 2021." *PC Magazine*, March 10, 2021. Accessed March 10, 2021. https://www.pcmag.com/picks/the-best-wordpress-web-hosting-services.

WordPress.org. "Support." Last modified 2021. Accessed March 10, 2021. https://wordpress.org/support/forums/.

Yang, Wenfan, Bin Zhao, Yan Quan Liu, and Arlene Bielefield. "Are Ivy League Library Website Homepages Accessible?" *Information Technology & Libraries*. 39, no. 2 (2020): 1–18. https://search.ebscohost.com/login.aspx?direct=true&AuthType=cookie,ip,cpid&custid=csl&db=aph&AN=143882437&site=ehost-live&scope=site.

CHAPTER 10

E-Books

LSS are able to assist and train users to operate public equipment, connect to the internet, use library software applications, and access library services from remote locations.

LSS perform basic troubleshooting of technical problems and resolve or refer those problems as appropriate.

LSS access and use basic assistive technologies, where appropriate, to ensure that all users have equitable access to technology.

Topics Covered in This Chapter
Basics
   Devices
   File Types
   Encryption
   Digital Rights Management
   Self-Publishing
Publishers
Content
   Trade
   Academic
Services
   Free Services
Assistive Technologies
Data and Statistics
Chapter Summary

Key Terms

Closed standard—The e-book file type is written for a specific e-book reader or app. For example, Amazon e-books are considered closed standard because they can only be read on the Amazon Kindle or by using an Amazon app on other devices.

DRM—An acronym for digital rights management, it restricts or limits how an e-book can be shared among people and devices.

Encryption—This is a part of a software program designed to guard the contents of the e-book files using algorithms and adjoining keys.

E-reader—This is a dedicated device used to download, read, and make notes about an e-book.

Monochrome—Black-and-white screen (or shades of gray) display of an e-reader that is easiest for viewing e-books.

Open standard—These are the file types that are available to use with any computing device and not specific to one e-book reader or vendor.

Trade books—These are books intended for the general public and are marketed with trade discount to bookstores and to libraries. Other types of books, such as textbooks, may not receive similar discounting.

BASICS

E-books, also called electronic or digital books, are a mainstream library service. E-books are available on any topic for any reading level. Chicago and APA style, as well as the Oxford English Dictionary and Merriam-Webster, have established *e-book* as the preferred spelling, but LSS will encounter other variations such as E-book, ebook, EBOOK, and Ebook.

Author Stephen King is recognized for having introduced e-books to the reading public.[1] In 2000 King provided his novella, *Riding the Bullet*, only in e-book format. With a fair amount of hype, his PDF e-book was free on Amazon or sold for $2.50 on other sites. It was downloaded more than four hundred thousand times in the first twenty-four hours upon release. His experiment challenged the traditional model of not only how people read, but how authors and publishers could profit on e-book sales.

As users became accustomed to e-books, many sought library e-book services for the following conveniences.

- E-books are quick and simple to download.
- E-books may be acquired 24/7 from the library.
- Multiple e-books can be downloaded on one device.
- Almost any mobile device can be an **e-reader**.
- Many e-book formats can be listened to using speech-to-text or built-in digital players.

LSS can be confronted by the many e-book options. The chapter continues with explanations of e-book devices, file types, rights management, and self-publishing.

Devices

People who access e-books may choose between using a dedicated e-reader or a personal mobile device. With the explosion of mobile device options, there is no longer required reading devices for e-books. Some people prefer a dedicated device, such as a NOOK, Kobo, or Kindle as an e-reader. Others may use a multipurpose device, such as a smartphone, iPad, or other tablet.

LSS should become familiar with various e-readers as patrons will seek help with their devices, especially if it is new or a recent gift. The following information about dedicated e-readers is useful.[2]

Top ranked—while new e-readers are still evolving, the more popular are Amazon Kindles, Rakuten Kobos, Onyx Book Notes, and Barnes & Noble NOOKs. E-readers sell for an average of $200, some under $100 and others upward of $500.

Screens—The company E-Ink has a long relationship with Amazon as the developer of its **monochrome** Kindle screen. Monochrome most resembles the print of a paper book. The optimum e-reader screen is six to seven inches with edge or backlighting to accommodate night reading. Where color screens tend to wash out or show reflections in sunlight, a monochrome screen is easier to read with adjustable brightness settings. Most e-readers offer both touch and keyboard screens.

Waterproof—Unlike paper books, some e-readers are waterproof and meant for beach or poolside reading.

Wireless connection—E-readers use Wi-Fi. Those that provide content, such as Kindle and Kobo, also have a built-in cellular wireless connection for direct access to their servers.

Storage—Most e-readers have enough internal capacity to store more than one thousand e-books.

Apps—Most e-readers have free, proprietary apps that can be downloaded to other devices. An e-book downloaded on an e-reader may be accessed via the app on another device.

A person may have multiple e-book apps on their device if they are users of e-books from various services. Those who use mobile devices instead of e-readers must download the apps that are compatible with e-book content file types.

File Types

There is no one file type for e-books. E-books are created in many file types or extensions. People choose the device and its workable e-book file types. The file extension is determined by the requirements of the e-readers and devices. The two e-book file standards are **open standard** and **closed standard**.[3] Open standard are not associated with any publisher or vendor and can be downloaded and read on both Apple and PC computers. One of the most common open file types for e-books is PDF or Adobe portable document format. PDF is the common file format for scanned pages, and many e-books in the public domain and not under copyright are available simply because they were scanned in their entirety from print books.

EPUB is the second open standard in e-book publishing that has great versatility. It can be easily converted to file types such as PDF and Mobi to be read on a Kindle. EPUB is also compatible with iBooks to be read on Apple devices.

Other open standards for e-books are HTML, hypertext markup language, and XML, eXtensible markup language. HTML and XML e-books have the following advantages.

- They can be read by multiple e-reader devices.
- Hyperlinks can be made to places within the e-book.
- Hyperlinks in the e-book content can link to external internet websites.

TXT or plain text works with almost any e-reader or computing device. TXT offers little to no formatting options and no file protection. It's most common in free e-books.

Closed standard files are specific to a brand of e-reader. Amazon's file type AZW is compatible only with its e-book reader, the Kindle. Amazon controls use of its e-books by publishing them specifically in AZW for its Kindle or Kindle app and transferring files over its network called WhisperNet. While Amazon uses closed standard, other e-book vendors are moving to the open standard of EPUB.

Using a program such as Calibre, LSS may be able to convert a file type to one that is best suited for a device. LSS gain practice by converting EPUB to PDF and using the various e-readers the library lends for its e-book collections (see figure 10.1). The more familiar LSS are with these processes, the better able they are to help patrons who are new users.

Figure 10.1.   E-book Reader. *mikkelwilliam / E+ via Getty Images*

Encryption

Providers of e-book content protect the use of their products and the copyrights of authors by purposefully encrypting e-book files. **Encryption** is a part of a software program designed to guard the contents of the e-book files using algorithms and adjoining keys. E-books are files of data. The encryption software is designed to scramble e-book data with one or more algorithms before it is transferred to the e-reader or device. Typically, each e-book file is encrypted using a unique encryption key within the software. Similarly, the software also generates a decryption key that can only decrypt that one set of encrypted data. The file encryption software itself is also protected by requiring the user to provide a valid username and password for using its encryption services.

Amazon, Barnes & Noble, and Kobo all use encryption protection on their closed standard files that prevents them from being read on other brands' e-readers. Encryption programs also are used to control the amount of time a patron is allowed to use a library e-book. When the e-book is overdue, the file encrypts and the user no longer has access to it. Typically, in order for the encryption to activate at a specific time, the e-reader or mobile device must be connected to Wi-Fi.

Digital Rights Management

Libraries, publishers, and authors have the right to manage their e-book digital content. This process is called digital rights management or **DRM**. DRM restricts or limits how an e-book can be shared among people and devices. Embedded in the e-book software, DRM controls are important to authors and publishers because it manages the authorized use and duplication of copyrighted works. DRM also protects the revenue to be made by e-books. It may limit the number of times a file may be read, watched, or listened to; what type and number of devices the file may be used on; and whether a full or partial copy can be made of the file. DRM works through encryption where permissions are defined and limited. Users are unable to circumvent DRM; the algorithms and keys are encoded and subject to change.

Self-Publishing

With the development of different file types and devices, self-publishing can be easily accomplished. Two companies that make self-publishing easy are Calibre and Amazon. Calibre has style helpers and scripts to generate a book's structure, allowing the author to concentrate on the content. Amazon Kindle Direct Publishing (KDP) provides instructions for uploading, entering details, and modifying an e-book before publishing. The detail page describes the e-book to potential buyers who can purchase self-published e-books on Amazon to be used on the Kindle.

PUBLISHERS

Libraries may legally lend print books to patrons under the "first sale" doctrine (17 U.S.C. § 109(a)). The library purchases one copy of a book and circulates it multiple times; however, at any given time only one patron has access to the copy.

The physical book belongs to the library, which is allowed to lend it without legal hurdles.[4] Libraries that want to circulate multiple copies must purchase each one. E-books are computer files that have the potential to be copied unlimited times and thus cannot be managed under "first sale" doctrine. Chapter 11 discusses digital copyright and how DRM comes into play.

Publishers are not required to sell e-books to libraries, nor are they restricted by what they charge. Many publishers jumped early into the library e-book market while others, concerned about loss of revenue, preferred to sell directly to individuals. Some publishers set such exorbitantly high prices for their e-books that most libraries could not afford to purchase. From late 2018 through 2019, four of the five largest publishers increased prices and changed their digital content licensing terms for libraries. There has been ongoing tension between librarians and publishers owing to the lack of a consistent and fair pricing model across the industry.[5]

Due to these issues, prior to the pandemic of 2020–2022 library usage of e-books had moderate annual growth of about 10 to 15 percent. As the pandemic escalated, the majority of schools, colleges, and libraries were closed or had limited curbside pickup for most of the year. Despite valiant efforts, circulation of books plummeted to unimaginable numbers, often with circulation down 75 percent of what would be normally expected. At the same time, library e-book circulation dramatically increased not only for the general public but for school use of all ages. As libraries closed their doors, some began shifting their print budgets to digital. In response, dozens of publishers began slashing library e-book and digital audio prices and easing restrictions. E-book usage increased upward of 50 percent as libraries and schools served their communities remotely. Almost overnight the pandemic numbers of patrons sought e-books from their libraries. Libraries could afford to purchase e-book content when publishers set reasonable prices.

It remains to be seen if the e-book demand continues to grow post-pandemic, and if publishers will return to their practice of unilaterally raising prices and changing terms without negotiation. LSS are often the first to hear patrons' requests for e-books and can discuss with supervisors if the library is meeting users' needs with its current e-book services.

CONTENT

Most e-books are digital versions of print books. Publishers and authors decide if the print book could also be successfully marketable as an e-book. The e-book version often is an exact copy of the print book, with or without embedded hyperlinks. Some e-books, however, are only created in digital format with embedded media, such as sound, animation, hyperlinks, or film. LSS think of e-books in the same collection categories as print books. While e-books are not physically on shelves, the content they deliver is classified and cataloged using standard cataloging tools, rules, and procedures.

Trade

Libraries obtain e-books from publishers, retailers, and wholesalers. Wholesalers are companies that sell many publishers' **trade books**. The term comes from wholesalers selling publishers' books to many trades, including businesses, schools, and libraries. Most libraries purchase most of their fiction and nonfiction trade books from wholesalers because of steep discounting they receive. One of the largest wholesalers for library books is Baker & Taylor, which has expanded its trade book market by also selling and hosting many of their publishers' e-books and other media to libraries. Publishers set e-book prices and contract with the wholesaler to make the sale and provide DRM. Baker and Taylor Axis 360 is an example of how libraries may obtain trade books in digital format.

Academic

Academic textbooks are published for purposes of teaching and learning. Schools and colleges particularly relied on academic e-books during the pandemic when buildings were closed. DRM control student and teacher access as well as for specific time periods, such as a specific semester or school year. Other benefits of academic e-books are as follows:

- Publishers make timely editing modifications to keep content accurate and current without the expense of costly publishing.
- Multiple copies of e-books can be easily made compared to print books.
- Publishers can keep better control of inventory.
- Schools may be able to spend less on textbooks and not have to carefully plan their inventory to meet shifting populations.

Follett is one of the largest wholesalers of academic textbooks for both K–12 and higher education. It represents more than 2,500 publishers of educational e-books, offering services such as bundles of e-books aimed for specific learning groups or subject content. Libraries and schools that use Follett e-books find DRM suited to their students' needs. Based on the proven success of e-textbooks, more likely than not there will be large shifts to digital for teachers and students acquiring texts (see figure 10.2).

Figure 10.2. Child Reading an E-book. *Roberto Westbrook via Getty Images*

SERVICES

Libraries of all types offer e-book services to their users without charge and with little staff overhead. In addition to Baker & Taylor 360 Axis and Follett, a few of the e-book services offered by libraries for the general public, specialties such as science or reference topics, and children are found in table 10.1.

Table 10.1.   Examples of E-Book Services

General Public	Specialty	Children
Overdrive	Wiley	Scholastic
RB Digital	ScienceDirect	TumbleBook
Hoopla	Springer	Teen Book Cloud
E-Book Central	InfoScience Books	Oxford Owl
EBSCO eBook Collection	Brill	ProQuest E-Book Central
cloudLibrary	Credo Reference	ABDO
Amazon (public library license)	Gale Cengage E-Books	Overdrive for Teens

It would be cost prohibitive for libraries to go it alone to provide all of the e-book content their communities need. Consortium purchasing shares the expense for libraries and maximizes e-book collections for users. E-book consortiums may be as small as partnerships between two libraries or school districts or as large as state-wide cooperatives. Libraries link patrons to statewide offerings via their websites, but they also seek regional consortium partnerships that will greatly expand the selection of e-books for their patrons with sufficient numbers of available titles.

Overdrive and RB Digital (formerly Recorded Books) are two services that many library consortiums provide their users. The number of volumes, titles, and DRM will vary depending upon the contract.

Each service has its own app to download e-books, e-audio, or other digital content. For example, Overdrive has an app called Libby that, when downloaded and used on a smartphone or tablet, transforms the device into a functional e-book reader where the user can keep track of pages read, highlight text, turn text to speech, tag embedded content, and many other helpful features. LSS who help patrons with downloading an e-book from a library service should be sure the patron has downloaded the appropriate app so that the e-book content can be displayed on the mobile device.

It is important for LSS who are helping patrons with personal devices to discuss the relationship between the e-book content, the owner's e-reader or device, and any required app. For example, a person with a Kobo e-reader can install the app Libby prior to downloading an Overdrive e-book, while Kindles use the Amazon website to download e-books from Overdrive.

Overdrive lends e-books for a wide variety of publishers. Librarians like Overdrive because they select individual titles to build their "own" library collection of e-books. Library staff has control over e-book collection development, unlike other vendors that provide their core collections.

LSS can familiarize themselves with the e-book vendors and services their library contracts with. Some print books may also offer complimentary access to the titles in e-book format. Know how to access each e-book collection and become familiar with the content in order to help others. Ask to see monthly library statistics for e-book usage and make it a personal goal to introduce the library's e-book collections to a few new users each week.

Free Services

There are many free e-book services available on the internet. Most of these titles are in the public domain, meaning their copyrights have expired or the authors have agreed to unlimited distribution.

- *Project Gutenberg*[6] has more than sixty thousand free e-book titles, many in multiple file types. The titles are in numerous languages, stored and hosted on servers all over the world. Anyone can access Project Gutenberg without cost or registration. The collection contains both fiction and nonfiction e-books. Project Gutenberg is particularly useful for its classic fiction titles.
- *Google Books* offers thousands of scanned books. Books without copyright restriction are offered in entirety. Copyright restricted books are for preview and partially viewable.
- *DOAB* is the Directory of Open Access Books. With more than thirty-five thousand e-books, DOAB is a community-driven discovery service that indexes and provides access to free scholarly, peer-reviewed open-access books and helps users to find trusted open-access book publishers. All DOAB services are free of charge and all data is freely available.
- Some vendors offer collections of free e-books, such as Kobo, Amazon, and Barnes & Noble.
- Educational institutions and nonprofits also offer free e-books, such as the Tufts University Perseus e-book collection of classics or the Smithsonian Digital Library.

LSS who explore free e-books for their own research and information will be able to introduce others to these useful collections.

ASSISTIVE TECHNOLOGIES

For those who are visually impaired, audio e-books allow independence in reading. Audio e-books are read by professional readers who read with clarity, tempo, and appropriate emotion. Characters in voice make listening to an e-book both interesting and exciting. Audio e-books, formerly known as books on tape, have been available for many years. Today's mobile digital devices allow people who are driving, walking, exercising, or engaged in other activities to be able to simultaneously listen to an e-book. Volume, accent, pace, and replay controls are all easy to manage. Audio e-books may have DRM, making it easy for library circulation. Most computing devices enable text-to-speech software where digital content is converted to sound. E-books in HTML file format can readily be converted to text-to-speech, and many vendors of e-books, such as EBSCO and Gale Cengage, provide listening capability with their easy-to-use players embedded in each e-book file. The text-to-speech voice recorder Read Aloud can read PDF, Google Docs, Google Play books, Amazon Kindle, and EPUB.

E-book files can be manipulated to increase font size, spacing, and often type to make them easier to view and read. For example, the very popular file type EPUB allows e-book text to automatically adjust to different screen sizes, including smartphones, netbooks, and e-reader devices. EPUB e-books also support embedded content such as a video that may convey content more easily than text.

DATA AND STATISTICS

E-books have the potential to provide abundant information about readers' preferences and habits, so much so that data obtained—often unbeknownst to readers—can greatly influence future book content and writing styles. The company Epic provides thousands of e-books and educational videos free to more than fifty million children in schools. Epic collects data on how long children engage in an e-book, how often they pick it up and put it down, and every time a child turns a page or types a search. There are privacy concerns and questions about collecting data on children and its influence on how authors create plot, characters, and setting. For example, their data shows owls score higher than koalas and Abraham Lincoln outranks Ben Franklin. Will an overuse of analytics lose the magic of creative storytelling?[7] There are serious concerns vendors who use such analytics could unreasonably influence the creative craft of children's literature.

Statistics analysis helps libraries understand how digital content is being used. Academic libraries that use COUNTER[8] agree to its open Code of Practice to facilitate the recording, exchange, and interpretation of online usage statistics for journals, databases, e-books, reference works, and multimedia databases at an international level. Vendors, content providers, and academic libraries pledge to abide by the code in order to ensure integrity in the collection and reporting of the statistical data they will share to make important decisions about the generation, sale, purchase, and use of digital content. LSS who work in academic libraries may seek more information about how staff use statistical data to make decisions about e-books and other electronic resources.

CHAPTER SUMMARY

LSS who are informed users of e-books are able to assist and train others to access library e-book services on a variety of e-readers and mobile devices from remote locations. LSS perform basic troubleshooting of technical problems with e-books and resolve or refer those problems as appropriate. They also know how to use the basic assistive technologies of e-books to ensure that all users have equitable access to this technology.

DISCUSSION QUESTIONS

1. What are the fundamentals of how e-book readers work and the file types they use?

2. Why may someone choose to use a dedicated e-reader rather than a computing device?
3. What are some of the key library e-book services and how do they benefit patrons?
4. Why should libraries analyze e-book data and statistics?
5. What are some of the assistive technologies found in e-books and why are they helpful?

ACTIVITY

The goal of this assignment is to explore several e-book providers and file types.

1. Download one e-book from each provider on personal devices.
2. Briefly annotate each book that you downloaded.
3. Provide patrons one "tip" to help new users.

Examples of E-Book Services

E-Book Provider	Title and Brief Annotation	Tip to Help New Users
Amazon		
EBSCO eBooks		
Google Books		
RB Digital		
OverDrive (or another service of the public library)		
Project Gutenberg		
ProQuest E-Book Central		

NOTES

1. The Digital Reader, "Amazon's First eBookstore Launched 13 Years Ago Today," last modified 2021, accessed March 24, 2021, https://the-digital-reader.com/2013/11/14/amazon-ebooks-14-november-2000/.

2. Sascha Segan, "The Best eReaders for 2021," *PC*, last modified March 3, 2021, accessed March 26, 2021, https://www.pcmag.com/picks/the-best-ereaders.

3. University of Pennsylvania, "E-Books at Penn: E-Book File Types," Penn Libraries, last modified 2021, accessed March 26, 2021, https://guides.library.upenn.edu/pennebooks/file_types.

4. American Library Association, "First Sale and Kirtsaeng v. Wiley & Sons, Inc.," *Copyright for Libraries: First Sale Doctrine*, last modified March 21, 2019, accessed March 27, 2021, https://libguides.ala.org/copyright/firstsale.

5. Richard Albanese, "A Reset for Library E-Books," *Publishers Weekly* 267, no. 41 (October 12, 2020), https://search.ebscohost.com/login.aspx?direct=true&AuthType=cookie,ip,cpid&custid=csl&db=f5h&AN=146401368&site=ehost-live&scope=site.

6. Project Gutenberg, "Welcome to Project Gutenberg," last modified 2021, accessed March 28, 2021, https://www.gutenberg.org/.

7. Ellen Gamerman, "Move Over, 'Charlotte's Web'—Kids' Books Look to Algorithm—Digital Publisher Uses Children's Online Searches to Determine Hits; Hoot the Owl," *Wall Street Journal*, March 25, 2021, eastern edition, sec. A, https://search.proquest.com/wallstreetjournal/docview/2504663769/8EBD62626F2D476BPQ/1?accountid=46995.

8. COUNTER, "The COUNTER Code of Practice for Release 5," last modified 2021, accessed March 28, 2021, https://www.projectcounter.org/code-of-practice-five-sections/introduction-to-counter-code-of-practice-release-5/.

REFERENCES, SUGGESTED READINGS, AND WEBSITES

Albanese, Richard. "A Reset for Library E-Books." *Publishers Weekly* 267, no. 41 (October 12, 2020). https://search.ebscohost.com/login.aspx?direct=true&AuthType=cookie,ip,cpid&custid=csl&db=f5h&AN=146401368&site=ehost-live&scope=site.

American Library Association. "First Sale and Kirtsaeng v. Wiley & Sons, Inc." Copyright for Libraries: First Sale Doctrine. Last modified March 21, 2019. Accessed March 27, 2021. https://libguides.ala.org/copyright/firstsale.

Counter. "The COUNTER Code of Practice for Release 5." Last modified 2021. Accessed March 28, 2021. https://www.projectcounter.org/code-of-practice-five-sections/introduction-to-counter-code-of-practice-release-5/.

The Digital Reader. "Amazon's First eBookstore Launched 13 Years Ago Today." Last modified 2021. Accessed March 24, 2021. https://the-digital-reader.com/2013/11/14/amazon-ebooks-14-november-2000/.

Janalta Interactive. "What Does File Encryption Software Mean?" *Techopedia*. Last modified 2021. Accessed March 26, 2021. https://www.techopedia.com/definition/29699/file-encryption-software.

Kovid Goyal. "About Calibre." Calibre Ebook Management. Last modified 2021. Accessed March 26, 2021. https://calibre-ebook.com/.

Project Gutenberg. "Welcome to Project Gutenberg." Last modified 2021. Accessed March 28, 2021. https://www.gutenberg.org/.

Segan, Sascha. "The Best eReaders for 2021." *PC*. Last modified March 3, 2021. Accessed March 26, 2021. https://www.pcmag.com/picks/the-best-ereaders.

University of Pennsylvania. "E-Books at Penn: E-Book File Types." Penn Libraries. Last modified 2021. Accessed March 26, 2021. https://guides.library.upenn.edu/pennebooks/file_types.

Wang, Lin, Hana Lee, and Da Young Ju. "Impact of Digital Content on Young Children's Reading Interest and Concentration for Books." *Behaviour & Information Technology* 38, no. 1 (January 2019): 1–8. https://search.ebscohost.com/login.aspx?direct=true&AuthType=cookie,ip,cpid&custid=csl&db=aph&AN=133507638&site=ehost-live&scope=site.

CHAPTER 11

Digital Rights and Responsibilities

LSS know basic principles and best practices to ensure the integrity of data and the confidentiality of user activities.

LSS know concepts and issues concerning the appropriate use of technology by different user groups.

Topics Covered in This Chapter

Fundamental Rights
   Privacy
   Confidentiality
Copyright Basics
Digital Millennium Copyright Act
Digital Rights Management
Chapter Summary

Key Terms

Advertisement tracking—Online shopping data is collected and used to sell. Many libraries use Google Analytics or other products to "anonymously" track their patrons' online use of library website views and engagement.

Confidentiality—This is the state of secrecy. In a library, patrons expect confidentiality of their personal computer use, searches, circulation data, and how they use digital information.

Fair use—Copyrighted material may be used for "criticism, comment, news reporting, teaching, scholarship, or research" without the user paying the producer or asking for permission.

First Sale Doctrine—Libraries have the right to resell, rent, lease, or lend the work without paying or asking permission of the copyright holder.

Privacy—This is the freedom from unauthorized public attention, observation, or intrusion. In a library, LSS provide privacy when they support the ability for patrons to be free from intrusion with space from others when using services and materials.
Public domain—This is the status of an item that is not protected under copyright and therefore its use belongs to the public at large.

FUNDAMENTAL RIGHTS

With the use of library digital information services come certain rights and responsibilities for both patrons and staff. LSS adhere to appropriate compliance with digital materials and support observance by library users.

LSS protect the rights to privacy and confidentiality for all library users. Libraries uphold the First Amendment, which guarantees all citizens freedom of speech, thought, and free associations. In a library, LSS provide **privacy** when they support the ability for patrons to be free from intrusion with space from others when using services and materials. In a library, patrons also expect **confidentiality** of their personal and circulation information. LSS uphold these freedoms of privacy and confidentiality when providing traditional and digital library services.

Privacy and confidentiality can be breached when technology systems are not secure from threat, sabotage, or attack. Where once libraries primarily thought about security in the context of keeping intruders from entering the building, today securing computers and networks is equally important. Because libraries use data systems and networks, patron privacy and confidentiality cannot be achieved unless all computing systems are secure. The sophistication of hackers and others who mean to cause harm to data and computing systems continues to accelerate. Libraries are not exempt. Every library should have in place processes with their IT management and vendors to protect and secure patrons' proprietary and private data from being compromised. Cybersecurity is essential to maintaining functional library digital systems.

Libraries have a primary obligation to safeguard users' personal data, including records of their online behavior and borrowing histories. LSS cannot be complacent.[1] Depending upon the library, administrators and others responsible for its IT and OT (Operational Technology) should work within their technology community, which may include its college campus, school district, or municipality to ensure security, privacy, and confidentiality of the library data and systems.

For example, a municipal or school library can achieve better website security if it is hosted with others rather than going it alone as a single customer. When the library website is hosted with other library or institutional sites and services, it benefits from a greater investment of cybersecurity and protections made by the group to keep all members' data and systems from harm by hackers.

Privacy

Technology both enhances and challenges the ability of LSS to protect privacy. Privacy is severely compromised when control of users' personal data, search history, and borrowing activities is compromised. Librarians need to keep in mind that technology companies are some of the most powerful companies in the world, and they obtain their money through user data. Some concerns of librarians both today and in the near future around users' privacy are as follows.

Cloud or third-party platforms: The library is the first party the patron provides her personal information to when applying for a library card. The patron assumes her information is stored on the library computers; however, the library may use a second-party host Integrated Library System (ILS) vendor who arranges for cloud storage of circulation data. The ILS may have contracts with third parties for cloud computing storage.

The library's responsibility for user privacy and confidentiality extends to licenses and agreements with outside vendors and contractors. Libraries that use and promote file sharing such as Google Docs, Dropbox, and other clouds should alert patrons that these are second- or third-party platforms and that the library cannot ensure their privacy or control the dissemination of their information. LSS may volunteer to review with other staff agreements with vendors that involve patron personal identifiable information (PII) to determine if privacy policies are in place, including for information of minors.

Internet of Things (IoTs)—Many of the IoTs libraries use or will be using in the future include smart building and events devices, radio frequency identification devices (RFID) to locate and manage collections, robotic book return, and drone delivery. IoTs wirelessly report data on the user's location and other activities.[2] LSS can work with other concerned staff to develop policies and procedures for disabling unnecessary data tracking from the library IoTs devices.

Advertisement tracking—Google, Facebook, Amazon, most social media, and the majority of commercial sites use **advertisement tracking**. It is not by coincidence that when we shop online, suggestions for similar or related products appear in our browser, email, and other accounts and places. Who we are and our shopping interests are being tracked, and likely our data is being purchased by others who want to sell. Many libraries are using Google Analytics or other products to "anonymously" track their patrons' online use of library website views and engagement. Discuss with the IT staff how the library evaluates for ad trackers, whether traffic sent to Google Analytics is anonymized, and how use of a virtual private network[3] for library self-service tasks provides patrons better privacy of their personal information.

Virtual Reality—Virtual Reality (VR) provides endless educational opportunities, especially in the area of participating by simulation in an academic, technology, or work experience that authenticates the real world. Many libraries with makerspaces are including VR in their array of STEAM opportunities. As centers of lifelong learning, libraries are quickly embracing VR for its experiential education because they understand emerging tech is information literacy. As VR becomes more affordable, scalable, and adaptable, this technology comes with concerns for patron privacy. For example, Meta owns a top VR headset and software maker.[4] LSS can discuss with library IT staff available options to better protect the privacy of VR users.

Confidentiality

Patrons expect their library dealings to be confidential. Patrons have both legal and personal expectations that what they read and view will not be shared with others. It is up to the patron to decide whether to share the latest library book title he read or the film she viewed. The ALA Library Bill of Rights, policy IV,[5] states in part, "Libraries should cooperate with all persons and groups concerned with resisting abridgment of free expression and free access to ideas." Further, the ALA Code of Ethics, policy 3,[6] states confidentiality extends to "information sought or received and resources consulted, borrowed, acquired or transmitted." Library resources could be a patron's database search records, circulation records, and interlibrary loan records, information about materials downloaded, or computer and internet use.

For example, databases and computer files are backed up and archived as a matter of standard IT practice. Library staff are bound by professional ethics to keep confidential both current and past patron circulation data. Libraries should purposefully dismantle any archiving of patron circulation data once the materials are checked in to help ensure confidentiality.

There are practical things LSS can do to help educate and support patrons' confidentiality when using technology at the library. Public computers can be arranged in a way that patrons have some measure of privacy from main floor traffic. Signage can be posted to remind people to be discreet with their personal passwords. LSS should scan for library computers not in use to be sure that the last person did not leave an account open.

The First Amendment freedoms of speech, thought, and association cannot be had without the support LSS give to ensuring privacy, confidentiality, and security of technology. However, there is a responsibility of patrons to use technology responsibly. The second part of this chapter discusses the responsibility of staff and patrons to know and apply copyright law when using digital materials.

COPYRIGHT BASICS

Digital assets, similar to any property, are subject to federal and state laws of ownership and copyright. Just as LSS would question ownership and understand copyright restrictions before using print materials, they also need to research ownership and copyright for digital assets intended to be shared or used in a digital collection. It is illegal to digitize a photograph by a known living photographer for use in a library digital collection without her permission. Written permission must be sought and kept on file. LSS should never abridge the U.S. Copyright Act or support others who aim to do so. Examples of copyrightable items include[7]

- art (pictorial, graphic, textual, and sculpture);
- literary works;
- dramatic works;
- musical works;
- sound recordings;
- motion pictures, film, and other audiovisual works;
- choreographic works; and
- architectural works.

All of these items have the potential to be created or converted into digital assets. Libraries are unique in their practice of lending items to the public. Because the

U.S. Copyright Act provides special sections for our services, it is permissible for libraries to lend copyrighted items unlimited times without giving compensation to authors. Libraries are also centers for research. Patrons use resources to enhance their learning. LSS should be familiar with the following three important sections of U.S. Copyright law that govern how libraries lend materials and promote learning:

- *U.S. Copyright Law, Sec. 107: Fair Use.* Copyrighted material may be used for "criticism, comment, news reporting, teaching, scholarship, or research" without the user paying the producer or asking for permission.
- *U.S. Copyright Law, Sec 108: Copying by Libraries and Archives*: Libraries and archives may reproduce and distribute one copy of a work under certain circumstances such as journal articles, book chapters, and so forth.
- *Section 109: The First Sale Doctrine*: The purchaser of a copyrighted work (library) has the right to resell, rent, lease, or lend the work without paying or asking permission of the copyright holder (see figure 11.1).

Copyright gives the creator of a work the right to control how the work is used and an economic incentive to create and share his or her ideas with others. Only items that are tangible or fixed, original, and minimally creative can be copyrighted. For example, paper, a computer disk, or an audio or videotape are all legitimate forms of fixation. Original means it precedes all others in time and that it is not derived from something else. Creativity need only be slight for the work to be eligible for protection. As a general rule, for works created after January 1, 1978, copyright

Figure 11.1. Copyright Protection. *Peter Dazeley / The Image Bank via Getty Images*

protection lasts for the life of the author plus an additional seventy years. Items not eligible for copyright are

- works, facts, and ideas in the public domain;
- words, names, slogans, or other short phrases—however, slogans, for example, can be protected by trademark law;
- blank forms; and
- government works, which include judicial opinions, public ordinances, administrative rulings, and works created by federal government employees as part of their official responsibility.

A copyright protects the right to limit copies of the work, the right to sell or otherwise distribute copies of the work for profit or gain, and the right to control who performs the protected work (such as a stage play or painting) in public. It is up to the person who holds the copyright to protect anyone from infringing on their work. In some instances the author chooses to give up or sell his or her copyright, such as the case of the Beatles, who sold many of the copyrights to their music to Michael Jackson. Once copyright has expired on a work, it is no longer protected and the rights to use and copy it belongs to the **public domain** with no permissions required for its use.

With the onset of technology, new copyright law was needed to regulate digital content. In 1998, the Digital Millennium Copyright Act was passed.

DIGITAL MILLENNIUM COPYRIGHT ACT

The Digital Millennium Copyright Act (DMCA) is incorporated into Title 17 of the U.S. Copyright Act to provide digital copyright protection. The ease of digitization created the potential for breaching copyright law in ways that were never possible just a generation ago. The act updated copyright law to address new situations presented by technologies and for the United States to conform to the policies of the World Intellectual Property Organization (WIPO).[8] Copyright law differs from country to country. WIPO sets standards for global cooperation and develops policies to work with and respect copyright among countries.

In the United States under the DMCA one cannot copy or sell copyrighted digital content such as computer apps, software, music, e-books, or digital media without the author's permission. Key reasons for the DMCA are to[9]

- prevent the circumvention of technological protection measures,
- set limitations on copyright infringement liability for online service providers,
- expand an existing exemption for making copies of computer programs, and
- provide a significant updating of the rules and procedures regarding archival preservation.

Today users seek e-books, digital media, databases, and other forms of technology from their libraries. It is important for LSS to know how to apply Sections 107, 108, and 109 with digital services.

Fair Use—U.S. Copyright Law, Sec 107: Copyrighted works can be used for non-profit or educational purposes. Libraries may fall into this definition depending upon the purpose of use. If the copyrighted work is out of print, it is more likely to be considered **fair use**. Considerations for fair use are

1. the purpose and character of the use if it is for commercial gain or for non-profit educational purposes,
2. the nature of the copyrighted work,
3. the amount and substantiality of the portion used in relation to the copyrighted work as a whole, and
4. the effect of the use upon the potential market for or value of the copyrighted work.[10]

Fair use requires brevity and spontaneity. The more one uses the work, the less likely it is considered fair. A good rule of thumb is not to exceed 10 percent of the work without gaining the author's permission. That would be 10 percent of an e-book, computer file, or document. Another guideline is not to use more than thirty seconds of a song or film without authorization.

Archives—U.S. Copyright Law, Sec 108: LSS may make a single copy of journal article or book chapter at the request of a patron or by another library. Title IV of Sec 108 updates digital preservation (1) to expressly permit authorized institutions, which include libraries, to make up to three digital preservation copies of an eligible copyrighted work; (2) to electronically "loan" those copies to other qualifying institutions; and (3) to permit preservation, including by digital means, when the existing format in which the work has been stored becomes obsolete.[11] At no time is the library to circulate multiple copies when they only purchased one. Section 108 ensures libraries can both circulate and maintain collections of digital resources. This section also encourages libraries to create archives of primary source and other materials in digital format for future research and use.

Currently Section 108 does not allow such duplication of musical works, pictorial, graphic, or motion pictures or other audiovisual works in their entirety for circulation. Libraries may make up to three copies in digital format for archival purposes and only to be used in the building under strict fair use applications of scholarship or research. Anticipate there may be future changes to the law; at the time of this writing Section 108 revision is in the Discussion Document phase (see figure 11.2).[12]

First Sale Doctrine—U.S. Copyright Law, Section 109: Under this section libraries have the right to resell, rent, lease, or lend the work without paying or asking permission of the copyright holder. Second 109 is a "hot topic" with regard to publishers and e-books. Publishers have legitimate concern that libraries purchase an e-book once and circulate it indefinitely, thus limiting the potential profit of the book. Some publishers have priced e-books for libraries at a much higher rate than for individuals (see chapter 10). Libraries and publishers are working together toward respectful understandings and solutions to this problem of first sale of digital e-books.

Table 11.1 presents examples of potential copyright situations that may occur in libraries and the appropriate response LSS may take.

Figure 11.2. Libraries Lend Materials. *SW Prodcutions / Photodisc via Getty Images*

Conversion equipment from analog such as analog VHS or sound cassette tapes to digital format is available for reformatting content. Digital equipment has the capacity to make almost unlimited copies. LSS should discuss with their supervisor the considerations of U.S. Copyright law when asked to convert an older format into digital or to make multiple digital copies to ensure that they are within legal boundaries of the DMCA.

Table 11.1. Potential Digital Copyright Situations

Potential Digital Copyright Situation	Appropriate LSS Response
Patron is using library equipment to scan and copy an entire popular print book to PDF so he can read it onscreen and not check it out.	LSS should intercede and tell patron this is not allowed under U.S. copyright, Sec 109, because the library can only circulate the paper copy it has purchased. Report activity to supervisor.
The library purchases only one copy of a popular children's software program and installs it on multiple computers in the children's room.	LSS should intercede and advise children's librarian that under Sec 108 libraries can only make one copy for theft or archival purposes. They cannot make multiple copies to get around multiple purchases.
Staff copy and post poetry of a local author on the library website for Poetry Month without permission of author.	LSS should intercede and advise webmaster or supervisor that poetry is fixed, original, and creative work. Author needs to give permission to have work posted online.
Staff scans all of the annual town reports as a digital collection.	LSS can help with this! Town reports are made by government employees as part of their work and are not subject to U.S. copyright law. If there are graphics or artwork in the reports, be sure it is copyright free.

DIGITAL RIGHTS MANAGEMENT

Digital rights management (DRM), introduced in chapter 10, is for controlling circulation of e-books. DRM is not copyright. Rather it is technology that provides protection for creators and authors of digital text, sound, video, and forms of media content from those who may want to make unlawful or unauthorized use of their files.

LSS work with DRM when they help patrons download e-books and upload files. DRM controls how libraries lend digital content, under what conditions, and for how long. Can subscription databases be accessed remotely or are they restricted to in-library use? Can the user share an e-book or other library file with someone else? DRM controls access, use, and distribution:[13]

- *Access*—how users obtain the digital content
- *Use*—what users do with content once they have access to it
- *Distribution*—how the content can be shared with others

It is not by chance that a user may have accessed a file but cannot copy or share it. In this case the DRM provides access but restricts unlawful use and distribution. LSS can ask supervisors about the DRM of the library digital content so that they can best inform and help patrons with digital content. DRM is purposeful in limiting or restricting copying e-books and supersedes "first sale" doctrine of libraries lending print books. In other words, libraries can only lend the one digital version of an e-book at a time. The library must purchase two copies if it would like to circulate two copies at the same time. It is illegal to make multiple copies of single copyrighted e-books and digital files.

DRM can be used to track readers' preferences. Its encrypted code can provide feedback to publishers and vendors about the popularity and consumption of digitized content. Some may argue that data gathering of this sort invades the user's privacy. Others who want such data may say that the data help provide future content that users will more likely seek. Patrons' privacy is a fundamental right that libraries seek to protect for print materials, yet the digital content they purchase or subscribe to for their patrons is embedded with DRM that may undermine or erode such rights. LSS who are informed about the DRM used in the library digital content can better understand the data that is being collected and how it is being used.

DRM can be specific to a device, such as an Amazon e-book being used on a Kindle. The device and DRM of the software work together to provide both benefits and restrictions on how the borrower or purchaser can access, use, and distribute the e-book. Other DRM are more general and not specific to a device. An example is "watermarking" a digital file with the owner's name and other identifying information so that it always appears in the file and can be traced.

In the next chapter topics of other digital rights, such as licensing of media, is discussed. LSS can support usage of networked and streamed media and audio sources when appropriately licensed.

CHAPTER SUMMARY

LSS who know and apply the basic principles and best practices to adhere to copyright help to ensure the integrity of data and the confidentiality of user activities. When LSS understand copyright concepts and issues concerning DRM, they can support appropriate use of technology and digital content by different user groups.

DISCUSSION QUESTIONS

1. What are key differences between privacy and confidentiality as they apply to patrons' expectations when they use library materials?
2. What are some concerns of librarians around technology and users' privacy?
3. What are key reasons for the need for the Digital Millennium Copyright Act?
4. What are potential copyright situations that may occur in libraries and the appropriate responses LSS may make?
5. What are the three controls of DRM for library digital content and why are they important?

ACTIVITY

Using the information in this chapter and the sources found below, create a handout or display on digital copyright for the library to be shared with staff and patrons. Explain the need for the Digital Millennium Copyright Act. What is permissible? What is not? Provide specific examples of situations that apply to users of library materials. Also explain in the handout DRM with examples of library digital information services where DRM is in use.

NOTES

1. Terrence K. Huwe, "Cybersecurity: Moving Targets, Shifting Strategies," *Computers in Libraries* 39, no. 9 (November 2019): 9–11, https://search.ebscohost.com/login.aspx?direct=true&AuthType=cookie,ip,cpid&custid=csl&db=aph&AN=139831899&site=ehost-live&scope=site.

2. Amy Carlton, "Top Tech Trends Focus on Privacy," *American Libraries* (blog), entry posted January 26, 2020, accessed October 29, 2020, https://americanlibrariesmagazine.org/blogs/the-scoop/top-tech-trends-focus-privacy/.

3. Carlton, "Top Tech Trends Focus on Privacy."

4. Carlton, "Top Tech Trends Focus on Privacy."

5. American Library Association, "Library Bill of Rights," *Issues & Advocacy*, last modified 2020, accessed November 2, 2020, http://www.ala.org/advocacy/intfreedom/librarybill.

6. American Library Association, "Professional Ethics," *Tools, Publications, and Resources*, last modified 2020, accessed November 2, 2020, http://www.ala.org/tools/ethics.

7. Purdue University, "Copyright Overview," Copyright Basics, last modified 2021, accessed April 1, 2021, https://www.lib.purdue.edu/uco/CopyrightBasics/basics.html.

8. WIPO, "Copyright. What Is Copyright?" World Intellectual Property Organization, last modified 2020, accessed April 1, 2021, https://www.wipo.int/copyright/en/.

9. Library of Congress, "The Digital Millennium Copyright Act," Copyright.Gov, last modified 2020, accessed November 2, 2020, https://www.copyright.gov/dmca/.

10. Library of Congress, "Fair Use and Its Impact on Audio Preservation and Access," National Recording Preservation Plan, last modified 2020, accessed October 10, 2020, https://www.loc.gov/programs/national-recording-preservation-plan/collections-management/fair-use-law-and-its-impact-on-audio-preservation/.

11. American Library Association, "Digital Millennium Copyright Act," *Issues & Advocacy*, last modified 2020, accessed November 3, 2020, http://www.ala.org/advocacy/copyright/dmca.

12. Library of Congress, "Revising Section 108: Copyright Exceptions for Libraries and Archives," U.S. Copyright Office, last modified 2020, accessed October 10, 2020, https://www.copyright.gov/policy/section108/.

13. Mirela Roncevic, "Digital Rights Management and Books," *Library Technology Reports* 56, no. 1 (January 2020): 5–30, https://search.ebscohost.com/login.aspx?direct=true&AuthType=cookie,ip,cpid&custid=csl&db=aph&AN=140438292&site=ehost-live&scope=site.

REFERENCES, SUGGESTED READINGS, AND WEBSITES

American Library Association. "Digital Millennium Copyright Act." *Issues & Advocacy*. Last modified 2020. Accessed November 3, 2020. http://www.ala.org/advocacy/copyright/dmca.

———. "Library Bill of Rights." *Issues & Advocacy*. Last modified 2020. Accessed November 2, 2020. http://www.ala.org/advocacy/intfreedom/librarybill.

———. "Professional Ethics." *Tools, Publications, and Resources*. Last modified 2020. Accessed November 2, 2020. http://www.ala.org/tools/ethics.

Carlton, Amy. "Top Tech Trends Focus on Privacy." *American Libraries* (blog). Entry posted January 26, 2020. Accessed October 29, 2020. https://americanlibrariesmagazine.org/blogs/the-scoop/top-tech-trends-focus-privacy/.

Huwe, Terrence K. "Cybersecurity: Moving Targets, Shifting Strategies." *Computers in Libraries* 39, no. 9 (November 2019): 9–11. https://search.ebscohost.com/login.aspx?direct=true&AuthType=cookie,ip,cpid&custid=csl&db=aph&AN=139831899&site=ehost-live&scope=site.

Library of Congress. "The Digital Millennium Copyright Act." Copyright.Gov. Last modified 2020. Accessed November 2, 2020. https://www.copyright.gov/dmca/.

———. "Fair Use and Its Impact on Audio Preservation and Access." National Recording Preservation Plan. Last modified 2020. Accessed October 10, 2020. https://www.loc.gov/programs/national-recording-preservation-plan/collections-management/fair-use-law-and-its-impact-on-audio-preservation/.

———. "Revising Section 108: Copyright Exceptions for Libraries and Archives." U.S. Copyright Office. Last modified 2020. Accessed October 10, 2020. https://www.copyright.gov/policy/section108/.

Purdue University. "Copyright Overview." Copyright Basics. Last modified 2021. Accessed April 1, 2021. https://www.lib.purdue.edu/uco/CopyrightBasics/basics.html.

Roncevic, Mirela. "Digital Rights Management and Books." *Library Technology Reports* 56, no. 1 (January 2020): 5–30. https://search.ebscohost.com/login.aspx?direct=true&AuthType=cookie,ip,cpid&custid=csl&db=aph&AN=140438292&site=ehost-live&scope=site.

Vaughan, Jason. "Library Privacy Policies." *Library Technology Reports* 56, no. 6 (August/September 2020): 1–53. https://search.ebscohost.com/login.aspx?direct=true&AuthType=cookie,ip,cpid&custid=csl&db=aph&AN=146048870&site=ehost-live&scope=site.

WIPO. "Copyright. What Is Copyright?" World Intellectual Property Organization. Last modified 2021. Accessed November 2, 2020. https://www.wipo.int/copyright/en/.

CHAPTER 12

Media and Streaming Services

LSS are able to assist and train users to operate public equipment, connect to the internet, use library software applications, and access library services from remote locations.

LSS know role of technology in creating, identifying, retrieving, and accessing information resources and demonstrate facility with appropriate information discovery tools.

Topics Covered in This Chapter

Streaming Basics
Consumer Streaming Services
   Global Market
   Fees
Libraries Provide Streaming Services
   Public Libraries
   Academic Libraries
   K–12 Schools
Public Performance Site Licensing
Hosting Services
Chapter Summary

Key Terms

Downstream—This is the direction of data when transmitted over the internet to end users from a central server point of origin.

Live streaming—This is when video of an event or performance is viewed as it occurs.

On-demand—Customers or institutions pay a subscription to have access to a large selection of media that users can view at their convenience.

OTT video streaming—Standing for "over the top," this type of streaming refers to film and television content provided via a high-speed internet connection rather than cable or satellite.

Pay-per-view—Customers or institutions pay a fee for a onetime viewing of a film.

Prerecorded streaming—This is media has been taped or recorded for viewing sometime after the event occurs.

Public performance site licensing—Under federal U.S. Copyright law, a license is required when showing a commercial film outside the home that provides compensation to those who hold the copyright.

Streaming—This is the process of using the internet as the transmission to view or host media from a host service to computing devices.

Upstream—The reverse of downstream, this is the transmission of data using the internet from the end user to the hosting service.

STREAMING BASICS

Streaming is the process of viewing or listening to media files over the internet from one computing source to another without storing them on the user's device. Streaming moves data in two directions called downstream and upstream. **Downstream** is the transmission of data to an end user from a central server or point of origin. An example of a downstream is when students view a critically acclaimed film from the university library Kanopy subscription service for a course assignment. The opposite direction of data flow is **upstream**. LSS who post library photos on Facebook upstream data to a central hosting service. Today viewing film or listening to audio from a central hosting service is referred to as streaming. The adoption by the public to using streaming exemplifies how when technology is easy to use, provides choice, and results in better products, people will rapidly change to acquiring new methods. Traditional broadcast companies earn revenue through embedded commercials that advertise every few minutes to their viewers. Today these companies grapple to compete with streaming services that offer the choice people desire and are willing pay for.

Unlike other types of downloading where files are stored on a personal device, such as a PDF e-book or a MP3 music file, streaming works because data is arranged in packets in such a way that they transfer almost instantaneously over the internet for viewing. When a user streams, they do not obtain ownership of the file, nor does the file remain in the device storage or memory.

Streaming[1] can be live or prerecorded. **Live streaming** is when the viewer watches video in real time as it occurs, as if they were present at a sport or another event. Zoom, Google Classroom, and other online services introduced many to live streaming during the pandemic.

Prerecorded streaming is media that was recorded previously. An example of prerecorded streaming is YouTube, whereby a viewer can stream from the YouTube servers any of its hosted video as often as desired, 24/7. Libraries participate in both live and prerecorded streaming. Often library programs are both streamed live and recorded for downloading later at patrons' convenience.

The higher the internet speed, the more successful streaming will be. People who live in urban and suburban areas are more likely to have faster and more reliable internet service than those who live in remote or rural areas. In a rural area, distance from the transmitting cell tower and the generation of internet will affect the robustness of streaming. Using 4G internet is adequate for most streaming, but those who are limited to 3G may not be able to reliably do so. Librarians considering streaming services should be aware that if most patrons have limited 3G or irregular 4G service, the subscription services are apt to not be useful.

Likewise to internet speed, streaming services require that users access their content via specific apps or programs. Some apps, like YouTube or Ted Talks, are available or installed when users select their content. Other streaming services require users to download an app or small program on their device that interacts with the hosting streaming service. The app is the tool that interprets or translates the data packets that are being transmitted over the internet to the user's device into viewable content (see figure 12.1).

People stream on a variety of equipment with a minimum of 4G internet capability such as TVs, tablets, computers, smartphones and watches, and gaming consoles.

Figure 12.1. Live Streamed Performance. *Glowimages via Getty Images*

CONSUMER STREAMING SERVICES

Some streaming services are free to users. Others charge users a subscription fee. Free services such as TED Talks and Google's YouTube are available to the public with the app accessible when the user selects a program and clicks "play." YouTube is owned by Google and markets through its advertising. Another model for free services is TED Talks, which is owned by the Ted Foundation,[2] a nonprofit organization whose goal is to foster the spread of ideas that could help create a better future by resolving global issues. Additionally to private and corporate donations, TED is supported by conference attendance fees, sponsorships, licensing fees, and book sales. Streaming enables people to learn from the expertise of TED speakers who are both live in front of audiences and prerecorded for anyone to access its archive of talks via the internet without cost.

The viewing public is bombarded daily with advertising to entice them to expand their television or computer watching by subscribing to fee-based streaming services. Two ways to acquire fee-based streaming is **pay-per-view** (PPV) and video on demand.[3] PPV does not require a subscription, but rather it may be offered through the television service, such as cable or satellite, that offer a PPV channel. PPV tend to be special programs such as sports, concerts, or unique events that are live streamed. Users check the TV guide on their PPV channel to purchase access to a specific show and learn when it will be viewed. When the show starts, viewers have access for however long the program is set to last. Once the show ends, access to the content expires.

A second streaming option, **on-demand**, has quickly gained great popularity and will likely continue to outpace traditional programming. For an additional nominal amount, often under $10 per month, viewers have access to hundreds of streamed preselected shows and movies and the dates that the shows are available to be viewed. Subscribers, including libraries, incur annual or monthly charges whether the service is used or not.

Global Market

LSS are made aware that the market of streaming digital content, while it serves the United States, is gearing toward the potential of billions of overseas viewers.[4] Where once Hollywood would dub or subtitle films in English and sell them to foreign markets, with a direct line to customers through the internet of global streaming platforms, Netflix, Disney, Amazon, and other companies are making significant investments to make culturally specific, local-language content to woo global subscribers. The rise in overseas production is spurring a historic boom of new films and TV series in many different languages. The emphasis on global content is creating more work and competition for international producers and storytellers, while also ushering in a new era in which Hollywood-made American content plays a smaller role in the worldwide entertainment industry.

In 2020 the number of streaming subscriptions exceeded 1.1 billion worldwide. About half of the new content Netflix is developing are productions based outside the United States, with roughly one-third of non-English-language content. Disney has approximately one-quarter of its new content in development based overseas. At Amazon, the volume of original, local-language content being produced has doubled each year since 2017. Libraries can expect to see more demand for content authentic to global cultures and languages in the future based on what people will be able to acquire from streamed services.

Fees

Likewise to the streaming services mentioned, customers have many more choices for on-demand subscription service. Google, Amazon, Apple, Hulu, HBO Now,

Hoopla, Acorn TV, and SONY are just a few of the large companies that vie for the general public market. While the regular YouTube viewing is free, YouTube TV and Sling TV are subscription brokers for many channels and streaming content. Consumers often have choice within the service. For example, in 2021 Hulu offered

- Basic: $6 a month for ad-supported on-demand streaming;
- Premium: $12 a month for ad-free on-demand streaming;
- Basic + Live TV: $65 a month for ad-supported on-demand and live TV streaming; and
- Premium + Live TV: $71 a month for ad-free on-demand and ad-supported live TV streaming.

Some providers bundle services. Disney Plus offers an option of bundled services with ESPN and Hulu. A family that subscribes to multiple services could add upward of $100 per month for media streaming.

LIBRARIES PROVIDE STREAMING SERVICES

Libraries may offer alternatives to consumer services by providing streaming services to their patrons. Streaming services target and appeal to specific audiences, and purposeful streaming services are commonly found in public, academic, and K–12 school libraries.

Public Libraries

During the pandemic, many libraries enhanced or initiated streaming services for their patrons as a way to offer remote quality digital content and to meet their users' needs. The majority of streaming is obtained through subscriptions. Similar to subscriptions of databases for journals and other content, media streaming services require a contract with the library. The library, in turn, provides access only to its registered patrons who use their library barcode or other access codes.

Users found during the pandemic that libraries offered streaming that was much more than entertainment. Libraries are shifting their budgets away from DVDs to purchase streaming services that offer a variety of content, including information and new learning. A survey of public libraries by Kanopy, an academic streaming service, found that

- the majority expect an increase in their video streaming budgets over the next three years;
- more than half reported that along with entertainment, patrons use streaming videos for personal enrichment and class assignments;
- half of public librarians say it is the library's responsibility to support K–12 curriculum with streaming video services;
- one-third report they are collaborating with schools in this effort; and
- all say diversity in the video collection is very important, yet only one-third say they are meeting patrons' needs in this area.[5]

Subscribing libraries enter a contract with the streaming service. The contract allows the library to provide access to the vendor's media to its cardholders under a set of lending rules that are agreed upon with the provider, such as offering patrons a limited seven-day pass for access or a restricted number of titles at one time. Some libraries lend Roku devices for patrons to access streamed content at home. A few of streaming video services that offer subscriptions for public library use are as follows.

- *IndieFlix*—This is a streaming movie service that offers unlimited access to pop culture favorites, box office hits, award-winning feature films, documentaries, and shorts.
- *Hoopla*—This is a digital media service of movies, music, audiobooks, e-books, comics, and TV shows offered by some local public libraries. Titles can be streamed immediately or downloaded to phones or tablets for offline enjoyment later.
- *Kanopy*—Popular with both public and academic libraries, Kanopy works with libraries to offer patrons films and documentaries across diverse subjects and disciplines.

LSS work directly with the public and are in a position to discuss with them their viewing requests and needs. It is important for LSS to share information about users' requests with supervisors. LSS may also research media streaming services other libraries use and present findings for supervisors to consider. What is clear is that the hard media of DVD is not a growing format for libraries to invest in. Rather, with the explosion of streaming media options, libraries can select services that align with the mission of being information providers that support lifelong learning.

Academic Libraries

Teaching with film is a proven and successful instructional modality. People are auditory and visual learners who learn from engaging in what they see and hear. Educators incorporate film in ways to expand students' knowledge base and to provide authentic visualizations of concepts, ideas, and events. Some library subscription database services provide mixed media, offering material in multiple formats such as text documents, sound recordings, video, and websites. Many EBSCO and ProQuest databases contain streaming video resources.

Kanopy is also popular with public libraries; the following are examples of media streaming services offered to students and professors in academic libraries that provide content to enhance learning.[6]

- *Academic Video Online*—This service provides access to thousands of video titles on the arts, humanities, science, and social sciences. The formats include documentaries, interviews, performances, news programs and newsreels, field recordings, commercials, raw footage, and award-winning films, all with accompanying transcripts. Collection highlights include BBC, PBS, Sony Pictures Classics, and Filmmakers Library.
- *Digitalia Film Library*—Digitalia is an international collection of primarily Spanish and Portuguese language streaming feature films, television series, and

documentaries in the original language, some available dubbed in English or with English subtitles.

- *Docuseek2*—This service provides streaming access to documentary and social issue films and videos from a variety of distributors, including Bullfrog, Icarus Films, and the National Film Board of Canada.
- *Film Platform*—This collection of streaming documentary films from across the world targets an academic audience. Films cover various topics of social, political, and cultural importance.
- *Films on Demand*—A collection of streaming videos from a variety of producers including California Newsreel, PBS, the BBC, National Geographic, Films for the Humanities and Sciences, and more, Films on Demand includes more than 35,000 videos covering a wide range of topics organized by broad subject area, as well as feature films in the world cinema collection.
- *Swank*—This service streams content to non-theatrical markets such as U.S. colleges and universities, K–12 public schools, and libraries.

Some of these services are also appropriate for students who are in the upper grades of high school. The range of media streaming content varies greatly from kindergarten through senior year.

K–12 Schools

Media streaming services for K–12 are purposefully created or bundled around curriculum. Curriculum is the content that is taught in each grade. K–12 schools are commonly divided into three groups: primary (grades K–4), middle school (grades 5–8) and high school (grades 9–12). So too would it be appropriate for media services to be bundled by these groups.

A few of the already mentioned services offer content to K–12 schools, such as the ProQuest and EBSCO databases. EBSCO provides three distinct databases: Primary Search, Middle Search, and MAS Ultra, that offer media streaming on many topics. Streaming can be found in EBSCO Reference Centers such as Science or History.

K–12 schools use online learning management tools where teachers share and direct student learning. Some of these professional tools provide access to online media such as Digital Campus through its partnership with Swank to offer media streaming on appropriate grade-level curriculum topics. K–12 libraries and schools may consider the following subscriptions:

- *Academic Video Online—This is a* comprehensive video subscription available to libraries delivering more than seventy thousand titles spanning the widest range of subject areas including anthropology, business, counseling, film, health, history, music, and more.
- *Education in Video*—This service provides teachers tools for use in the classroom, including lessons taught in actual classroom settings.
- *Films on Demand*—This is a comprehensive collection of nearly five thousand high-quality educational videos available for streaming to the computer desktop. Titles cover a wide range of topics organized into twenty subject folders. Individual Learning Objects for each title subdivide the videos into smaller segments.

- *History in Video*—This online collection gives faculty and students access to critically acclaimed documentaries from filmmakers worldwide.

Likewise to subscription databases, there are many free options for media streaming for both schools and colleges that LSS can explore and recommend to students and teachers.[7] These range from public access programming to nonprofit foundation content such as the following.

- *American Library*—The Library of Congress provides streaming access to films and videos covering a wide range of topics including American music, film, and civil rights, in the Library of Congress Digital Collections.
- *Annenberg Media*—Teachers use these educational streaming videos to enhance their lessons. Teachers must set up individual accounts to access the videos on this site free of charge.
- *Civil Rights Digital Library*—This includes archival moving images, reference resources, and instructional resources for educators.
- *KidLitTV*—A winner of the Parents' Choice Gold Award, KidLitTV has been selected as an American Association of School Librarians Best Digital Tool for Teaching and Learning. KLTV is available in more than seven hundred thousand schools worldwide via its website and video distribution partners, providing fun new ways to reinforce an appreciation of reading.
- MIT World—This is a free and open site that provides on-demand video of significant public events at MIT. MIT World's video index contains more than eight hundred videos.
- PBS—There are several exemplary media programs produced by PBS used in education including the American Experience, Frontline, NOVA, and Point of View. The archives of these public access television programs are available for streaming and used by many educators with their students (see figure 12.2).

Figure 12.2.   Site License Permits Audience Viewing. *kali9 / E+ via Getty images*

PUBLIC PERFORMANCE SITE LICENSING

LSS know media licensing is required for libraries that wish to show a film or video as a performance either in DVD or by video streaming. Librarians who host public events with media as the focus should be aware of the need for annual **public performance site licensing**. This special license, required by U.S. copyright, requires a license regardless of whether the library charges a fee to attend a movie performance. A public performance is the viewing of a movie that is shown outside of someone's home. The revenue generated from the licensing is distributed as a form of compensation to copyright owners and the studios and people who create the film. Without having such license, it is illegal for libraries to use film without specific permission. Unlike the use of a movie for a onetime classroom lesson, the license allows libraries to legally show movies inside the library for entertainment, fundraising, or other types of programming. Movie Licensing USA and Swank Motion Pictures[8] are two brokers who act as liaisons between those who offer public performances and the filmmakers who are to be compensated. Annual public performance site licensing offers libraries

- 24/7 coverage of showing film in the library building or grounds;
- unlimited movie screenings in your library regardless of whether it is the library or an outside organization showing the film;
- copyright coverage for any movie obtained from a legal source such as rental, personal collections, and so on; and
- continuous coverage with automatic renewal, multiyear pricing, and multibranch discounts.

Libraries may choose to purchase single-event licenses for a onetime showing of a film as a public performance. Most libraries need to have the site license to be able to have the flexibility to offer multiple programs that engage their community. LSS can ask administration about the public performance site license to learn about how the license is renewed and other information about its usage.

HOSTING SERVICES

OTT video streaming[9] is a form of video broadcasting that goes "over-the-top" of traditional broadcasting technology, such as satellite or cable, and uses the internet to deliver content instead. Accessing video via OTT is convenient for viewers. Here is how OTT technology looks in action:

1. Broadcasters upload video content to an OTT video host.
2. The video host transmits the data to remote servers via a content delivery network.
3. Viewers select the content they want to stream on the user-facing video gallery.
4. The video player on the device delivers the video content via the internet from the video streaming server.

The apps we download or that are embedded in the service are necessary to connect the user device to the OTT video host. Once done, the app works with the Content Delivery Network (CDN) to deliver and then open the packets of data from the OTT host. All of this appears seamless for the viewer, who clicks "play" and begins to watch the film. Academic and large municipal libraries provide cable access to their communities. If they have upgraded to be an OTT host, the content resides on the library or university propriety servers.

The most-used OTT video hosts are YouTube and Vimeo, which are free and have familiar platforms. YouTube has abundant advertising and has limited, if any, customer support. Vimeo's basic service is free, but it is fee-based for things such as customization, use of tools, and analytics. Libraries that wish to have security protection and technical support for their hosted videos should seek hosting services that are fee-based with contractual obligations. A few fee-based OTT video hosts[10] libraries may consider are

- Panopto—a secure hosting service used by business and academics,
- Brightcove—used by many known companies and institutions,
- IBM Watson Media—reliable hosting to reach worldwide audiences of any size,
- JW Player—offers a flexible platform of video services,
- Qumu—recognized for supporting live streamed and on-demand video services, and
- Microsoft Stream—video hosting that is part of Microsoft 365.

LSS can assist in researching OTT video hosts by obtaining recommendations from librarians who use streaming hosts. They may also speak with marketing and sales representatives to compare cost and services.

CHAPTER SUMMARY

In less than a decade DVDs have rapidly been replaced in both homes and libraries with streaming video. LSS are able to assist and train users to select streamed content offered either free or through the library subscriptions by connecting to the internet and downloading appropriate apps. LSS know how streaming is currently changing how people across the globe retrieve and access audio and visual information resources and are able to help others in its use.

DISCUSSION QUESTIONS

1. How does media streaming work? What are the differences between downstream and upstream?
2. What are the differences between live and prerecorded streaming?
3. Why has on-demand gained popularity?
4. How will the global market for streamed video influence what libraries offer their patrons?
5. What are the benefits of public performance site licensing to the movie industry and why should libraries renew their licenses each year?

ACTIVITY

This chapter discusses many quality free media streaming services. Explore each of these services. Create a display or brochure for three services that you would like to introduce to patrons in the library you work in or frequent. Include in your information how to access the streaming service, whether an app must be downloaded, the target audience level, and subject content of the service. Who would the service appeal to and why? Share your display or brochure with a friend or family member who will follow your instructions. Ask for feedback on how to improve your display or brochure so that it is professional and accurate.

NOTES

1. Verizon, "Streaming," last modified 2021, accessed April 22, 2021, https://www.veri zon.com/info/definitions/streaming/.
2. TED Conferences, "How TED Works," *TED: Ideas Worth Spreading,* last modified 2021, accessed April 22, 2021, https://www.ted.com/about/our-organization/how-ted-works.
3. MTC, "What's the Difference between Pay-Per-View and On Demand?" last modified 2021, accessed April 25, 2021, https://www.mdtc.net/whats-the-difference-between-pay-per -view-and-on-demand/.
4. R. T. Watson, "Streaming Wars Lead to Shows Born Abroad," *Wall Street Journal,* April 23, 2021, eastern edition, B1, https://search.proquest.com/newspapers/streaming-wars-lead -shows-born-abroad/docview/2516676922/se-2?accountid=46995.
5. "Pandemic Leads to More Library Video Streaming," *USA Today Magazine,* March 2021, 8, https://search.ebscohost.com/login.aspx?direct=true&AuthType=cookie,ip,cpid&cust id=csl&db=aph&AN=149742453&site=ehost-live&scope=site.
6. Yale University, "Streaming Video Collections," Yale University Library, last modified 2021, accessed April 25, 2021, https://guides.library.yale.edu/streamingvideo.
7. Miami Dade College, "Streaming Video Options for Educators," Learning Resources, last modified 2021, accessed April 25, 2021, https://libraryguides.mdc.edu/c.php ?g=392611&p=3076517.
8. Swank Motion Pictures, Inc., "License Options," Public Libraries Movie Licensing, last modified 2021, accessed April 26, 2021, https://www.swank.com/public-libraries/licens ing-options/.
9. "Comparing the Top 10 OTT Video Hosting Solution Providers in 2021," *Dacast* (blog), entry posted April 5, 2021, accessed April 25, 2021, https://www.dacast.com/blog/best-5-vid eo-hosting-solutions-for-ott-service-providers/.
10. Panopto, "Comparing the Top Video Platforms of 2021," last modified February 15, 2021, accessed April 25, 2021, https://www.panopto.com/blog/comparing-the-top-on line-video-platforms/.

REFERENCES, SUGGESTED READINGS, AND WEBSITES

"Comparing the Top 10 OTT Video Hosting Solution Providers in 2021." *Dacast* (blog). Entry posted April 5, 2021. Accessed April 25, 2021. https://www.dacast.com/blog/best-5-video -hosting-solutions-for-ott-service-providers/.
LaFountain, Cal. "Parchment Community Library: Digital Oral Histories and Format's Menacing Eraser." *Computers in Libraries* 38, no. 6 (July/August 2018): 24–27. https://

search.ebscohost.com/login.aspx?direct=true&AuthType=cookie,ip,cpid&custid=csl&db
=aph&AN=130673783&site=ehost-live&scope=site.

Miami Dade College. "Streaming Video Options for Educators." *Learning Resources*. Last modified
2021. Accessed April 25, 2021. https://libraryguides.mdc.edu/c.php?g=392611&p=3076517.

MTC. "What's the Difference between Pay-Per-View and On Demand?" Last modified 2021.
Accessed April 25, 2021. https://www.mdtc.net/whats-the-difference-between-pay-per
-view-and-on-demand/.

"Pandemic Leads to More Library Video Streaming." *USA Today Magazine*, March 2021,
8. https://search.ebscohost.com/login.aspx?direct=true&AuthType=cookie,ip,cpid&custid
=csl&db=aph&AN=149742453&site=ehost-live&scope=site.

Panopto. "Comparing the Top Video Platforms of 2021." Last modified February 15, 2021.
Accessed April 25, 2021. https://www.panopto.com/blog/comparing-the-top-online-vid
eo-platforms/.

Pitsker, Kaitlin. "Drowning in Streaming Fees." *Kiplinger's Personal Finance* 73, no. 10 (October 2019): 62–66. https://search.ebscohost.com/login.aspx?direct=true&AuthType=cookie
,ip,cpid&custid=csl&db=.

Shumaker, Dave. "Beyond Coping: Libraries Stepping Up to Meet Community Needs
during the Pandemic." *Information Today* 38, no. 2 (March 2021): 12–14. https://search
.ebscohost.com/login.aspx?direct=true&AuthType=cookie,ip,cpid&custid=csl&db=aph
&AN=148900242&site=ehost-live&scope=site.

Swank Motion Pictures, Inc. "License Options." Public Libraries Movie Licensing. Last modified
2021. Accessed April 26, 2021. https://www.swank.com/public-libraries/licensing-options/.

TED Conferences. "How TED Works." *TED: Ideas Worth Spreading*. Last modified 2021. Accessed April 22, 2021. https://www.ted.com/about/our-organization/how-ted-works.

Verizon. "Streaming." Last modified 2021. Accessed April 22, 2021. https://www.verizon.com
/info/definitions/streaming/.

Watson, R. T. "Streaming Wars Lead to Shows Born Abroad." *Wall Street Journal*, April 23,
2021, eastern edition, B1. https://search.proquest.com/newspapers/streaming-wars-lead
-shows-born-abroad/docview/2516676922/se-2?accountid=46995.

Yale University. "Streaming Video Collections." Yale University Library. Last modified 2021.
Accessed April 25, 2021. https://guides.library.yale.edu/streamingvideo.

PART III

Social Networks, Mobility, Education, and Future

CHAPTER 13

Social Networks and Mobile Solutions

LSS demonstrate flexibility in adapting to new technology.

LSS are able to assist and train users to operate public equipment, connect to the internet, use library software applications, and access library services from remote locations.

Topics Covered in This Chapter

Social Media
    Personal Social Media and Communities
    Business Social Media
    Library Social Media
Social Media Marketing
    Tools
Mobile Solutions
LibGuide Community
Chapter Summary

Key Terms

App—An abbreviation for a short version of a software program or "application," these were first popularized by Apple because full-version web programs could not be reasonably viewed on smartphones and mobile devices.

Platform—This is a term used synonymously for a social media product. The library Facebook and Twitter accounts are platforms.

Private live streaming—These are video services that restrict access to live media to a select group of people rather than the entire public.

Push notifications—These are brief text messages that appear on a user's mobile device to alert them to headlines of newsworthy items, current happenings, or events. Libraries can use this method to notify patrons of upcoming special programs, etc.

RSS feed—An acronym for the term *really simple synchronization*, this is a way for users to subscribe to view new content on a website, blog, or social media.

Social media tools—These are apps or other means that libraries can use to receive feedback about their social media, easily publish new content, and analyze how platforms are being used by patrons.

This chapter is about how libraries reach users who are on the go with social media and mobile apps. Social media is a familiar and quick way to promote programs and events and make connections with users. Mobile apps, used on smartphones and other compact devices, provide essential services from the library website at any location with Wi-Fi or cellular providers.

SOCIAL MEDIA

It is essential today for libraries to purposefully reach users with multiple technologies that include a highly functional website and multiple social media. An important distinction between the library website and social media has to with access and promotion. The library website primarily provides access to important resources such as the online catalog, digital databases, e-books, magazine and journal subscriptions, and other products and services. On the other hand, libraries use social media as a tool to market, advertise, publicize, and bolster promotion of library events, programs, and materials.

Personal Social Media and Communities

The adage "no man is an island" bears truth; humans need to be and thrive when they are in a community with others. Communities are purposeful groupings of people who support each other for common purposes. Our most primary community is our family. Examples of other important communities can be friends, neighborhoods, and memberships in social, political, athletic, religious, or educational institutions.

People of all ages use web 2.0 personal social media to stay connected with family and their friends. They also use social media to keep up with current events, shop, participate in discussions, and network with others. Content is user generated, meaning that those in a social media community can view, share, contribute, and link to discussions, calendars, photos, media, information, and ideas. The Pew Research Center compiles data on many types of technology use, including social media. The following facts from Pew provide a baseline of social media use in the United States.[1]

- Seventy-two percent of the public uses some type of social media.
- Approximately 70 percent of adults between the ages of eighteen and sixty-four use at least one social media.
- YouTube and Facebook are the most widely used online platforms.

- Smaller shares of Americans use sites such as Twitter, Pinterest, Instagram, and LinkedIn.
- A greater percentage of women use Facebook and Instagram than men.
- A greater percentage of men use LinkedIn than women.
- Seven in ten Facebook users—and around six in ten Instagram and Snapchat users—visit these sites at least once a day.
- Prior to the pandemic, Pew found that roughly eight in ten teens ages thirteen to seventeen (81 percent) say social media makes them feel more connected to what's going on in their friends' lives.
- Two-thirds of teens say these platforms make them feel as if they have people who will support them through tough times.
- By relatively substantial margins, teens tend to associate their social media use with positive rather than negative emotions, such as feeling included rather than excluded (71 percent vs. 25 percent) or feeling confident rather than insecure (69 percent vs. 26 percent).

Undoubtedly, social media usage increased for all ages with the pandemic. Librarians understand that social media is a powerful way to promote the library and its services to teens and adults. LSS can share such data from Pew and other sources with supervisors to better understand the demographics around social media and the importance to create appropriate content by gender, age, or interests.

Personal social media connotes freedom of expression, but with this freedom comes concerns about validity or reliability of information. At the time of this writing, there is great controversy over personal social media censorship. Wikis and blogs are types of social media where a forum or information item is hosted for others to share and add their own opinions and expertise to the topic. LSS should remain cautious suggesting unverified social media as sources of information because there exists potential for unchecked bias and misinformation. Librarians rightfully monitor and select information from social media sites carefully for these concerns. In general, personal social media aim to support those who wish to

- find and connect with people;
- share interests with a community of those with similar objectives;
- plan and host events, both real and online;
- share photos, movies, and videos;
- discuss and seek advice from others;
- buy and sell goods and services;
- share creative works and seek feedback from a like-minded community; and
- seek physical and behavioral help from virtual healthcare practitioners.[2]

Business Social Media

Business social media accounts focus on marketing the enterprise and promoting the people who work in it. Many libraries use business accounts of social media to keep their community of patrons abreast of library events. Following a model for business social media, library social media provides the following.

- *Focused objectives*—These objectives may be promoting new databases, book or media titles, services such as employment support, upcoming children's and adult programs, local history collections, and so on. LSS can discuss with library administration the objectives it has to use social media to enhance its presence in the local or academic community.
- *Engagement*—Active engagement is crucial for keeping followers interested in library happenings and services as well as building customer relations. LSS can help by brainstorming topic ideas to start meaningful threads related to the benefits of using the library.
- *Strategy*—Effective professional social media requires a detailed strategy that incorporates what, when, where, and how to post your content. Creating a successful social media strategy requires knowing the library community through surveys, data gathering, and an understanding of its target audience. LSS can volunteer to be a member of the team that develops a workable strategy to keep the library social media meaningful, vibrant, and current.
- *Promotion*—Libraries with business social media accounts can use their promotional aspects to market to the community. LSS who are social media users can work with others to explore the tools associated with the account to send alerts and other communications to users.
- *Content*—Library content should look and sound professional, include high-quality graphics, and be consistent with other communications such as newsletters, flyers, and so on. LSS can look at other libraries' social media for ideas on what content to include and how to present it in a way that will engage users.
- *Networking*—Some social media provides a means to network with other library professionals. Explore sites such as LinkedIn and Pinterest to seek and share ideas as well as discuss common areas of professional interest with other LSS both local and afar.

Library Social Media

Social media products are called **platforms**. Facebook, Twitter, Instagram, and YouTube are all platforms. Social media enhances the presence of the library with its community. A few of the more common social media platforms used by libraries are as follows.

- Facebook Business Accounts—Libraries can create a free business account to post photos, events, posts on focused topics, hours, directions, and other common information. To access a library business account, one is not required to have a personal Facebook account (see figure 13.1).
- Twitter—Libraries of all sizes, including the Library of Congress, reach out to librarians and customers on Twitter to share quick updates and posts on focus topics.
- Instagram—Libraries share photos and short video with users about its news items, programs, special events, and other happenings that promote and inform about library people and occurrences.
- Pinterest—This social media is aimed for creativity and sharing. LSS can share or gain ideas for library displays, promoting books, seasonal decorations, sig-

Figure 13.1. Facebook, Preston Public Library. *Preston Public Library, CT*

nage, summer reading, programming, and many other day-to-day or special events and activities.

- YouTube—One of the most successful and earliest social media is YouTube. Here anyone can create a video or film and post it online without cost. Likewise, the millions of videos are searchable by any internet user and streamed quickly to the user's device. Libraries upload programming and other film to YouTube to share with their community of users.
- Snapchat—Teen librarians hold book and focused discussions, plan events, and otherwise engage teens on Snapchat, the most used photo and video sharing social media by teens. Snapchat is somewhat similar to Instagram and has become the key means of communication for individuals aged thirteen to thirty-four. Libraries that want to reach teens should consider Snapchat for its looser and less polished appearance that appeals to younger users.

From social media has sprung new terms or ways to enhance the library presence. A few of the terms LSS become familiar with are as follows.[3]

- *Crowdsourcing*—posts that are created with the intention of generating feedback from library followers such as to like, comment on, or tag others in a particular post.
- *Humanizing*—posts that emphasize the human character, warmth, humor, or amusement such as historic or archival photos used to convey these sentiments.
- *Interacting*—posts with photographs or videos at library-associated events.
- *Orienting*—posts that situate the library within its larger community such as geographic information, location of local artifacts, and so on.
- *Placemaking*—posts that capture the atmosphere of the library through its physical space and furnishings, such as permanent artwork, architecture, or sculpture.
- *Showcasing*—posts that highlight the library resources, services, or coming events.

LSS can explore their library social media, compare its platforms with these terms, and discuss with their supervisor how employing these ideas could increase the following of the library social media.

SOCIAL MEDIA MARKETING

A new industry is social media marketing. In lieu of traditional advertising, social media marketing uses online methods to promote businesses and nonprofits, such as libraries. The goal of social media marketing is to increase awareness of a product or service by prompting users to like, share, recommend, or +1 a product or service. For example, phrases such as "Like us on Facebook" or "Follow us on Twitter" encourage users to promote a product or service online.

A library uses several platforms of social media marketing to connect with their patrons in order to increase awareness of its programs and services. LSS may become involved with monitoring one of the library platforms to ensure its content is current and accurate. Other ways LSS can help with a platform is to maintain social media profiles of staff or users, read, listen, and engage followers in library programs and services, analyze use of the platform, and use the platform to market new and old library services.

Tools

LSS can explore the different types of **social media tools** used by those with business accounts to help enhance a platform. Three kinds of tool categories that can be used separately or together are as follows.

- Listening tools—include suites such as Salesforce Marketing Cloud that monitor many different social media platforms to find out what people say about the business or library. This information is helpful to create content users will find relevant to their needs.
- Publishing tools—help to post content to the platform. HootSuite and Percolate allow one to share content easily, posting across multiple platforms at once. LSS can set a posting schedule, making it easy to share content regularly.
- Competitive analysis tools—used to track metrics that matter to the library administration about the use of its platforms.[4]

Many libraries use the free Google My Business tool to make finding the library hours, directions, and links to its website noticeable and easy with a Google search. Analytics are also free, which provide library administration data about the number of people who open the library website or click on other data from this prominent sidebar. Google also offers free Google Alerts to provide notification whenever the owner's website or social media are accessed. These free Google products quantify the access and offer feedback about how often and in which categories content on the library website and social media are utilized. In addition to Google Alerts, librarians may consider free accounts with Hootsuite or TweetDeck to monitor success of the library's social media platforms.

Facebook, Twitter, and other platforms have tools to scan for mentions, consolidate social media accounts, and schedule posts. Using a free tool targets the particular platform. If the library uses multiple platforms and would like to consolidate and view data efficiently, it should consider the purchase of a commercial tool for listening, publishing, and comparison analytics.

A critical role of LSS is to help users navigate information, technology, and social media.[5] Know the differences between personal and business social media. Be part of the social media team that strategizes to apply the elements of a business model to its library marketing. Suggest appropriate social media platforms to reach both potential and regular customers. Successful library social media promotes the use of its services and programs to its community of users.

In order for library social media to be successful, it must have a following of people who check it regularly. Steps LSS can use to create library followings for its social media are

1. learn how to use basic design tools such as Canva to produce eye-catching designs;
2. design content that matches the library's aesthetic or branding—if your library's interior has bright colors, use the same colors on the social media page;
3. cross post on all of the library social media platforms;
4. encourage followers to share posts in their social network communities;
5. be consistent in style with more graphics and less text; and
6. have a consistent and professional tone that is friendly and may use appropriate light humor.[6]

Social media thrives in a mobile environment. The next section discusses how libraries use apps and mobile solutions to promote and deliver services.

MOBILE SOLUTIONS

Social media has been fueled by the growing use of smartphones, tablets, and small computing devices that are commonly used to access social media services on the go. Similar to websites, most social media platforms also provide custom apps to view and post updates while on the go.

Computer software programs are applications. The word **app**, first popularized by Apple, is an abbreviated form the word "application." Apple created apps for its iPhone and tablets because (1) early devices could not hold as much memory as desktop computers and thus needed smaller software packages to perform functions; (2) the majority of websites are designed to be viewed on a computer monitor—smaller devices do not have the same screen size to view the entirety of most websites and apps offer a modified version of the regular-sized webpage to fit the screens of smaller devices; and (3) apps are significantly less expensive to develop and less costly for users to purchase, thus spurring their popularity and market share.

To maximize the impact of digital information services, LSS can help customers access library e-content. Many libraries offer well over one hundred different e-resources. A simple yet important process LSS can do, either alone or with others, is to access every library-sponsored website, social media, and database on a smartphone and tablet to ensure the view is functional and readable (see figure 13.2). For those that are not, the next step is to work with IT staff to determine if the product or service has an app. If so, download the app and compare the view. In other words, replicate what users may encounter when they access any library service or database

Figure 13.2.   Accessing Library Using Smartphone. *SDI productions / E+ via Getty images*

on a mobile device. If the product offers an app, this is information the library can include on its instructions to users in its promotion. For example, LSS who work in libraries that offer Overdrive for e-books can point customers to its mobile app and help them search and download from the e-book collections.

Apps are necessary to access library services on mobile devices. As time goes on, so does the number of apps the library requires users to have to fully engage in its communications and services increase. LSS may offer to create a spreadsheet of all mobile apps library users should know about with a short description. This spreadsheet can be used to create a webpage and social media pages to inform users of them. The list would contain all of the library apps, for example:

Libby—an Overdrive app required to download e-books from the library
EBSCOhost—an app that provides access to EBSCO databases on mobile devices
Flipster—an app used to access full magazines from the library digital collection
Feedly—an RSS app used to receive important library news and notifications
Mango Languages—a language-learning app

Libraries may also use apps to provide security or authorization for special programs. This is referred to as **private live streaming**. Private live streaming restricts access to a select group of people rather than the entire public. For example, if the library is offering a live streamed program with a famous author with young children participating, it may consider protecting underage participants' identity and privacy by using a private streaming service. In order for those to either watch live or view later, the viewer would have to register with the service by phone or email. A verification code is then sent to the viewer that is good for only a restricted period. The service gives permission and access to viewers. It also has a record of the viewers, thus discouraging any unauthorized or potentially sinister use. There are many private streaming apps, such as Band, dacast, Vimeo Livestream, and Kaltura, to name just a few. LSS may explore and present information to supervisors about private live stream services, particularly as libraries post-pandemic will continue to offer online programming.

The combination of mobile devices and apps are changing how libraries offer services. If customers can engage in a library service on their smart device, the library should plan on how to enhance the experience. Mobile devices have shifted the onus of performing many basic library tasks from staff to users. For example:[7]

- *Checking out materials*—Many ILS offer a mobile user–friendly version of the full software. LSS can confirm that the library has purchased this option and promote its use with patrons.
- *Accessing e-books and other e-resources*—LSS are in the right place to help and support new users to locate and download e-books, audio, and databases to their smart devices. Pointing out where new users can find appropriate apps and guiding them through the process will support continued use of the library digital information services.
- *Reading library news*—Today many get their news from their mobile devices. So too can they obtain library news through well-designed library websites, social media, electronic newsletters, and subscriber **RSS feeds**. RSS stands for really simple synchronization and is a way for users to subscribe to view new content on a website, blog, or social media.[8] News is fetched by a user's RSS feed app reader, which converts the files and the latest updates from these sources into an easy-to-read text format. An RSS feed takes the headlines, summaries, and update notices, and then links back to the online source. LSS can explore feed-reading app options, such as the popular Feedly, and discuss with their supervisor ways to link the library website and social media into an RSS feed. Patrons can obtain the free RSS app and subscribe to library and other sources, such as the municipal news. RSS provides access to real-time headlines updates without actually visiting the website, blog, or social media. Links are provided to the feed headlines for full articles.
- *Receiving library notifications*—**Push notifications** are the short blurbs that seem to magically appear on a smartphone or email notifying us of such things as school closings, sports scores, weather alerts, or even an invitation to download a discount coupon. Notifications come from many places, including to those on social media such as Facebook or Pinterest. The user has the control to limit or restrict notifications. Many people appreciate notifications as they receive immediate news of the event or happening. Libraries may use notifications for many reasons, such as to alert users of a live video of a special upcoming program, a new service, a promotion opportunity, or a change in daily operations. OCLC is just one vendor source that offers customized mobile apps for library notifications. As suggested for RSS feed apps, LSS can explore options for push notification apps that library administration may find useful for both promoting events or services and providing news to library users.
- *Asking a question*—While the phone is still an efficient way to remotely ask a question of reference or other library staff, many today turn to apps or social

media to do so. Many librarians use text or short messaging systems (SMS) messaging to communicate with users who find a text message from a smartphone a quick way to pop a question. Depending upon the type of question and anticipated response, queries to specific people or audiences may be made using email, Facebook Messenger, Instagram, or a Twitter direct message (see figure 13.3). More general type questions or less time-sensitive ones may be asked on blogs or mobile communication apps such as WhatsApp or Telegram. LSS can help staff with managing the overwhelming task of monitoring online questions that come from these and other places. Just as they may be responsible for listening to phone voice messages, they can offer to check one or two of the library social media sites each day to be sure questions are found and forwarded to appropriate staff. One service that can successfully consolidate library chat, text messages, email, and voice messages is LibAnswers.[9] It has an option to manage social media questions as well. LSS can view the LibAnswers website to see if it could be useful to the library. If so, they may offer to be part of a free trial with this solution for libraries whose remote questions from users come from an ever-growing array of social media and mobile apps and devices.

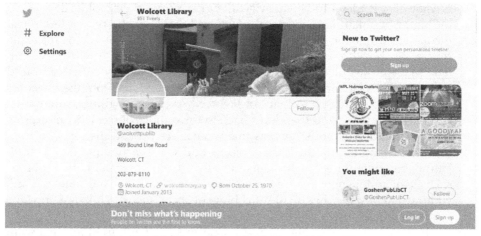

Figure 13.3.   Twitter, Wolcott Public Library. *Wolcott Public Library, Wolcott, CT*

LIBGUIDE COMMUNITY

LibAnswers is a product from the company that offers LibGuides, popular web-based content management system for library resources and information is discussed in chapter 9. Just as Pinterest and other social media are designed to share creative ideas, so are librarians encouraged to share their LibGuides with others both inside and outside of their library customers. Many, many librarians expend their talent and professional knowledge to create exemplary LibGuides on academic subjects, focused topics, and instruction methods. If the library is in agreement, they may join the LibGuide Community[10] to have their guides searchable and shared through the community website. At the time of this writing, more than two hundred thousand librarians in more than five thousand libraries in one hundred countries have agreed to have their guides shared with the public. The number of guides is staggering; it approaches one million. The public is encouraged to use these guides either by linking directly to the guide or copying specific sources.

The LibGuide Community is a showcase of the willingness of librarians to share exemplary information sources. Using social media as a model, the community of librarians shares its professional work to improve information opportunities for all.

CHAPTER SUMMARY

LSS demonstrate flexibility in supporting the library use of social media to communicate to their users and promote its services. Those who are knowledgeable of and familiar with mobile devices and apps are able to assist and train users to access library services from remote locations. LSS have an important role in planning, implementing, and supporting the use of social media and mobile apps in order to enhance the library programs, events, and information resources in its community.

DISCUSSION QUESTIONS

1. How do the purposes of library website and library social media differ?
2. In what ways can LSS support the library social media platforms?
3. Why may an app be needed on a mobile device when there is a full desktop software program?
4. What are some library staff tasks that now can be done via apps or social media? How does library service differ using these technologies from face to face with a librarian?
5. How does social media enhance the work of LSS? Provide two specific examples from platforms mentioned in the text.

ACTIVITY

Create a spreadsheet of the mobile apps and social media found at the library you work in or frequent. Next to each title provide a short description and one- or two-line description of its purpose for library users.

Access the websites and social media of three peer or cohort libraries. These libraries should serve a similar demographic and number of patrons as your library. Create separate sheets of their social media and apps.

Find three platforms or apps that these libraries use and that yours does not that would benefit your library users. Write a one-page memo to your library administrator justifying why the library should consider having these platforms and how they could be used to the patrons' benefit.

NOTES

1. Pew Research Center, "Social Media Fact Sheet," *Internet & Technology*, last modified April 7, 2021, accessed May 19, 2021, https://www.pewresearch.org/internet/fact-sheet/so cial-media/.

2. Patrick Oney, "Evolution of Social Media," *How Social Media for Business Is Different from Personal Social Media* (blog), entry posted July 8, 2020, accessed May 20, 2021, https://www.cc-sd.edu/blog/how-social-media-for-business-is-different-from-personal-social-media.

3. Jylisa Doney, Olivia Wikle, and Jessica Martinez, "Likes, Comments, Views: A Content Analysis of Academic Library Instagram Posts," *Information Technology & Libraries*. 39, no. 3 (2020): 1–15, https://search.ebscohost.com/login.aspx?direct=true&AuthType=cookie ,ip,cpid&custid=csl&db=aph&AN=146072338&site=ehost-live&scope=site.

4. Unmetric, "What You Need to Know about Social Media Tools," last modified 2021, accessed May 21, 2021, https://unmetric.com/resources/social-media-tools.

5. Julius C. Jefferson Jr., "Making a Difference," *American Libraries* 52, no. 5 (May 2021): 4, https://search.ebscohost.com/login.aspx?direct=true&AuthType=cookie,ip,cpid& custid=csl&db=aph&AN=150118872&site=ehost-live&scope=site.

6. Jessica Hilburn, "Dad Jokes and Storytime Posts: How to Create a Fun, Informative Library Social Media Presence," *Information Today* 37, no. 3 (April 2020): 12–14, https://search.ebscohost.com/login.aspx?direct=true&AuthType=cookie,ip,cpid&custid=csl&db =aph&AN=142482454&site=ehost-live&scope=site.

7. David Lee King, "Chapter 3: Mobile Outside the Library," *Library Technology Reports* 57, no. 2 (March/April 2021): 18–23, https://search.ebscohost.com/login.aspx?direct=true& AuthType=cookie,ip,cpid&custid=csl&db=aph&AN=148951873&site=ehost-live&scope=site.

8. RSS America, "How Do RSS Feeds Work? What Is RSS?" last modified 2021, accessed May 22, 2021, https://rss.com/blog/how-do-rss-feeds-work/.

9. Springshare, "LibAnswers +Social," last modified 2021, accessed May 23, 2021, https://springshare.com/libanswers/.

10. Springshare, "LibGuides Community," last modified 2021, accessed May 23, 2021, https://community.libguides.com/.

REFERENCES, SUGGESTED READINGS, AND WEBSITES

Dacast. "Top 10 Private Streaming Platforms for Broadcasting Secure Live Stream Events [2021 Update]." *dacast*. Last modified 2021. Accessed May 22, 2021. https://www.dacast.com /blog/7-live-streaming-solutions-for-private-events/.

Doney, Jylisa, Olivia Wikle, and Jessica Martinez. "Likes, Comments, Views: A Content Analysis of Academic Library Instagram Posts." *Information Technology & Libraries*. 39, no. 3 (2020): 1–15. https://search.ebscohost.com/login.aspx?direct=true&AuthType=cookie,ip ,cpid&custid=csl&db=aph&AN=146072338&site=ehost-live&scope=site.

Hilburn, Jessica. "Dad Jokes and Storytime Posts: How to Create a Fun, Informative Library Social Media Presence." *Information Today* 37, no. 3 (April 2020): 12–14. https://search.ebscohost.com/login.aspx?direct=true&AuthType=cookie,ip,cpid&custid=csl&db =aph&AN=142482454&site=ehost-live&scope=site.

Jefferson, Julius C., Jr. "Making a Difference." *American Libraries* 52, no. 5 (May 2021): 4. https://search.ebscohost.com/login.aspx?direct=true&AuthType=cookie,ip,cpid&cust id=csl&db=aph&AN=150118872&site=ehost-live&scope=site.

King, David Lee. "Chapter 3: Mobile Outside the Library." *Library Technology Reports* 57, no. 2 (March/April 2021): 18–23. https://search.ebscohost.com/login.aspx?direct=true&Auth Type=cookie,ip,cpid&custid=csl&db=aph&AN=148951873&site=ehost-live&scope=site.

Oney, Patrick. "Evolution of Social Media." *How Social Media for Business Is Different from Personal Social Media* (blog). Entry posted July 8, 2020. Accessed May 20, 2021. https://www.cc-sd.edu/blog/how-social-media-for-business-is-different-from-personal-social-media.

Pew Research Center. "Social Media Fact Sheet." *Internet & Technology.* Last modified April 7, 2021. Accessed May 19, 2021. https://www.pewresearch.org/internet/fact-sheet/social-media/.

RSS America. "How Do RSS Feeds Work? What Is RSS?" Last modified 2021. Accessed May 22, 2021. https://rss.com/blog/how-do-rss-feeds-work/.

Springshare. "LibAnswers +Social." Last modified 2021. Accessed May 23, 2021. https://springshare.com/libanswers/.

———. "LibGuides Community." Last modified 2021. Accessed May 23, 2021. https://community.libguides.com/.

Unmetric. "What You Need to Know about Social Media Tools." Last modified 2021. Accessed May 21, 2021. https://unmetric.com/resources/social-media-tools.

CHAPTER 14

Learning and Digital Information Services

LSS know the general trends and developments in technology applications for library functions and services.

LSS access and use basic assistive technologies, where appropriate, to ensure that all users have equitable access to technology.

Topics Covered in This Chapter

Fundamentals
  Learning
  Education
  Information
Digital Learning Environments
Online Learning
  Learning Tools and Systems
Assistive Technologies
School Media Center
Chapter Summary

Key Terms

Assessment—This is the method, such as observations, tests, etc. used to measure what students are able to do after being instructed in a specific process, skill, or curriculum.

Asynchronous—This type of online learning does not require real-time interaction; instead, content is available for students to access when it best suits their schedules, and assignments are completed to deadlines.

Curriculum—This is the content or subject matter taught by instructors.

Digital Learning Environments—These are libraries or educational institutions that provide access to digital information services, use analytics to map how documents are used, and sponsor collaboration, personalization, and interoperability.

Hybrid—This type of learning is a combination of asynchronous, synchronous, and face-to-face formats.

Instruction—This is the method and pedagogy used to teach new knowledge and skills to students.

Interoperable—This is the ability for various databases and digital collections to be searched and accessed seamlessly by the user.

Online learning management system—This is a software program that provides a secure platform for teacher and student sharing of files that promote learning.

PlumX metrics—This is an example of a data research system that librarians use to determine how people interact and use databases and other digital information services.

Synchronous—This type of online or distance education happens in real time, often with a set class schedule and required log-in times.

FUNDAMENTALS

Our learning begins from the moment we are born. Lifelong learning is the process of acquiring knowledge and skills through experiences, study, or education. Library digital information services enhance learning by providing content and context for learning. This chapter provides a broad overview of education as well as strategies for LSS to use to enhance the use of digital information learned in chapters 1 through 13. Fundamental to the mission of libraries are learning, education, and information.

Learning

There is distinction between learning and education. Learning is a process that results in a change of knowledge or behavior as a result of experience.[1] We create experiences through daily observations or contacts with people, facts, or events. While the majority of experiences are not held in long-term memory, those that are contribute to learning. For example, while many of the nuances of shopping last week are not memorable, the experience of a loud alarm sounding at the exit may be a learning experience to be sure clerks deactivate security tags from your purchases before you leave a store.

Regardless of age, learning has the following key attributes.[2] Learning is

Active—People learn when they are mentally engaged in experiences, conversations, and observations. We learn when we are in physical contact with our world and interact with people and things. Active learners make connections between prior knowledge and new ideas gained from active experiences.

Built on prior knowledge—Using what we know as a base, new learning has the potential to enrich or change what we know to be true.

Social—We learn from and by being with others. Learning involves people, the things they use, the words they speak, the cultural context they're in, and the actions they take.

Authentic—We learn best when we are in need-to-know or want-to-know situations.

Dependent on motivation and engagement—Mental effort and persistence are necessary to learn complex ideas, new skills, and abstract concepts, such as mathematics, language, and other academic topics.

When any of these five components is missing, the process of learning is compromised. LSS who work in schools may attest that it is very difficult for an unmotivated student to learn. They may also confirm that students who actively learn with others can successfully acquire new knowledge and skills.

Learning can be individual or collaborative. LSS respond to both types of learning by providing instructions and library resources appropriately. In makerspaces and focused programs, libraries provide stimulating activities, a social environment with real-life situations or projects. These components help to stimulate motivation and engagement of the learner to make connections to their prior knowledge as a base to build new learning experiences in the library.

Education

Education is a complex business that has its own sets of mandates, standards, certifications, theories, and methods. While every LSS has had the experience of being a student, most LSS are unfamiliar with the educational processes that guide formal schooling in the United States and other countries. Insights to these processes are important to apply to digital information services as libraries provide resources, technology, instruction, and in many other ways aid education. As a consequence, LSS also have an important role in supporting education in their daily work.

Education is the process of receiving or giving systematic instruction. Education may be informal or formal. People casually learn from each other in informal settings, such as one LSS showing another LSS how to place and renew holds. Formal education, on the other hand, typically requires a regular commitment in a structured setting such as a school or university with an instructor or educator guiding the learning.

LSS participate in and support others in both informal and formal education. Formal education typically has a defined age or time period, such as middle school, or cumulating recognitions, such as a certificate or degree, that mark achievement. In order to "pass" from one level to another, certain learning goals, knowledge, or skills need to be mastered. Mandated by the states and supported by the federal government, all children in the United States (and many other countries) are required to have a minimum amount of formal education. One way to measure the success of a country is by its educational systems and student achievement. Libraries are key educational supports to both informal and formal education.

There are three key criteria for formal education: **instruction**, **curriculum**, and **assessment**:

Instruction—the methods and pedagogy of how to teach.

Curriculum—the content, topics, or subjects of what is taught and to be learned.

Assessment—the methods of measuring what students are able to do after being instructed in a specific curriculum.

Not unlike a juggler with three balls in the air, if any of these three components are not coordinated and in place, new learning is compromised. The teacher has well-designed and often multiple methods of instruction to teach the curriculum of the lesson. He uses examples and engages all of his students in a game to reinforce concepts. Before moving on to new curricula, he provides students both written and oral assessments to measure their knowledge and ability.

A key difference between instruction and assessment is what the student knows and is able to do as a result of her engagement with the curriculum. The instruction teaches us *how* to do something. The supervisor who teaches a new LSS how to use a suite of new databases provides the instruction. But after the instruction, is the LSS *able* to successfully search and select specific content? The way to find out is by assessment. The supervisor observes the LSS's search strategies and provides coaching when needed. When the supervisor assesses that the LSS accurately and confidently is able find a variety of articles using advanced search features, he deems his instruction successful.

LSS can better support users' education when they are able to identify whether the need for information is for instruction, curriculum, or assessment. Digital information services are essential for each of these areas. Teachers use digital information services to prepare their lessons and to develop curriculum. Students use digital information services to write research papers and other types of assessments. The days when a textbook was the primary or only source for instruction, curriculum, and assessment are past. Today it is necessary for educators to use a variety of both print and digital information sources, and the library is an essential partner to this end in both schools and the larger community who continue their education informally.

Information

Information is essential to both the learning process and educational structures. Learners both use and create information that is knowledge obtained from investigation, study, or instruction. Information is a broad term that includes facts, data, communications, or reception of knowledge or intelligence. The time of day is an information fact. Likewise, high-level secret understandings obtained from espionage is also information. Information is what we know or what we want to know. LSS work with many types of information—oral, visual, print, or digital. LSS also can be most helpful to users when they categorize information sought:

Persuasive—This is information that is based in opinion or judgment, meant to sway the opinion of the reader.
Informative—This is information that is primarily factual and unbiased. Think of most nonfiction as being informative.
Entertainment—This information has an appeal that supports humor, intrigue, fantasy, relaxation, or escape from work or routine.

People use the library to find new information to enhance their learning or understanding. Finding information can be planned or spontaneous. How often in our search for information do we come upon other ideas that spur our interest? Without robust and dynamic sources of information, learning and education would be flat. LSS know that the library for many is an essential source of both current and historic information.

Digitization has revolutionized the way people share, store, retrieve, and use information. Not that long ago the only way to find words in a text was through its index. Today library discovery systems simultaneously search hundreds, if not thousands, of databases for key words. LSS help users search, select, and use digital information from seemingly endless sources.

As seen in previous chapters, digital information services used in learning and education are subscription databases, e-books, digital collections, primary sources, audio and visual media, websites, social media, and now library discovery systems and platforms. A certainty is the demand for digital information services will continue to outpace any print sources and that ongoing advances in technology will put information closer to the world's fingertips. LSS work in an exciting environment where information is the commodity and the overwhelming options require staff to be lifelong, educated learners who keep pace with these and other digital information services to better serve their customers (see figure 14.1).

Figure 14.1. Digital Learning Environment. *Thana Prasongsin / Moment via Getty Images*

DIGITAL LEARNING ENVIRONMENTS

We learn in a variety of environments that range from mega groups to the individual. Learning models most commonly used are in person or face to face, fully online, and hybrid, where classes switch between in person and online. A **Digital**

Learning Environment (DLE) supports all of these types of learning models in the following five ways.[3]

1. All instructional models use information that is accessible and supports student success.
2. Analytics are used to assess student readiness, map progress, advise, and trigger interventions to ensure student success.
3. Both within and outside of the educational institution, collaboration is encouraged and supported.
4. Digital information sources are **interoperable** in that they work together seamlessly for both student and instructor.
5. A digital information environment is student centered and supports personalized experiences with both content and learning choices.

While schools and universities may make a formal commitment to use a DLE framework, libraries that acquire and support digital information can have staff adapt these five DLE components. The following are questions with strategies founded in DLE theory that LSS may employ to support patrons' use of digital information.

Question: Are library databases accessible?
LSS support accessibility to digital information services.

   a. The LSS works with supervisor and other staff to create clear instruction sheets and videos that show how to use each database the library offers.
   b. Outside of the library building, LSS accesses each library database on a mobile device and with password to determine if there are any problems with remote access.

Question: How do librarians use data to know if digital services are being used?
LSS is familiar with the analytics features of each library database.

   a. Ask supervisor whether monthly use for each database is being captured and offer to do so for the library administration if not.
   b. Become familiar with features of databases, such as **PlumX metrics**, that provide insights into the ways people interact with articles, conference proceedings, book chapters, and many more information types found in the online environment.
   c. PlumX metrics data is categorized by citations, usage, captures, mentions, and social media. Discuss with supervisor which of these categories hold data that is most important for staff to know how databases are being used. Work with staff to promote underused databases.

Question: What ways can users collaborate over digital information?
LSS promote a DLE where new learning and ideas are shared.

   a. Are there appropriate spaces in the library for collaboration where users can share, debate, view, and otherwise use digital information?
   b. LSS may create a proposal for a program or workshop where the library digital information services are used to solve a real-life or other interesting problem.

Question: Do library digital information sources complement each other?
LSS learn about state and local digital libraries and services that are interoperable.

    a. LSS work with and learn features and functions of databases supplied by each vendor such as EBSCO, ProQuest, Gale, and so on, so that they can share best practices with others.
    b. LSS who work in libraries that have discovery systems learn the basic and advanced search features so that they can guide others for best use.

Question: Do digital information services offer personalized experiences?
LSS learn features of digital information services that support research and efficiency.

    a. LSS discuss with reference staff ways they can suggest to patrons how to create reading lists, create a citation account, save files, and other functions that support patrons' ongoing research or use of databases.
    b. LSS create their own personal accounts where digital information services allow them to explore and learn the benefits of each product's features.

The library that is a DLE prioritizes how people learn. Best learning takes place when the need is authentic and people can relate what is new to what they already know. Digital information services provide the information that is the basis of learning. LSS can do much to support the library having a DLE where learning is social and supportive. DLE provide the resources for people to engage in solving problems or working through new ideas. The DLE provides digital tools, resources, materials, and related technologies that support the many pathways of teaching and learning (see figure 14.2).[4]

Figure 14.2. Online Learning. *Eva-Katalin / E+ via Getty images*

ONLINE LEARNING

The pandemic occurred during the writing of this text. Within days of its onset, towns and states closed their schools and universities. Unexpectedly and astonishingly, education across the country—and around the world—went from traditional classroom to online. Online learning typically is one of three types: **asynchronous**, **synchronous**, or **hybrid**.[5]

Asynchronous: This type of online learning does not take place in real time. Students are provided with prerecorded lectures by the professor or teacher, supporting content, and scheduled assignments. Interaction may take place through discussion boards, blogs, and wikis, but it may also happen in email, texts, online meetings, or phone calls. Asynchronous online learning environments are effective for students who seek flexibility.

Synchronous: These types of courses require the instructor and all enrolled students to interact online simultaneously. They are similar in some ways to a webinar; participants interact through text, video, or audio chat. Synchronous learning environments enable students to participate in a course from a distance in real time.

Hybrid: Hybrid courses, also known as blended courses, are learning environments that allow for both in-person and online interaction. Typically, hybrid courses meet in person several times during a semester in combination with online sessions.

These types of online learning can also apply to online library programming. A synchronous library program would be interactive in a Zoom or other session with a known author. Viewers would preregister and be able to ask questions or otherwise interact verbally with the guest speaker at appropriate times. The program could also be used asynchronously if it were prerecorded and available on YouTube or another hosting service for those who could not participate live but would like to hear the author's presentation when convenient for them. An example of hybrid learning could be a second invitation to the author to come to the library for an in-person follow-up workshop for those who participated synchronously.

Learning Tools and Systems

Schools and universities provide their teachers and students access to **online learning management systems** that serve as common and secure online space for only the instructor and her students. These management systems can be used in a traditional classroom for some features, such as the online gradebook, uploading assignments, or providing students active links to specific digital resources. Other DLE management systems are used as the primary medium for online learning where professors provide either live or prerecorded lectures, discussions, chat, assignment feedback, and so on. Some commonly used management systems are Blackboard Learn, Google Classroom, Canvas, Moodle, Schoology, and Edmodo, to name a few. LSS who work in school or academic libraries can become familiar with the management system used by the institution in order to be able to help new users who may not be familiar with its functions.

LSS support online learning when they are users themselves of digital e-books, academic journals, educational media, podcasts, subscription databases, digital collections, and all of the other types of digital information services discussed in this text. LSS can help others when they are proficient with common tools such as Google Docs, Office suite, Adobe suite, Pages, Writer, and other word processing, spreadsheet, and presentation software.

ASSISTIVE TECHNOLOGIES

Digital information services, coupled with assistive technology, open the opportunity for all people, regardless of disability, to become consumers and users of information. LSS have an important role in making digital information accessible to users by being able to select functions and features of hardware or software that convert text to speech, enhance audio and video for hearing and visually impaired, simulations, and other educational tools with features that reduce barriers to information for disadvantaged or disabled users.

An assistive technology device is "any device, piece of equipment, or product system whether acquired commercially off the shelf, modified, or customized, that is used to increase, maintain, or improve functional capabilities of a child with a disability."[6] Devices range in complexity from "low-tech" highlighters and modified paper to "high-tech" laptops and software. Assistive technology services support both adults and children with disabilities. LSS may support such users with selecting, acquiring, or using an assistive technology device. LSS may seek training in the use of devices so that they, in turn, may help others.

SCHOOL MEDIA CENTER

There are more school media centers than any other type of library in the United States.[7] In a recent national count there were approximately one hundred thousand school libraries compared to ten thousand public, three thousand academic, and five thousand special libraries. Extrapolating from this data, the majority of LSS work in K–12 school libraries at a time when certified. Over the next decade, almost 70 percent of school library media specialists across America are expected to leave their jobs, many due to retirement, according to the American Library Association.[8] States regulate teacher preparation and certification requirements in all areas and subjects, including school library media. Most states require a graduate degree in Library Information Science (or comparable coursework) as well as successful teacher preparation, including coursework and student teaching, in order to be certified as a school media specialist. Fewer people are training for the profession, thus leaving a critical void. At the same time, the role and responsibly of a school media specialist has grown to include technology. In many schools the media specialist is also the technology coordinator or specialist for the building.

Schools are relying on LSS to help fill the void of professional personnel. It is essential that LSS who work in schools have the knowledge and skills, in addition to library and technology, of an educator. Many school LSS are former teachers who are valued particularly for their educational background. In elementary and middle schools, it is not uncommon that LSS have sole responsibility for the library, if not the library and school technology.

It is essential for LSS who work in schools to be knowledgeable and able to guide teachers and students to digital information services. If there is not a school media specialist in the building, LSS can seek support from others in the district as well as public library professionals. A few suggestions LSS can consider to expand the use of digital information services in their library (school, academic, or public) follow.

1. Ask teachers for copies of their course syllabus each semester or year. Not only do syllabi contain outside readings, but they are maps to guide the student through the course. LSS can learn much about the course content curriculum, future assignments, and expected readings through a syllabus. Using this knowledge, LSS can make suggestions to teachers for library databases, e-books, and so on that complement course objectives.

2. Be curious about what teachers may need. Often the teacher has very limited time and cannot explore the library digital collections. For example, an email or webpage from LSS to the Social Science Department with five suggested databases will be appreciated by teachers who, in turn, may require their students to use the state digital library databases of the history reference center, biography reference bank, and the history reference e-book collection for a research assignment.

3. Teach others about state library digital collections and databases. If a public library card or student ID is required for remote access to such, create a bookmark and mass produce it with the information so that both teachers and students know how to obtain remote access to digital resources they may think are only available at the school.

4. Be knowledgeable of and promote to teachers digital library services and technology that support special needs. In chapter 12 assistive or adaptive technologies were discussed. Students with disabilities require digital information services that support audio, visual, and cognitive challenges.

Much is asked of LSS who work in school libraries and grapple to fulfill the professional role of librarian, technologist, and teacher. Seek informal mentoring from teachers and school administration. Participate in professional school, technology, and library workshops and conferences. Avail yourself to other librarians, forming a network of support and learning. When LSS are able to use digital information services in their own learning, they, in turn, can demonstrate and help others with the information needs that enhance learning.

CHAPTER SUMMARY

This chapter provides an overview of how learning, education, and digital information services are intertwined. Our future lies with how people are able to use digital information to solve problems and for the benefit of society. LSS who know the general trends and developments in digital information services and technology applications enhance library functions and services for users. LSS who access and use all of the digital information services of their library and learn how to use basic assistive technologies help to ensure that all users have equitable access to information for formal and informal learning.

DISCUSSION QUESTIONS

1. What are the key elements of the learning process and why is each one important?
2. How is education different from learning? How is it similar?
3. What are Digital Learning Environments and how can LSS help to create them in the library?
4. How do synchronous, asynchronous, and hybrid online learning vary?
5. Why is it critical for LSS who work in school libraries to be knowledgeable and able to use assistive technologies and digital information services?

ACTIVITY

Prepare a summary report that could be shared with supervisor or librarians on the use of digital information services of the library LSS work at or frequent. Create a spreadsheet that lists each library database or service, its target audience, and main topic or content. Describe how the database can support patron information and enhanced learning.

Once the spreadsheet of this data is created, compare it to how you perceive the library databases and digital information services are currently used. Discuss your observations with the reference librarian, and, if possible, ask to see PlumX metrics or other statistics for a sampling of the databases. Identify which databases or services are underutilized. Propose three suggestions for introducing these databases to potential users.

NOTES

1. University of California–Berkeley, "What Is Learning?" Berkeley Center for Teaching and Learning, last modified 2021, accessed June 3, 2021, https://teaching.berkeley.edu/resources /learn/what-learning.

2. University of California–Berkley, "What Is Learning?"

3. University of Wisconsin System, "What Is a DLE?" Digital Learning Environment (DLE), last modified 2021, accessed June 5, 2021, https://www.wisconsin.edu/dle/strategy/.

4. William & Mary, "Digital Learning Environment," eLearning Initiatives, last modified 2021, accessed June 5, 2021, https://www.wm.edu/offices/apel/working-groups/digital-learn ing-environment/index.php.

5. Fordham University, "Types of Online Learning," Online Learning, last modified 2021, accessed June 6, 2021, https://www.fordham.edu/info/24884/online_learning/7897 /types_of_online_learning.

6. Department of Defense, "Special Education: Assistive Technology," Department of Defense Education Activity, last modified 2021, accessed June 7, 2021, https://www.dodea.edu /Curriculum/specialeducation/assisttech.cfm.

7. American Library Association, "Number of Libraries in the United States," last modified 2021, accessed June 7, 2021, https://libguides.ala.org/numberoflibraries.

8. University of Vermont, "Career Options," *School Library Media Specialist,* last modified 2021, accessed June 7, 2021, https://learn.uvm.edu/program/school-library-media-studies/career-options/.

REFERENCES, SUGGESTED READINGS, AND WEBSITES

American Library Association. "Number of Libraries in the United States." Last modified 2021. Accessed June 7, 2021. https://libguides.ala.org/numberoflibraries.

Department of Defense. "Special Education: Assistive Technology." Department of Defense Education Activity. Last modified 2021. Accessed June 7, 2021. https://www.dodea.edu/Curriculum/specialeducation/assisttech.cfm.

Fordham University. "Types of Online Learning." Online Learning. Last modified 2021. Accessed June 6, 2021. https://www.fordham.edu/info/24884/online_learning/7897/types_of_online_learning.

University of California–Berkeley. "What Is Learning?" Berkeley Center for Teaching and Learning. Last modified 2021. Accessed June 3, 2021. https://teaching.berkeley.edu/resources/learn/what-learning.

University of Vermont. "Career Options." *School Library Media Specialist.* Last modified 2021. Accessed June 7, 2021. https://learn.uvm.edu/program/school-library-media-studies/career-options/.

University of Wisconsin System. "What Is a DLE?" Digital Learning Environment (DLE). Last modified 2021. Accessed June 5, 2021. https://www.wisconsin.edu/dle/strategy/.

William & Mary. "Digital Learning Environment." eLearning Initiatives. Last modified 2021. Accessed June 5, 2021. https://www.wm.edu/offices/apel/working-groups/digital-learning-environment/index.php.

CHAPTER 15

Future of Digital Information Services

LSS know the general trends and developments in technology applications for library functions and services.

LSS demonstrate flexibility in adapting to new technology.

Topics Covered in This Chapter

Accessibility
Digital Collections
    Preservation for the Future
Digital Fluency
Digital Equity
    Seattle
    Cambridge
Trends and Developments
    Internet of Things (IOTs)
    Robotics
    Virtual Reality (VR)
    Artificial Intelligence (AI)
Continuous Learning
Chapter Summary

Key Terms

Accessibility—Every user has equal opportunity to locate, obtain, use, and understand open and unbiased information.

Broadband—This is a type of high-speed internet connection such as digital subscriber line (DSL), cable, fiber, wireless, or satellite.

Digital equity—This occurs when all individuals and communities have the information technology capacity needed for full participation in our society, democracy, and economy.

Digital fluency—This occurs when people have the ability to apply digital technology to enhance the quality of their lives, improve productivity and communication, solve problems, and streamline processes.

Digital literacy—This is the ability to successfully use information and communication technologies to find, read, view, evaluate, create, and communicate information, requiring both cognitive and technical skills.

Inclusion coalition—Libraries, schools, community-based organizations, local governments, housing, and others who cooperatively address equitable access and use of digital information.

Internet of Things—Commonly referred to as IoTs, these are "smart" devices that have inbuilt technology that cause the device to operate and communicate with other devices over a network.

Memory institutions—These are museums, libraries, archives, historical societies, arboreta, and other heritage sites that serve as repositories of public knowledge, history, and culture.

ACCESSIBILITY

It was shown during the pandemic that technology made it possible for students to learn and adults to work from almost anywhere. When cities and buildings closed, people around the globe were able to remotely access, manage, and use information as well as communicate and collaborate with others because of technology. Libraries were essential to these efforts because of their digital information services, collaborative practices, and communication and infrastructure networks that supported both learning and the workplace. Based on current trends and future developments, this chapter will attempt to predict some of the ways LSS will continue to work with digital information services in the future.

The pandemic took nations by surprise. Government leaders, employers, and teachers unexpectedly struggled to find ways to use technology to maintain productivity. Overnight the internet and its digital services provided the means to work, communicate, learn, collaborate, and use information to solve problems. In schools and communities, libraries were pivotal in their services and supports to these efforts.

The experiences of the pandemic are being integrated into the future of society. Businesses are reevaluating the need to have all workers on site simultaneously. Educators found that offering the choice of different digital learning environments—in person, fully online, and hybrid—can be beneficial to both students and the institution. LSS help to make digital information services accessible and interoperable so that searching and selecting information from databases and electronic collections appear seamless to users.

**TEXTBOX 15.1: DIGITAL INFORMATION
IS ACCESSIBLE WHEN IT IS . . .**

- capable of being reached or obtained;
- affordable;
- easy to deal with;
- capable of being used or seen;
- available to everyone;
- capable of being understood or appreciated;
- open and unbiased, presenting new ideas; and
- easily adapted for and used by people with disabilities.

One of the fundamental considerations of digital information services is **accessibility**. Textbox 15.1 lists ways in which information is accessible.[1]

LSS can greatly impact the use of library digital information services when they place high value on these important attributes to provide information to any and all patrons.

A future trend with one aspect of accessibility that will continue to influence how libraries provide information is around internet access and mobile technology. Key findings by the Pew Research Center about how people will use the internet show that in 2021, 91 percent of adults in the United States have home **broadband** or smartphones—or both.[2] Broadband describes a type of high-speed internet connection such as digital subscriber line (DSL), cable, fiber, wireless, satellite, and so on. Smartphones, while they can be connected to home Wi-Fi, have a primary cellular mobile plan so that people can have phone and internet on the go. Two key findings from the Pew survey that inform how people will use the internet in the future are:

- *Smartphone dependency:* Some 15 percent of U.S. adults are "smartphone-only" internet users, that is, they have a smartphone but do not have a home broadband connection.
- *Interest in getting broadband:* Fully 71 percent of non-broadband users say they are not interested in having such a connection at home.

In other words, the future trend is that home broadband will be less in demand as mobile technology grows. One important way the future will be shaped is how the world accesses and uses information. Libraries need to continue to explore ways for digital information services to be fully accessible and usable with mobile technologies.

DIGITAL COLLECTIONS

Ask any LSS who has worked for twenty or more years how their work has changed over time. Key to these significant changes are the processes of digitization that revolutionized print libraries into information centers that provide almost instantaneous access and delivery of a wide variety of digital information services. LSS today guide users to the library collections of e-books, databases, multimedia, and networks.

Technology has changed how libraries provide access to their collections. From California to Maine, state libraries offer online catalogs, digital collections, and other vital digital information services to their residents. Many digital information services are also available to anyone with an internet connection. For example, the California State Library in its digital collections freely offers in the Internet Archive intriguing collections of primary sources on the early film industry.[3] Across the world using digitization and metadata, libraries, museums, and historical societies share millions of images, film, sound, and multimedia of historic, scientific, literary, and just plain entertaining information.

When library buildings shuttered for the pandemic, e-book and e-magazine use skyrocketed. Libraries that are members of e-book consortiums provided access to patrons to download e-books from home twenty-four hours a day. Reading habits shifted from print to digital in schools and the general public.

Preservation for the Future

Preservation through digitization has value beyond the local community. The Library of Congress (LOC), world leader in setting standards for digitization, has a clear and simple Digital Strategy that LSS are urged to read and embrace.[4] The LOC envisions its digital collections as a means to connect all Americans to the services of the Library of Congress. It also has three main goals, in part, as follows.

1. *Throw open its treasure chest*—The LOC will continue to build a universal and enduring source of knowledge and creativity by expanding and continuing its aggressive digital acquisitions program which prioritizes the LOC's unique treasures. It will improve search and access services that facilitate discovery of materials in both physical and digital formats.
2. *Bring the LOC to users*—The LOC will bring digital content to users by making more of its material available in its websites and apps. Structuring its information to be machine-readable will make the LOC's primary source material available to more people in more places and accessible to a broader diversity of users.
3. *Invest in the future*—The LOC will encourage experimentation and offer the training, tools, infrastructure, opportunities, and organizational support needed to enable staff to try new approaches and adapt to a changing information landscape.

While the LOC has budget, staff, and resources compared to none, any library staff can find meaning in the LOC's Digital Strategy and apply these three goals to their own library digitization collections initiatives. LSS who obtain either formal or on-the-job training in digitization are invaluable to the effort of the library to convert its treasures, like the LOC, to digital formats to be accessible on the internet to the local community, the state, and the world.

Likewise, the national Institute of Museum and Library Services (IMLS) has digital initiatives as one of its highest priorities. The IMLS is an independent federal agency that provides library grants, museum grants, policy development, and research. Grants administered and awarded by state libraries are often from IMLS, making it a most important agency to libraries and museums.

IMLS has three focused themes for its digital technology grants.[5] All have the ability to shape digital information services in the future:

1. *Expanding digital access:* IMLS supports projects that increase digital inclusion, broadband access, and digital literacy, giving communities access to information on a wide spectrum of topics, such as education, workforce development, public safety, and health.
2. *Digitizing collections:* New technologies help museums improve how they collect, preserve, and enable the use of cultural collections. IMLS supports projects that expand the capacity of museums to serve as **memory institutions**.
3. *Facilitating open research:* Researchers and scholars rely on digital technologies like open-source software, as well as open science, open scholarship, and open data. IMLS supports grants that build the technology used for research and scholarly communications.

There is a plethora of ideas and information at the IMLS site. LSS are encouraged to read more about each of these goals, but also, from its homepage, find and read successful grants in their state and others. By reading successful grants, LSS can glean ideas of what type of digitization projects are more likely to be endorsed by library administration and possibly funded by outside sources. As the LOC implies, all libraries have treasures waiting to be digitized, accessible, and shared.

In addition to reviewing successful grants, LSS can help ensure a successful future of digitization by being a member of a team that explores digital collection platforms. No library wants to invest in developing collections only to find that its software, choice of file format, or storage plan is flawed.[6] Smart decisions with respect to selecting a digital collections platform are a first phase of a digital collections launch. Form relationships with state and other experts in digitization not only to learn from them about the technical aspects of digitization but also to envision how future collections can be reliably and fully searched, shared, and used.

DIGITAL FLUENCY

As discussed in chapter 1, digital literacy is the ability to use information and communication technologies to find, evaluate, create, and communicate information, requiring both cognitive and technical skills. More commonly, **digital literacy** is using technology to support the processes of reading, viewing, writing, and speaking. For example, the U.S. Department of Education and other agencies that fund digital literacy initiatives support students' success in using technology that supports academic achievement and college and career readiness.[7] These initiatives enhance the integration of technology into instruction and leverage learning outside the classroom. Digital literacy initiatives may use technology to help students learn English, improve reading and math skills, explore new careers, or complete a training program.

Digital literacy skills enable one to access, view, and read text. Additionally, required in the near future will be digital fluencies in information analytics, ethics, and strategies to apply information for social, economic, and political good. **Digital fluency** is the ability to apply digital technology to enhance the quality of our lives, improve productivity and communication, solve problems, and streamline processes (see figure 15.1). People who are digitally fluent know how to maximize new and emerging technologies in order to work, learn, and be contributing members in a digital society.[8] Digital information fluency uses higher-level critical thinking to make predictions, evaluate, or be creative.

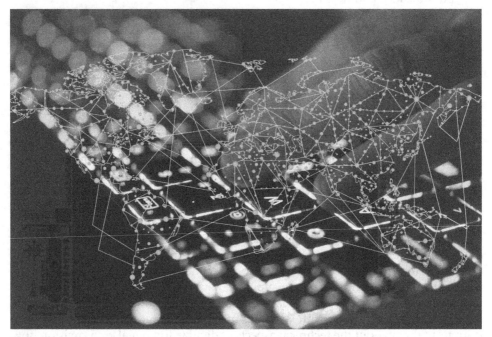

Figure 15.1.   Digital Fluency. *Manuel Breva Colmeiro/ Moment via Getty Images*

The research demands of academic libraries have resulted in new and interoperable library discovery and management systems and other digital information services that support learning. Predictions are that content and accessibility of future digital information services will differ from what we know today.[9] These changes will require new sets of digital fluencies and literacies that will prepare students for jobs in civic service and the public good that go beyond knowing today's technical skills of access.

Libraries must do more than support digital literacy. Every staff member should strive to be digitally fluent. Ways LSS can enhance digital fluency so that they, in turn, may help others are found in textbox 15.2.

TEXTBOX 15.2: WAYS LSS CAN ENHANCE DIGITAL FLUENCY

- LSS are curious to learn new technologies independently, in workshops, or classes.
- LSS are skilled and confident in using a wide variety of digital tools to express their ideas and create projects.
- LSS are adept at understanding research studies and other academic sources. When LSS are motivated by their own need or interest to learn how credible research is created and explained, they, in turn, may help others interpret commonly used statistics, surveys, demographic, and other research data.
- LSS are knowledgeable and practiced in evaluating the credibility of sources in any print or digital format.
- LSS are thoughtful and careful about their own digital footprint and what they share online, knowing it may make a first impression based on their social media and other interactions online.
- LSS keep current and discuss with others technology ethical and social issues, such as cyber threats, digital inequity, etc. LSS strive to work at the highest level of digital professionalism.

CDs and VHS formats had their day, and LSS are alert to new ways people will acquire and use digital information services in the future. As methods to digitize advance, so will new content formats. Libraries will continue to be the curators of virtual content and will guide the preservation of 3D video and new media.[10] Digital fluencies, based in the liberal arts and sciences, cultivate approaches to data that require critical thinking and ethics. Digital information will support users to be continuous learners who are able to make judgments on changing social and economic contexts.

LSS and those who work in libraries will find dual emphasis on digital fluency in both technical aspects of library work and supporting users in applying information that enhances civic and public good. Not only will they support the searching and selection of information, but they will also need to be equipped for themselves and to help others analyze and apply information critically and appropriately. Besides the current trend in data analysis and business analytics, in the near future we will be expected to be able to fluently visualize, analyze, apply, and comprehend data for the benefit of others.

DIGITAL EQUITY

The digital divide deepens every day, negatively affecting people who do not keep pace with technology. Socioeconomic and demographic factors are associated with the divide, including inability to afford internet service, educational level, age, and rural and social isolation. Without use of the internet, people will not access digital information services. These information services are essential for improved health, finances, education, and personal and mental growth. The internet supports primary social engagement through social media, email, and online meetings or visits. Today grandparents who do not Skype or use Facebook are likely excluded from the special moments in their families' lives. Without the internet, people cannot access their personal health care digital information service, which has become a primary way to receive diagnostic and testing results or make necessary appointments. A poignant example of this is that during the pandemic those on the bottom of the divide struggled to make appointments to be vaccinated.

LSS are aware of the digital divide and the importance of the library having sufficient computers and Wi-Fi for those who lack technology at home. LSS can help minimize the divide for individuals when they instruct a new user about a digital information service or database. Taking the initiative to introduce a library computer user to a new database or even a helpful shortcut in a small way contributes to minimizing the divide and making digital information services more equitable.

Two cities, Seattle, Washington, and Cambridge, Massachusetts, on opposite coasts, strive for **digital equity** for their residents. Regardless of where LSS work, there is digital inequity in their communities that can begin to be mitigated following the examples from Seattle and Cambridge. Key to both cities is the understanding that digital inequity is not solely a technology concern. Achieving digital equity resides in resolving the socioeconomic and demographic attributes that are at the root of problem.

Seattle

The city of Seattle recognized digital inequity more than twenty-five years ago and began its work to foster digital inclusion in 1996.[11] Its current plan was developed by more than one hundred community leaders, nonprofit organizations, businesses, and the public who work toward eliminating the divide through the following goals.

- *Outreach and accessibility*—Make it easy for residents to know about, find, understand, and use appropriate services and information.
- *Skills training*—Create and deliver educational opportunities for all residents to gain the technology skills for successful employment.
- *Connectivity*—Ensure there are sufficient options for internet connectivity for all disadvantaged residents, small business, and communities.
- *Devices and technical support*—Likewise, ensure there are affordable, available, and sufficient technology devices for all disadvantaged residents, small businesses, and communities.
- *Inclusive engagement and empowerment*—Develop digital tools and the use of tools to maximize diverse, inclusive, civic engagement, sense of community, and participation in decision making.

Seattle strives to achieve digital equity with skills training, abundant connectivity and devices, and ongoing technical support. LSS participate and support these same strategic areas in their daily work when they help their community of users successfully search, locate, and use digital information services on either their own or library devices.

Cambridge

The City of Cambridge, home to both Harvard University and the Massachusetts Institute of Technology, strives to close the gap of digital inequity for its disadvantaged residents.[12] The Cambridge Housing Authority internet survey found that many older and disadvantaged residents face significant challenges related to internet affordability, device maintenance, and computer skills.

In response to the pandemic, Cambridge launched a pilot program to assist more than four hundred families in obtaining low-cost internet service, accelerated the Cambridge Public Schools laptop and hotspot provision efforts, and supported the Cambridge Public Library first-ever technology lending programs. Its current plan is to expand these existing programs, create new initiatives, and learn from successful digital equity efforts in other cities. Some of the key recommendations of its plan to close the digital gap are to

- establish a digital equity and **inclusion coalition**,
- create a digital equity fund emphasizing device and skills programs,
- engage local philanthropic organizations for broadband equity initiatives,
- partner with organizations that provide low-cost devices and training to Cambridge residents,
- expand loaner programs,
- establish a digital skills training corps,
- expand public Wi-Fi and charging stations in core areas, and
- facilitate additional providers of low-cost service to more Cambridge Housing Authority developments.

Both Seattle and Cambridge are proactive in their resolve to be cities where residents have digital equity. Much can be learned across the country from their efforts. What is common to both cities' plans is the need to not only provide affordable and robust internet access and devices to the disadvantaged, but, most importantly, to equally make skills and technology training available to those who are being left behind for socioeconomic or demographic reasons. Seattle and Cambridge recognize that digital equality to information services improves the health, education, and economy of their residents that extends to the cities. LSS have the opportunity to help to resolve digital inequity in their own communities by assisting disadvantaged users with informal support or training of library digital information services.

TRENDS AND DEVELOPMENTS

It is a bold attempt to predict the future; however, there are technology trends and developments today that will surely influence the future of digital information services.

The future of libraries is here as well as ahead of us. The future is happening piece by piece around us. LSS have the ability to influence the future by being essential providers and informal educators of digital information services. Technologies such as IoTs, robotics, virtual reality, and artificial intelligence have the potential to greatly enhance or change digital information services in the future.

Internet of Things (IOTs)

An **IoT** is a "smart" device that has inbuilt technology that supports actuators that cause the device to operate and communicate with other devices over a network. Libraries use IoTs to improve patron services at circulation, maintain building temperature and security, or share resources within a consortium. Devices are "smart" because they run on intelligent and creative software applications. Along with the capacity to communicate, many IoT devices also include an array of sensors that provide useful information. LSS in the future may work with information discovery and management systems that are highly programmable and will be customized by staff and users to perform many of the functions that take manual intervention today.

Robotics

Where once LSS went into the archives to retrieve a specific volume and issue, today LSS retrieve journal articles through database searching. It is conceivable that robotics, or machine learning, will augment, if not replace, many of the steps of digital information retrieval that are done by staff today. Users may use voice assistance to describe to a "robot" or computer the type of information they seek. Selection and document delivery could be done robotically.

Virtual Reality (VR)

Those who play computer games accept simulation and fantasy of virtual worlds. Digital information services may in the future also provide simulation. For example, a user may need information on how to set a formal dining table. It is conceivable a document or file with this basic information could be converted and retrieved in multiple options—different for special occasions, using specific colors, and so on. The coupling of digital information and VR is an intriguing idea! Simulations could also be virtual where the key information of a digital document is extracted and visualized into a "how to" video (see figure 15.2).

Figure 15.2.   Digital Information Using Virtual Reality. *Nastasic / E+ via Getty Images*

Artificial Intelligence (AI)

There is great potential for AI to augment how people search and retrieve digital information services. Many use AI when they "speak" to their smartphones or Alexa to retrieve information or perform a basic command. As AI becomes more developed and libraries and other information providers create more metadata for the semantic web, users will be able to discuss their needs for critical information with smart devices that have a high level of AI.

CONTINUOUS LEARNING

The predictions of influences on future digital information services will spur LSS to use library technology in new ways. Both formal and informal technical learning is necessary to keep current with innovation. Formal learning occurs through courses, webinars, or workshops with planned curriculum. Informal learning occurs through many paths, such as reading professional journals, conversations and supports with others, mentoring, self-guided tutorials, deliberate practice, or hands-on experiences and applications. LSS should aim for combinations of both formal and informal learning to stay abreast with digital information services and the potential libraries have to use them with patrons. The speed of technology innovation does not allow LSS to ignore the need for continuous learning. LSS enhance their value to their employer as well as continue to have passion for their work when they are active innovators and users of library technology and digital information services.

Learning is lifelong. We do not stop learning because we have graduated from a school or program. We learn something new every day. LSS can focus some of their new learning toward future digital information services. Best learning is both analytical and experiential. Analyze and reflect how you learn and use digital information services and apply your most successful methods to help others have digital equity.

CHAPTER SUMMARY

This final chapter is about the general trends and developments in technology applications for library digital information services and how they may change in the future. Digital equity is critical to the social, economic, educational, and health success of all people and places. LSS who demonstrate flexibility in adapting to new technology influence the critical and essential role libraries have to be providers of digital information services to their communities.

DISCUSSION QUESTIONS

1. How can LSS make digital information services more accessible?
2. What is digital fluency and what are some examples of it?
3. What is digital equity and why is it imperative to achieve it?
4. How can LSS be a part of the solution to digital inequity?
5. What predictions do you have for digital information services based on technology innovations today?

ACTIVITY

Does your town or city have a plan for digital equity? If so, access a copy and create a short report to share with library administrators describing how the public and school libraries in the town can be a contributing member. For example, if the plan suggests a lending program of computing devices and hotspots, how would your library go about participating in this effort?

If your town does not have a digital equity plan, read Seattle's or Cambridge's plans (see references for citations), and write the report making suggestions from these plans that would enhance digital equity in your town.

NOTES

1. Merriam-Webster, "Accessible," last modified 2021, accessed June 12, 2021, https://www.merriam-webster.com/dictionary/accessible.

2. Pew Research Center, "Mobile Technology and Home Broadband 2021," *Internet & Technology*, last modified June 3, 2021, accessed June 12, 2021, https://www.pewresearch.org/internet/2021/06/03/mobile-technology-and-home-broadband-2021/.

3. California State Library, "Collection," last modified 2021, accessed June 12, 2021, https://archive.org/details/californiastatelibrary.

4. Library of Congress, "Digital Strategy for the Library of Congress," last modified 2021, accessed June 12, 2021, https://www.loc.gov/digital-strategy#we-will-invest.

5. Institute of Museum and Library Services, "Digital Initiatives," last modified 2021, accessed June 12, 2021, https://www.imls.gov/our-work/priority-areas/digital-initiatives.

6. Tom Adamich, "Turning Digital Collections into Dynamic Access Points," *Computers in Libraries* 41, no. 5 (June 2021): 21–24, https://search.ebscohost.com/login.aspx?direct=true&AuthType=cookie,ip,cpid&custid=csl&db=aph&AN=150658711&site=ehost-live&scope=site.

7. U.S. Department of Education, "Digital Literacy Initiatives," Literacy Information and Communication System, last modified 2021, accessed June 12, 2021, https://lincs.ed.gov/state-resources/federal-initiatives/digital-literacy#students.

8. Virginia Tech, "Develop Your Digital Fluency Competency," *Career and Professional Development*, last modified 2021, accessed June 12, 2021, https://career.vt.edu/develop/DigitalFluency.html.

9. Scout Calvert, "Future Themes and Forecasts for Research Libraries and Emerging Technologies," Association of Research Libraries, last modified August 2020, accessed June 12, 2021, https://www.arl.org/resources/future-themes-and-forecasts-for-research-libraries-and-emerging-technologies/.

10. Calvert, "Future Themes."

11. City of Seattle, "Digital Equity," *Seattle Information Technology*, last modified 2021, accessed June 13, 2021, http://www.seattle.gov/tech/initiatives/digital-equity.

12. City of Cambridge, "City of Cambridge Releases Comprehensive Digital Equity Study," last modified April 20, 2021, accessed June 13, 2021, https://www.cambridgema.gov/news/2021/04/cityofcambridgereleasescomprehensivedigitalequitystudy.

REFERENCES, SUGGESTED READINGS, AND WEBSITES

Adamich, Tom. "Turning Digital Collections into Dynamic Access Points." *Computers in Libraries* 41, no. 5 (June 2021): 21–24. https://search.ebscohost.com/login.aspx?direct=true&AuthType=cookie,ip,cpid&custid=csl&db=aph&AN=150658711&site=ehost-live&scope=site.

California State Library. "Collection." Last modified 2021. Accessed June 12, 2021. https://archive.org/details/californiastatelibrary.

Calvert, Scout. "Future Themes and Forecasts for Research Libraries and Emerging Technologies." Association of Research Libraries. Last modified August 2020. Accessed June 12, 2021. https://www.arl.org/resources/future-themes-and-forecasts-for-research-libraries-and-emerging-technologies/.

City of Cambridge. "City of Cambridge Releases Comprehensive Digital Equity Study." Last modified April 20, 2021. Accessed June 13, 2021. https://www.cambridgema.gov/news/2021/04/cityofcambridgereleasescomprehensivedigitalequitystudy.

City of Seattle. "Digital Equity." Seattle Information Technology. Last modified 2021. Accessed June 13, 2021. http://www.seattle.gov/tech/initiatives/digital-equity.

Institute of Museum and Library Services. "Digital Initiatives." Last modified 2021. Accessed June 12, 2021. https://www.imls.gov/our-work/priority-areas/digital-initiatives.

Library of Congress. "Digital Strategy for the Library of Congress." Last modified 2021. Accessed June 12, 2021. https://www.loc.gov/digital-strategy#we-will-invest.

Merriam-Webster. "Accessible." Last modified 2021. Accessed June 12, 2021. https://www.merriam-webster.com/dictionary/accessible.

Pew Research Center. "Mobile Technology and Home Broadband 2021." *Internet & Technology.* Last modified June 3, 2021. Accessed June 12, 2021. https://www.pewresearch.org/internet/2021/06/03/mobile-technology-and-home-broadband-2021/.

U.S. Department of Education. "Digital Literacy Initiatives." Literacy Information and Communication System. Last modified 2021. Accessed June 12, 2021. https://lincs.ed.gov/state-resources/federal-initiatives/digital-literacy#students.

Virginia Tech. "Develop Your Digital Fluency Competency." *Career and Professional Development.* Last modified 2021. Accessed June 12, 2021. https://career.vt.edu/develop/DigitalFluency.html.

Glossary

Accessibility—Every user has equal opportunity to locate, obtain, use, and understand open and unbiased information.

Accession—This refers to the act of acquiring and including items in a digital collection according to library policy.

Advertisement tracking—Online shopping data is collected and used to sell. Many libraries use Google Analytics or other products to "anonymously" track their patrons' online use of library website views and engagement.

Algorithm—This is a set of rules that a computer needs to complete a task. Search engine software is embedded with such rules and procedures in order to index sites from the web.

Analog—Libraries circulate books, tapes of sound and film, and other continuous formats. Recorded in a continuous line with a beginning and end, analog media formats have rapidly been replaced with digital.

App—An abbreviation for a short version of a software program or "application," these were first popularized by Apple because full-version web programs could not be reasonably viewed on smartphones and mobile devices.

Archives—Highly organized and selective places of storage, archives are often associated with museums and libraries, for records, media, and artifacts of significant importance.

Archivists—These people are specially trained to identify documents, texts, media, and artifacts of lasting value and preserve, store, and provide access to records and artifacts of importance.

Artifacts—These are two- or three-dimensional objects that have artistic, cultural, personal, or historic value that are preserved for future generations.

Assessment—This is the method, such as observations, tests, and so on used to measure what students are able to do after being instructed in a specific process, skill, or curriculum.

Assets—These objects include digital photos, videos, and song files that reside on computing storage devices or cloud networks for fast access and reliability.

Asynchronous—This type of online learning does not require real-time interaction; instead, content is available for students to access when it best suits their schedules, and assignments are completed to deadlines.

BIBFRAME—These are the new and emerging standards for cataloging library items established in the United States by the Library of Congress that expand the use of metadata.

Binary code—Using the numbers zero and one (0 and 1), this code used in programming operates computers and other digital devices.

Broadband—This is a type of high-speed internet connection such as digital subscriber line (DSL), cable, fiber, wireless, or satellite.

Bundling—Multiple databases, typically all from a single vendor, are sold as a unit to the library customer.

Census—In the United States, this is the official ten-year count or survey of its population that records various details of individuals and establishes the number of congressional districts.

Closed standard—The e-book file type is written for a specific e-book reader or app. For example, Amazon e-books are considered closed standard because they can only be read on the Amazon Kindle or using an Amazon app on other devices.

Cloud computing—Libraries use this type of storage system for digital collections of remote servers that ensure offsite backup and reliability.

Cognition—These are the processes of thinking and how the human brain stores and processes information to make sense of the world.

Collection analysis—This process determines what materials patrons find desirable, what materials are not, and where gaps exist in subjects or content.

Confidentiality—This is the state of secrecy. In a library, patrons expect confidentiality of their personal computer use, searches, circulation data, and how they use digital information.

Consortium—Multiple libraries, museums, or other institutions create a formal and legal partnership to fund, staff, and accomplish the mission and goals.

Content Management Systems—Also known as CMS, these are tools that provide patrons better access to library digital information services. CMS are used to create, edit, manage, and host websites.

Curation—This is the process of selecting and caring for important artifacts and objects so that they can be displayed, grouped, or digitized as part of a specific collection or around a theme.

Curriculum—This is the content or subject matter taught by instructors.

Digital collections—These are clusters of digital assets that are commonly grouped and linked around a topic or theme for improved organization and access for users.

Digital equity—This occurs when all individuals and communities have the information technology capacity needed for full participation in our society, democracy, and economy.

Digital fluency—This occurs when people have the ability to apply digital technology to enhance the quality of their lives, improve productivity and communication, solve problems, and streamline processes.

Digital Learning Environments—These are libraries or educational institutions that provide access to digital information services, use analytics to map how documents are used, and sponsor collaboration, personalization, and interoperability.

Digital library—This is a specialized form of library that encompasses electronic collections of visual, text, audio, or film digital assets that are accessed by users over a computer network.

Digital literacy—This is the ability to successfully use information and communication technologies to find, read, view, evaluate, create, and communicate information, requiring both cognitive and technical skills.

Digitization—This is the process of transforming physical material into a digital (electronic) form by scanning or imaging.

Direct Object Identifier—Commonly referred to as the DOI, this is a set of numbers, letters, and symbols that uniquely and permanently identifies an article or document. The DOI links the item to the web. The DOI may be used in bibliographic citations.

Discovery—This is the ability to search library catalogs, databases, and other resources simultaneously.

Distributed web—As opposed to a centralized, top-down internet, this configuration is a peer-to-peer network where users' computers can be accessed to speed up searching.

Downstream—This is the direction of data when transmitted over the internet to end users from a central server point of origin.

DRM—An acronym for digital rights management, it restricts or limits how an e-book can be shared among people and devices.

Dynamic IP Range—Consecutive numbers randomly assigned to library computers speed database searching with devices preregistered on the library network.

Element—This is an identifying term or phrase that describes a point of information about an artifact, document, image, or media.

Encryption—This is a part of a software program designed to guard the contents of the e-book files using algorithms and adjoining keys.

Enumeration Districts—A term also referred to as "EDs" by the Bureau of the U.S. Census, these are the areas that could be covered by a single census taker or enumerator in one census period.

E-reader—This is a dedicated device used to download, read, and make notes about an e-book.

Fair use—Copyrighted material may be used for "criticism, comment, news reporting, teaching, scholarship, or research" without the user paying the producer or asking for permission.

Federated search—This type of search cross-indexes multiple databases simultaneously with results viewed in one screen as an efficient way to search many products at once.

File format—TIFF and JPEG are the commonly used formats for scanned files for library digital collections. The format tells a software program how to display the contents in the file.

First Sale Doctrine—Libraries have the right to resell, rent, lease, or lend the work without paying or asking permission of the copyright holder.

Graphical User Interfaces—More commonly known as GUIs, this is a component of a web browser that enables images, video, and other media to be viewed from websites.

Hybrid—This type of learning is a combination of asynchronous, synchronous, and face-to-face formats.

Inclusion coalition—Libraries, schools, community-based organizations, local governments, housing, and others who cooperatively address equitable access and use of digital information.

Index—Search engines compile an index of websites and URLs that, in turn, are where the results of a search derive.

In-kind—These are the staff, equipment, and other resources the library already has in place that, if a grant is funded, will help make the project successful.

Instruction—This is the method and pedagogy used to teach new knowledge and skills to students.

Internet of Things—Commonly referred to as IoTs, these are "smart" devices that have inbuilt technology that cause the device to operate and communicate with other devices over a network.

Interoperable—This is the ability for various databases and digital collections to be searched and accessed seamlessly by the user.

Library Support Staff—LSS or library paraprofessionals are involved in library operations at all levels. The range and complexity of their duties varies with each position, the size and type of the library, and each library's specific needs.

License agreement—This contract between the library and the database company provider specifies how long and under what conditions library patrons may use the subscription database or resource.

Link rot—This is a slang term for hypertext links or URLs that are broken and thus web sites or pages cannot be found.

Linked data—With one search, connections will be made to other databases that are associated with a topic. No longer will the internet be a collection of documents, but rather it will be based on relationships among data.

Literacy—This is the ability and skills of a person to read, write, and perform mathematics. The term also defines having knowledge and expertise in a particular field of study.

Live streaming—This is when video of an event or performance is viewed as it occurs.

MARC 21—These are the current cataloging standards established by the Library of Congress.

Memory institutions—These are museums, libraries, archives, historical societies, arboreta, and other heritage sites that serve as repositories of public knowledge, history, and culture.

Metadata—This includes both basic bibliographic information such as the title, author, publisher, date, etc. and wider and more thorough descriptions and associations about the attributes of library resources.

Metatag—This is a top line of computer code on a webpage for inputting searchable subjects that will enhance the ranking of the page. These lines of code influence search engine results by matching the user's search terms with the subjects found in these lines of code. Library programmers can influence the ranking of their websites using metatags.

Monochrome—Black-and-white screen (or shades of gray) display of an e-reader that is easiest for viewing e-books.

Navigation—This refers to the connecting links within a website that allow users to move from one webpage to another.

Needs assessment—This process is used to gather data that will help to determine the strengths and shortcomings of the library collections.

Nonlinear text—This refers to words or sentences that are neither in consecutive order nor follow a left-to-right, line-by-line arrangement. Nonlinear text may be words in any vertical or horizontal manner and may not appear connected to each other.

OCR—Optical character recognition is the process of scanning an item and turning it into digitized code.

On-demand—Customers or institutions pay a subscription to have access to a large selection of media that users can view at their convenience.

Online learning management system—This is a software program that provides a secure platform for teacher and student sharing of files that promote learning.

Open access—These are scholarly articles, commentaries, research reports, etc. that are made free to anyone on the web.

Open standard—These are the file types that are available to use with any computing device and not specific to one e-book reader or vendor.

OTT video streaming—Standing for "over the top," this type of streaming refers to film and television content provided via a high-speed internet connection rather than cable or satellite.

Paper deterioration—This refers to the crumbling and degradation of paper, an essential material for library collections, which is exacerbated by environmental, mechanical, and chemical processes.

Pay-per-view—Customers or institutions pay a fee for a one-time viewing of a film.

Performance metrics—These are figures and data representative of a library's actions, abilities, and overall quality of materials.

Platform—This is a term used synonymously for a social media product. The library Facebook and Twitter accounts are platforms.

PlumX metrics—This is an example of a data research system that librarians use to determine how people interact and use databases and other digital information services.

Portal—This is a website designed to be a starting point or opening to information on the web because it simplifies searching by consolidating and organizing links from different digital libraries and other sources.

Prerecorded streaming—This is media has been taped or recorded for viewing sometime after the event occurs.

Preservation—Librarians and archivists use methods to restore artifacts to as close to the original state as possible and share with the public images through digitization.

Primary sources—Artifacts, documents, sound recordings, film, clothing, inventions, and other objects and materials that are authentic and present first-hand accounts or direct evidence.

Privacy—This is the freedom from unauthorized public attention, observation, or intrusion. In a library, LSS provide privacy when they support the ability for patrons to be free from intrusion with space from others when using services and materials.

Private live streaming—These are video services that restrict access to live media to a select group of people rather than the entire public.

Public domain—This is the status of an item that is not protected under copyright and therefore its use belongs to the public at large.

Public performance site licensing—Under federal U.S. Copyright law, a license is required when showing a commercial film outside the home that provides compensation to those who hold the copyright.

Push notifications—These are brief text messages that appear on a user's mobile device to alert them to headlines of newsworthy items, current happenings, or events. Libraries can use this method to notify patrons of upcoming special programs, etc.

Remote access—This provides a patron the ability to externally access and use a library subscription database from outside of the library.

RSS feed—An acronym for the term *really simple synchronization*, this is a way for users to subscribe to view new content on a website, blog, or social media.

Search entry—Acting like a search engine for a specific discovery service, this is the program used to simultaneously find items in the library ILS, subscription databases, and open access resources on a subject or keywords.

Secondary sources—These materials interpret and analyze primary sources. Written by those who have special expertise on topics, providing historical context or critical perspectives.

Semantic web—Also referred to as Web 3.0 or the web of data, this is a framework that allows different applications and programs to share data such as dates, numbers, formulas, and more.

Silo—Communication within an information silo is self-contained and always vertical, making it difficult or impossible for the system to branch out horizontally and work with unrelated systems.

Simultaneous use—More than one patron may access a subscription database at the same time.

Social media tools—These are apps or other means that libraries can use to receive feedback about their social media, easily publish new content, and analyze how platforms are being used by patrons.

Spiders—This is search engine software that crawls through the internet to build its indexes based on algorithms and other criteria.

Streaming—This is the process of using the internet as the transmission to view or host media from a host service to computing devices.

Subscription databases—These are collections of searchable and authoritative documents, articles, images, sound, media, websites, or other information formats clustered around a broad theme or subject.

Synchronous—This type of online or distance education happens in real time, often with a set class schedule and required log-in times.

Technology standards—Clear expectations of outcomes of achievement define what students should know how to do with technology to support their learning.

Tertiary sources—These sources are even more removed from the original than secondary sources as they index, abstract, organize, compile, or digest other sources

Trade books—These are books intended for the general public and are marketed with trade discount to bookstores and to libraries. Other types of books, such as textbooks, may not receive similar discounting.

Trial—This is an agreed-upon length of time when a library can try a database without cost with its patrons to help evaluate whether it meets an information need.

Uniform Resource Locator—More commonly referred to as the URL, this is the internet address of a webpage.

Upstream—The reverse of downstream, this is the transmission of data using the internet from the end user to the hosting service.

UX—Meaning user experience, in a library these are the interactions a user has to accomplish a task with its products and services, including the library website. UX takes into account how successful the interactions were and how the user felt about them.

Videography documentation—Documentation is an ongoing process of community filming; LSS support the documentation and preservation of local heritage by helping to create a local film archive.

Visual literacy—This is the ability to interpret information and inferences from photographs, pictures, or illustrations, whether they are still or animated.

Web accessibility—This occurs when there are websites, tools, and technologies that provide equal opportunity for everyone to interact with and contribute to the web.

Web browser—A key component of the search process that enables users to retrieve and view the websites once they are located.

Web directories—Similar to LSS creating library bibliographies, directories are databases of preselected websites on a theme or subject that serve to provide quick access to informative websites.

Index

404 error, 92

abstract awareness. 1–11
academic literacy. 5
Academic Video Online, 160–161
access. *See* remote access
accessibility, 196–197. *See also* web accessibility
accession, 45, 52
acquisitions, 20, 24
advertisement tracking, 143, 145
aggregated searches, 33
AI. *See* Artificial intelligence
ALA Code of Ethics, 146
ALA Library Bill of Rights, 146
ALA-LSSC Competency standards, xiii
ALA-LSSC. *See* American Library Association Library Support Staff Certification
Alaska Digital Library, 36
Alaska State Library, 36
algorithm, 92, 95, 97, 135, 209
Amazon, 132–135, 158
American Library Association Library Support Staff Certification, xiii, xviii
American Memory, 66
Analog. 3–4, 150, 209
Ancestry, 83
Annenberg Media, 162
app, 132–133, 138, 157, 164, 169–170, 175–178, 209
application software. *See* app
archival supplies, 78

archives, xvi, 52, 67–68, 70, 75, 79–85, 149, 209
archivist, 75, 79–81, 114, 209
artifacts, xvi, 45–50, 52–54, 60, 65–67, 75–79, 84–85, 209
artificial intelligence, 95, 203, 205
assessment, 183, 186, 209
asset. *See* digital asset
assistive technologies, 98, 117, 125, 131, 139, 191, 193
Association for Library Collections and Technical Services, 53
asynchronous, 183, 190, 210
audio e-books, 139

autobiography, 51
Bank of America Philanthropic Solutions, 85
BIBFRAME, 53, 105–107, 110, 210
binary code, 3–4, 201
Blackboard, 190
Bloom's Taxonomy. 100, 102
Boolean, 99–100
broadband, 195, 197, 199, 203, 210
Brookings Institution, 68
browser. *See* web browser
bundling, 31, 38, 210
business directories, 93–94
business social media, 171–172, 175

census, 76, 82–83, 201
Center for Research Libraries, 68

Chronicling America, 66
Church of Jesus Christ of Latter-Day Saints, 83
Civil Rights Digital Library, 162
closed standard, 132–135, 210
cloud. *See* cloud computing
cloud computing, 45, 53, 145, 210
CMS. *See* Content Management Systems
cognition, 3, 7, 210
collaboration, 47, 53,64–65,84
collection analysis, 17, 19–20, 210. *See also* needs assessment
collection development policy, 18, 61
comprehension, 8–9
concrete awareness, 10–11
confidentiality, 143–146
Connecticut Digital Archive, 53
Connecticut Digital Collections, 84
consortium, 25, 59, 64, 68, 70, 138, 210
content management system, 117–118, 125, 178, 210
CONTENTdm, 126
continuous learning, 205
copyright, xvii, 26, 60, 62, 110, 113, 135–136, 139, 143–144, 146–152, 156, 163, 211, 214
Cornell University Library Digital Library Collections, 69
Council on Library Resources, 64
crowdsourcing, 173
curation, 60, 62, 67–68, 210
curriculum, 161, 183, 185–186, 205, 210
cybersecurity, 144

data, 18–20
database. *See* subscription database
deacidification, 77
design elements, 121–123
digital access, 199
digital asset, xvi, 60–66, 69, 146
digital collection, xvi, 45, 47, 52–53, 60–64, 67, 70, 78, 83–85, 109, 118, 126, 146, 197–199, 210
digital divide, 201–202
digital equity, 196, 201–203, 205–206, 210
digital fluency, 196, 199–201, 205, 210
digital information services, 5–6, 123, 184–192, 196–197, 203, 205
digital learning environment, 184, 187, 196, 210

digital libraries, xvi, 64–65, 67–68, 110–111. *See also* state digital libraries
digital literacy, xv–xvii, 3, 5–7, 9, 13, 196, 199–200, 211
Digital Millennium Copyright Act, 148, 152
Digital Prairie, 36
Digital Public Library of America, 53, 70
Digital Rights Management, 132, 135, 151, 211
Digitalia Film Library. 160
digitization, xiii–xiv, 52–54, 60, 76, 187, 197–199, 211
digitization grants, 84
Direct Object Identifier, 31, 211
Directory of Open Access Books, 139
Directory of Preservation Organizations and Resources, 78
discount purchasing, 25
discovery. *See* discovery services.
discovery services, xvi, 32–41, 107
distributed web, 91, 101–102, 211
DMAC. *See* Digital Millennium Copyright Act
DOAB. *See* Directory of Open Access Books
DRM. *See* Digital Rights Management
Docuseek2, 161
DOI *See* Direct Object Identifier
domain, 99–199
downstream, 155–156
DPLA. *See* Digital Public Library of America
Dropbox, 145
Dublin Core, 62, 110, 114
dynamic IP range, 18, 26, 211

e-book devices, 132–133. *See also* e-reader
e-books, xiii–xiv, xvii, 82, 118, 132–141, 149, 151, 176–177, 198
EBSCO, 23, 26, 35–36, 40–41, 138–139, 160–161, 176
EBSCO Novelist, 36
education, 184–187
Education in Video, 161
electronic holds, 33–34
elements, 109–110
Encoded Archival Description, 114
encryption, 132, 135, 211
enumeration district, 76, 82, 211
Epic, 140
e-reader, xvii, 132–135, 138, 211
Europeana, 70–71

Facebook, 61, 145, 156,170–174
fair use, 53, 143, 147, 149, 211
federated search, 18, 23, 33, 35,38, 211
Feedly, 176–177
file format, 45, 53, 60, 110, 133, 139, 199, 211
file sharing, 145
film platform, 161
Films on Demand, 161
First Amendment, 144, 146
First Sale Doctrine, 135–136, 143, 147, 149, 151, 211
Flipster, 176

Gale Cengage, 22, 33, 138–139
genealogical records, 47, 52, 83
Google Analytics, 94, 123, 145, 209
Google Books, 98, 139
Google Classroom, 98, 156, 190
Google Docs, 98, 139, 145, 191
Google My Business, 94, 99, 123, 174
grants and grant writing, 84–85, 199, 212
Graphical User Interfaces, 92, 117, 211
Greenstone, 110–111
Groton History Online, 84
GUI. *See* Graphical User Interfaces

handwriting, 9
Henry Ford. *See* The Henry Ford
historical societies, 47, 64, 78–79, 81, 83–85, 196, 198, 212
History in Video, 162
Hoopla, 138, 159, 160
hybrid, 184, 187, 190, 196, 211

ILS. *See* Integrated Library System
IMLS. *See* Institute of Museums and Library Services
inclusion coalition, 196, 203, 212
index, 32–33, 92, 95–98, 107–108, 212
information literacy, 5
Information Technology. *See* IT
in-kind, 76, 85, 212
Instagram, 61, 171–173
Institute of Museum and Library Services, 61, 84
instruction, 40, 184–188, 199, 212
Integrated Library System, 19, 37–40, 120, 145
intellectual freedom, 18

intellectual property rights, 62
Internet Archive, 101, 198
Internet of Things, 5, 145, 196, 204, 212
internet search, xvi, 33, 50, 107
internet speed, 156–157
interoperability, 63, 184, 188–189, 196, 200, 210, 212
IoT. *See* Internet of Things
IT, 146, 175

J. P. Getty Institute, 67

Kanopy, 156, 159–160
Kentucky Department for Libraries and Archives (KDLA), 35
keyboard, 6, 98, 124, 133
keyboarding, 9

learning, xvii, 27, 147, 160–161, 184–189, 205. *See also* online learning
LibAnswers, 178
Libby, 138 176
LibGuide Community, 41–42, 178–179
LibGuides, 41, 93, 126, 178
Library Discovery Services, xvi, 32–40
Library of Congress, 46, 52, 65–66, 77, 82, 106, 108, 162, 172, 198
Library Support Staff, xiii–xv, xviii
license agreement, 18, 26, 212
lifelong learning, 25, 68, 145, 160, 184
link rot, 92, 212
linked data, 105, 112–113, 212
live streaming, 155–156, 212. *See also* private live streaming, streaming
local digital collections, 10, 32, 35, 84
LSS. *See* Library Support Staff

Mango Languages, 176
MARC 21, xvi, 37, 53, 106–110, 212
mathematical literacy, 6
media, 156, 160, 190
media literacy, 5.
media streaming, 159–162
memorabilia, 76
Memory Institutions, 196, 199, 212
Meta, 145
metadata, xvi, 22, 32, 62–63, 65–66, 84–85, 106–114, 212
metadata management, xvi, 109
metatag, 106, 109, 212

metrics. *See* performance metrics
misinformation, 171
MIT World, 162
mobile apps, xvii, 170, 176–178
mobile solutions, xvii, 175
monochrome, 132–133, 212
morphological processing, 8
museums, 47, 50, 61, 66–68, 70, 78, 81, 84, 107, 110, 113, 196, 198–199

NARA. *See* National Archives and Record Administration
NASA Space Technology Institutes, 68
National Archives, 70, 81–82
National Archives and Record Administration. *See* National Archives.
National Digital Library, 66
National Endowment for the Humanities, 85
navigation, 117, 119–123, 212
Nebraska Library Commission, 22, 26
needs assessment, 18, 20–21, 213. *See also* collection analysis
NEH. *See* National Endowment for the Humanities
new literacies, 6
New York State Archives, 83
nonlinear text, 4, 8, 213

OCLC, 20, 34, 40, 110, 126, 177
OCR, 45, 54, 213
Oklahoma Department of Libraries, 36
on demand, 155, 158–159, 161–162, 164, 213
Online Archive of California, 84
Online Computer Library Center. *See* OCLC
online learning, xiv, 118, 161, 183–184, 190, 210, 213
open access, 32–38, 40, 107, 113, 139, 213
Open Directory Project, 92
open research, 199
open standard, 132–134, 213
optical character recognition. *See* OCR
orthographic processing, 8
OT, 145. *See also* third party
OTT video streaming, 155, 163–164, 213. *See also* streaming video
over the top, 163. *See also* OTT video streaming
Overdrive, 138, 176

pandemic, xiv, 60, 136–137, 156, 159, 171, 177, 190, 196, 198, 202–203
paper deterioration, 76–77, 213
PastPerfect, 62, 110
patron personal identifiable information, 145
pay-per-view, 156, 213
PBS, 160–162
peer review, 21, 27, 34, 39, 139
peer-to-peer network, 92, 101, 211
performance metrics, 18, 23–24, 213
Performing Arts Encyclopedia, 66
Pew Research Center, 170, 197
phonological processing, 8
Pinterest, 171–172, 177–178
platform, 62, 70, 111, 119–120, 145, 158, 161, 164, 169–175, 187, 213
PlumX Metrics, 23–24, 184, 188, 213
portal, 60, 70, 118, 126, 213
PPV. *See* pay-per-view
prerecorded streaming, 156, 213
preservation, xvi, 76, 78–81, 85, 148–149, 198, 201, 213
pricing, 24–25, 163
primary source, xvi, 46–55, 76, 84–85, 149, 187, 198, 213
privacy literacy, 6
private live streaming, 169, 176, 213
Project Gutenberg, 139
ProQuest, 25, 34–35, 38, 160–161, 189
public domain, 133, 139, 144, 148, 214
public performance site license, 155–156, 163, 214
Purdue University Libraries, 68
push notification, 177

radio frequency identification device, 145
RB Digital, 138
reading comprehension, see comprehension
reliability, 21–22, 34, 171
remote access, 18, 26, 60, 188, 192, 214
reputation, 21, 23
reviews, 19, 22–24
RFID. *See* Radio frequency identification device
rights management. *See* Digital Rights Management
robotics, 203–204
Roku device, 160
RSS feed, 126, 170, 177, 214

scanning technology, xvi, 54–55
school library. *See* school media center
school media center, 191
search engine, xvi, 32–33, 91–93, 95–102, 106–109, 112, 125, 209, 212
search query, 23, 32, 97, 99
secondary source, 46, 51, 214
self-publish, 132, 135
semantic processing, 8
semantic web, 106, 112–114, 205, 214
short messaging systems (SMS). *See* Text
silo, 118, 120, 214
simultaneous use, 18, 26–27, 214
smartphone, 7, 133, 138, 140, 157, 168–170, 175–178, 197, 205
Smithsonian, 67, 109, 139
Snapchat, 171, 173
social media, xvii, 24, 36, 118, 170–173, 175–179, 202, 214
social media marketing, 174
social media tools, 170, 174
social network, xiv, 17, 169–173
Society of American Archivists, 81
Songs of America, 66
spiders, 92, 97, 214
standards, *See* technology standards
state digital libraries, 35, 52, 83
state digital libraries. *See also* digital libraries
statistics, 19, 23–24, 63, 106, 138, 140–141, 201
STEM. *See* STEAM
STEAM, 145
streaming, 156–159, 214. *See also* live streaming, OTT
streaming video, 60, 155–156, 159–160, 163. *See also* OTT video streaming
streaming services, xiv, xvii, 159–161, 163, 213
subscription databases, xv, 18–21, 23–27, 32–37, 83, 187, 214
superficial awareness, 10–11
Swank, 161, 163
synchronous, 184, 190, 214
syntactic processing, 8

tablet, 133, 138, 157, 160, 175
technology standards, 4, 7, 214
TED Talks, 157
tertiary source, 46, 51, 214
The Henry Ford, 78

third party, 145
trade books, 132, 136–137, 214
training, 27, 40–41, 68, 78–81, 125, 191, 198–199, 202–203
trial, 18, 20–23, 42, 178, 215
tutorials, 27, 205
Twitter, 8, 171–172, 174, 178

U.S. Copyright Act, 146–148
Uniform Resource Locator, 92, 96, 112, 215
URL. *See* Uniform Resource Locator
upstream, 156, 215
User experience. *See* UX
UX, 118, 121, 215

vendor, 22, 24, 33–35, 37–41, 120, 138–140, 145
video hosting service, 164
videography documentation, 76, 215
virtual reality, 145, 204
visual literacy, xv, 4–6, 10–13, 215
visual media, 10, 187
Voice Search Engine Optimization, 98
VR. *See* Virtual Reality
V-SEO. *See* Voice Search Engine Optimization

Wayback Machine, 101
Web 3.0, 106, 112, 214
web accessibility, 118, 123–125, 215
web browser, xvi, 92, 95–97, 215
web directories, 92–95, 215
webinars, 27–28, 40, 190, 205
WebJunction, 20
website design, 62, 121–122
website services, xvii, 118
wi-fi, 26, 60, 113, 133, 135, 145, 170, 195, 197, 202–203
wireless. *See* wi-fi
WordPress, 125
World Digital Library, 70
World Intellectual Property Organization, 148
WorldCat, 34–37

YouTube, 27, 41, 98, 156–157, 159, 164, 170, 173, 190

Zoom, 156, 190

About the Author

Marie Keen Shaw is the program coordinator for the Library Technical Assistant certificate program at Three Rivers Community College in Norwich, Connecticut, where she has also been an adjunct professor since 1999. She teaches courses in cataloging and classification, digital resources, reference services, and management strategies. She has served on the boards of the Connecticut Library Consortium and the Connecticut Digital Library. She currently serves in a leadership role on the board of the Groton Public Library in Groton, Connecticut. Marie received her doctorate of education from the University of Connecticut in educational leadership and adult learning, a sixth-year degree from Southern Connecticut State University in educational leadership, and her MS from Purdue University in library and information science and educational media. A retired certified high school library media specialist and curriculum instructional leader, she has been a speaker at state library and educational media conferences in Rhode Island, Illinois, and Connecticut. Marie is coauthor of *Management and Supervision: An Introduction for Support Staff* (2019) and *Communication and Teamwork: An Introduction for Library Support Staff* (2019). She is the author of the books *Using Technology in the Library Workplace* (2021), *Cataloging Library Resources: An Introduction* (2017), *Library Technology and Digital Resources: An Introduction for Support Staff* (2015), and *Block Scheduling and Its Impact on the School Library Media Center* (1999). Her doctoral dissertation *Teacher's Learning of Technology: Key Factors and Process*, was accepted by the University of Connecticut, 2010.

CPSIA information can be obtained
at www.ICGtesting.com
Printed in the USA
BVHW011632120322
630947BV00002B/5